AF559960

THE FICTION OF AMITAV GHOSH

A CRITICAL COMMENTARY

THE FICTION OF AMITAV GHOSH

A CRITICAL COMMENTARY

Edited by
Vivekanand Jha

Published by

ATLANTIC

PUBLISHERS & DISTRIBUTORS (P) LTD

7/22, Ansari Road, Darya Ganj, New Delhi-110002
Phones : +91-11-40775252, 23273880, 23275880, 23280451
Fax : +91-11-23285873
Web : www.atlanticbooks.com
E-mail : orders@atlanticbooks.com

Branch Office
5, Nallathambi Street, Wallajah Road, Chennai-600002
Phones : +91-44-64611085, 32413319
E-mail : chennai@atlanticbooks.com

ISBN 978-81-269-1793-8

Printed in India at Glorious Printers, A-13, D.S.I.D.C.,
Jhilmil Industrial Area, Delhi-110095

Dedicated to

My Mother
Late Srimati Ram Jyoti Devi

Preface

The essayist, journalist, writer, anthropologist and novelist, Amitav Ghosh is a gem, gifted and blessed author of Indian writing in English and he is the touchstone of genius, versatility and eternal and an incessant source of inspiration. He is a role model for amateur, ambitious and budding writers of India writing in Indian English. He is a widely read and travelled man, and right from India to Sri Lanka, Iran, Egypt, United Kingdom, United States and Bangladesh have remained his spots of exploration and experimentation in his comprehensive and burgeoning writing career. The son of a Lieutenant Colonel in Indian Army, he was born with a silver spoon in his mouth and he encased all the amenities and facilities at his disposal in bolstering his academic acumen and literary career. Since Amitav Ghosh has travelled all around the world, his susceptibility and sensibility have been shaped by the socio-cultural heritage of India in particular and the rest of the world in general.

Amitav Ghosh has received several awards, honours and due recognition for his exceptional and exemplary endowment in the field of fiction, non-fiction, travelogue, history, anthropology and journalism. He has authored seven volumes of fiction and five volumes of non-fiction. Most of the novels authored by him turned out to be best sellers and he has been crowned with a number of coveted awards: The Prix Medicis Étrangère (1990); The Ananda Puraskar (1990); Sahitya Akademi Award (1990); Nomination for American Society of Magazine Editors Award (1999); The Arthur C. Clarke Award (1996); The Pushcart Prize (1999); Grand Prize for Fiction; Frankfurt eBook Award (2001); Crossword Book

Award (2005); Finalist, Kiriyama Prize (2006); Padma Shri Award (2007); Grinzane Cavour Prize (2007); Asian-American Literary Award (2007); Shortlisted, Man Booker Prize (2008); Crossword Book Award (2009); Indiaplaza Golden Quill Award (2009); Dan David Prize (2010); and Blue Metropolis International Literary Grand Prix (2011). But more than receiving a host of honours and awards, Amitav Ghosh is deemed sincere, significant, non-conformist and popular. He turned down the Commonwealth Writers' Prize in 2001 because the prize only recognized the writers and writings in English.

The novels of Amitav Ghosh are postulated by personal, nonconformist and extraordinarily contrived themes on the issues and aspects of subaltern, pre-colonialism, colonialism, post-colonialism, modernism and postmodernism. Both his fiction and non-fiction are teemed with homogeneous amalgamation and blend of variegated cultures, traditions and languages and the major thematic preoccupations of his writings are based upon impressive themes of travel, opium war, migration, historical facts, communal cruelty, political turmoil, corruption, caste politics, love, loss, travellers, diasporic exiles, struggle and strife. The epic like *Ibis* trilogy of which two-thirds of journey have already been explored with a great deal of fanfare, exuberance and achievement, remains so far the most ambitious and go-getting project of his life.

Turning towards the primary objective, it is heartening and stirring to see women taking a quantum leap and making galloping success in all walks of life, and they are peerless in their representations in language and literature too. The voice of women authors applauding the fiction of Amitav Ghosh reverberates in this anthology also, and out of twenty-four contributors of this anthology fifteen are women's voices. This is a revolutionary upsurge of feminine participation in the area of Indian English literature.

Now it's time to have a cursory glance on the core thematic thrust of every contributor of this anthology. The commencement of the book has been done with a tribute poem to Amitav Ghosh by me. The session of articles is inaugurated by Dr. Neerja Arun who dwells into the treatment of history as presented by the shadows in the novel, *The Shadow Lines.* The paper by Indira Nityanandam richly thrashes out the significance of time and space in the novel, *The Calcutta Chromosome.* Deepak Thakur throws light on contemporary theory and analyses the theme of the subaltern in the novel, *In an Antique Land.* The article by Anju Bala Agrawal studies Ghosh's female characters who are the hallmark of female consciousness and are capable of paddling their own canoe. The paper by Dinesh Kumar opulently takes up the issues of migration, gender and nationality that dominate the novel, *The Hungry Tide.* My own article exhaustively traces out the working of imageries and other figures of speech in the novel, *River of Smoke.*

Rajnish Mishra highlights skillful narration of opium trading by Amitav Ghosh in the novel, *River of Smoke.* Vishwanath Bite digs out both medieval and contemporary treatment of the theme in the novel, *In an Antique Land.* Ch. Swathi incorporates various issues of marginality, forgotten and neglected history and people representing them with respect to the novel, *Sea of Poppies.* Vandana Rajoriya warrants the attention of readers on stark realities of life and struggling of both men and women characters for their survival in the novel, *The Glass Palace.* A. Sujatha converses the role played by opium in India with respect to socio-environmental perspective in the novel, *Sea of Poppies.* Dalvir Singh Gahlawat and Suman Yadav elucidate the issues of demarcation which may cause even a sense of insecurity among the people with respect to the novel, *The Shadow Lines.* Prof. Saykar Satish Govind centres his attention on the themes of partition and communal conflict in the novel, *The Shadow Lines.* Neeta Dhumal has weaved collectively the sufferings of orphan, dispossessed and distressed characters of the novel, *Sea of Poppies.* Prof. Shyam Chothani highlights orthodox experimentation and discovery in the novel, *The Calcutta Chromosome.*

In my second article, I have put together all the epigrammatic and proverbial quotations with their pertinent contexts of the novel, *River of Smoke*. Meeting the touchstone of theory of subaltern, Prof. Ambarish Sen showcases the woes and worries of marginalized people, marginalized groups and the lower classes. Prof. Somdatta Bhattacharya analyzes working of psyche of Calcutta city in the novel, *The Shadow Lines* and *The Calcutta Chromosome,* whereas Rashi Saxena presents Amitav Ghosh as post-colonial fictional writer. Prof. Priyanka Vaidya discusses the novel, *The Circle of Reason* as a bildungsroman, picaresque and detective novel. Prof. (Mrs.) Rituparna Datta Roy analyses the novel, *The Hungry Tide* written in the Bengali tradition of the river-novel. L.V. Padmarani Rao and Ms Githa Bhojane sketch out the plot of the novel, *The Glass Palace* with special reference to a hundred years of pre-colonial, colonial and post-colonial Burmese history. Rajnish Mishra has again shown a great deal of skill and erudition in depicting the historical and communal facts that have been plaguing both India and Pakistan for years. Prof. Rupali Jain substantiates the positive aspects of globalization which play a pivotal role in bringing together the East and the West in the light of the novel, *The Hungry Tide.* In my third article, I have pointed out both legitimate and immoral elements of love and sensuality of the novel, *River of Smoke.*

The denouement of this comprehensive and exhaustive critical anthology is accomplished by the inclusion of Amitav Ghosh in conversation with another author Lila Azam Zanganeh, which has further bolstered usefulness and effectiveness of the anthology. I am grateful and indebted to promising and talented novelist, Zanganeh for allowing me to publish her conversation with Amitav Ghosh. The revealing interview rich in contents and information will be pretty useful for the students, researchers and scholars in going deep into Ghosh's novels. It will benefit students, researchers, critics, scholars, authors and academicians of Indian English Fiction in pursuing their endeavours and goals.

I take this opportunity to express my gratefulness to all the contributors for their warm and affectionate support in making this anthology one of the best anthologies ever written on

Indian English Fiction. However, simultaneously, the cases of plagiarism in English literature cannot be denied as it is on its zenith in the age of electronics and internet and some of the authors are in the tradition of indulging in such heinous and malicious endeavours.

Although every effort has been made to avoid such transgression and incongruity, yet their utter asceticism cannot be taken for granted. Therefore, the Editor and the Publisher will not be responsible for any copyrighted breach and embarrassment that may bang in due course of time. The individual author will be held responsible for any act of infringement in his/her article if it is reported. All the thoughts, observations and examinations expressed by the authors in this book are entirely their own and the Editor is only a link to communicate between authors and readers.

I express my insightful thanks to my well-wishers as well as detractors as both play a prerequisite part in pursuing and procuring my purpose. I must convey my deep sense of gratitude and thanks to Mr. Manish Kumar Gupta, Managing Director, Atlantic Publishers & Distributors (P) Ltd for the interest evinced in publishing this book.

Vivekanand Jha

Contents

1

A Tribute Poem to Amitav Ghosh

Vivekanand Jha

An emblem of beauty and wisdom
Fresh perfection treads in tandem.

Even in the teeth of *The Hungry Tide*
The horse of success you ride.

Even in the *Incendiary Circumstances*
Your pen steadily advances.

Your destination knows no doubt and confusion
As you embarked journey upon *The Circle of Reason*.

Over your face, no trace of *The Shadow Lines*
Even at fifty-five you enjoy an age of prime.

Even *In an Antique Land*
Beat the 'Magic-Realism' band.

By emancipating women in *The Calcutta Chromosome*
Bring happiness in every hearth and home.

Even those you provide solace
Who pelt stones on *The Glass Palace*.

No colonialism, opium or coffee
Can ebb out the wave of *Sea of Poppies*.

Your creativity is spreading like a tree of oak
As now you have swimmed across *River of Smoke*.

Least is being shortlisted for *Man Booker Prize*
You shall be basking in many more sun rise.

2

Transcending Generations with Time-Slip Fantasy through *The Shadow Lines*

Neerja Arun

The cultural process moved with extraordinary pace during early twentieth century of united and thereafter divided India. It posed two vital questions: one with traditional point of view and the other with contemporary view. It can be termed as the flash back and the present narrative technique used by Amitav Ghosh in *The Shadow Lines*. It is completely legitimate to inquire into the dynamics of the cultural process in twentieth-century India, yet in the very posing of this question there lurks a contradiction from the traditional point of view, an understanding of "process" is inextricably linked with an understanding of "progress". This sequence is narrated by Ghosh not as progress but as continuous and unexpected "renewal" of the cultural landscape.

Indeed, this "renewal" is not at all concerned with novelty or newness, but instead with a return to old forms. The revolutionary culture "grew back" in place of the tradition swept away by the revolution. This is well defined by the grandmother's journey to Bangladesh in order to bring her uncle to Kolkata. The unceasing desire to view the process as one of progression is the result of a failure to understand this system of renewal.

The present paper dwells into the treatment of history as presented by the shadows in the novel. The technique used is that of the time-slip fantasy. Time-slip fantasy is a particularly popular genre of literature with many children in grades six and seven. It is sometimes referred to as historical fantasy, time-warp fantasy, time-travel or past-time fantasy. Its strong attraction lies partly in the fact that it crosses three distinct genres (fantasy, historical fiction and contemporary realism) and takes the reader to a time that is quite distinct from current time, one that might be perceived as being less complex than today. It enables the reader to step back from contemporary life and see the struggles of human existence from a more distanced, reflective perspective. At the same time, the reader remains fully engaged with the characters and the issues with which the characters are faced. In time-slip fantasy, the travel across time is generally spurred by some unhappiness experienced by the protagonist. Contemporary readers in the 'middle years' can certainly identify with the need to get away from the routines of life when they grapple with issues that are beyond their control; issues such as body image, bullying, anxiety, divorce, death and adolescence itself.

With this perspective it is natural that Amitav Ghosh has combined history, story and narrative into the strings of shadows. The researcher Amitav has been superposed by Amitav, the novelist. The characters are integrated into events which have the capacity to lead to prominent historical event. The stark difference which result *The Shadow Lines* as a novel of intricate relations and not a historical novel lies in the fact that there are two narrators: the grandmother and the narrator. Both have their own perspectives. The historical perspective is much stronger than the contemporary viewpoints. The human relations, their responses to each other's emotions and the outcome, everything has a lead to past events which took place in the history of India.

The authors have been engaging their imagination in reliving the past through a number of narratives, but this is also true that the best narrative remains the history itself. Pre-independence and post-independence Indian history may be conceptualized as a process of ceaseless cultural erasing and re-writing. Both the continuity and the dissimilarity among the stages of India's history stem, not so much from a simple reexamination of "cultural heritage", but from its endless erasing and re-writing. Whether, it is the erasing or the re-writing that constitutes the dominant approach at given moment determines the strategy for constructing the past and, consequently, imagining the future, including the production (and over-production) of social expectations, the creation of what is commonly called "the historical perspective", the whole teleology of social development, and the like. The event itself has little meaning as compared to the shadow of such events.

Amitav Ghosh has presented *The Shadow Lines* more in the revolutionary culture. Unfulfilled aspirations and careful demands have become the recurrent themes. In Ghosh's local library, the unnamed narrator makes archival researches into the street riots in Calcutta, 1964, because no one but him seems unable to recollect the events: "they had dropped out of memory into the crater of volcano of silence" (230). In the light of other events that happened in post-Partition Dhaka or postcolonial India, the riots were rather small events, but what matters most to him is that they did happen: according to "the edition of Saturday, 11 January 1964, and sure enough, there it was: huge banner headline which said: Curfew in Calcutta, Police Open Fire, 10 dead, 15 wounded" (224). Rather than ascertaining whether the author tells us an historical fact.

These two models of cultural construction combined a comprehensive set of strategies for dealing with the past. Each of these attempts to carry out modernization and at the same time to recoup the past has retained both the object of erasing and re-writing as the dominant strategy for dealing with the past. The very reason that the narrator narrates in first person is to relate with each event as a personal issue. "Every word write about those events of 1964 is the product of struggle with silence" (218), for "once the riots had started they produce thousands of words of accurate description. But once they were over 45 and there was nothing left to describe they never speak of it again" (228).

The narrator in the novel has no name. The narrator's grandmother, Thamma is an important character in the novel. She is a bold middle-class Indian woman. She was born and brought up in British India. She felt that it was necessary to kill Englishmen who were reborn in bloodshed during wars and "all she wanted was a middle-class life in which like the middle class the world over she would thrive believing in the unity of nationhood and territory, of self-respect and national power; that was all she wanted, a modern middle class life, a small thing that history had denied her in its fullness and for which she could never forgive it" (151-52).

In Dhaka, the grandmother was growing like a honey comb. Her home was inhabited by so many branches of the family that they had become confused about their relationships. In the memory of grandmother, there was a crowded house, everyone living and eating together, her grandparents, her parents, she and Mayadebi, her Jethmoshai, her father's elder brother and his family.

When my father was about six, both my grandmother's parents died, a months of each other. My grandmother returned to Dhaka only twice after that, and then only to make sure that the rooms she and Mayadebi had inherited were still in intact. On both occasions she decided to go across and talk to her uncle and aunt but the house was full of painful memories now and both times she fled back to Mandalay after spending barely a day in Dhaka (124).

A radically new situation has emerged in post-independence culture in India. The cultural trauma has been resolved, history once again began anew. The strategy for dealing with the past has taken the form of a particular kind of nostalgia which is free from the old reflexive actions. The narrator refers to his investigation of the riots as "a voyage into land outside space", and it is "a land of looking-glass events" (224). By "looking-glass events", he means mutual reflexivity between the sphere of one's own and the sphere of our own. Notably, his concept of reflexivity derives from Tridib, who has ever told him "that one could never know anything except through desire, real desire, which was not the same thing as greed or lust; pure, painful and primitive desire" which "carried one beyond the limits of one's mind to other times and other places" (29). Tridib's "imagination with precision" is based on "real desire" or "pure, painful, primitive desire", by which one can imaginatively, albeit precisely, situate oneself in "other times and other places". The reflection between one and oneself contrasts markedly with the distinction between self and other. What is achieved by the praxis of reflexivity is hence depolarization, through which it becomes feasible to accelerate decentralization and decolonization. It is then worth drawing parallel between the narrator's depolarization and the polarization by his grandmother and cousin, Tha'mma and Ila.

As stated earlier, the narrator transforms his private story into the public history. Such transformation is also exemplified by Tha'mma. When she was schoolmistress, she wanted to make terrorist attack on the colonial government of the Empire. "It was for our freedom", she reflects, "7 would have done anything to be free" (39; emphasis added). Tha'mma has struggled for both personal and national freedom; that is, "her" private ideal of freedom is entirely defined by "our" public ideal of freedom. It is in this very point that her struggle for national freedom presents sharp contrast to Ila's desire for personal freedom: she leaves Calcutta for London simply because she wants to be free. Free of what? This is precisely the narrator's question, and "Free of *you*! she shouted back. Free of your bloody culture and all of you" (87).

The cultural process, of course, is multi-layered, but we nevertheless must discern the leading tendencies and make them the focus of our attention. That which is found on the periphery does not give birth to style. Only that which gives birth to and represents the stylistic system is important. In his article "Literary Fact" Tynianov noted that "every abnormality, every "mistake", every "irregularity" of the poetic norm is, potentially, a new constructive principle. One needs to keep in mind, however, that there are many "mistakes", "abnormalities" and "irregularities", and there is only one "poetic norm". In each case a picture of the future shows through in the present, along with the stains of the past.

In this way, reworked forms prove to be not just secondary, but ternary derivatives. There was a chance that Sots-art exploits Realism not so much thematically as aesthetically; through Socialist Realism it exploits the hated avant-garde. To quite similar cases from Soviet history and literature, the point is not that it is impossible to read the poetry of Prigov if one does not know Soviet ideological language, or that it is necessary to have a knowledge of Socialist Realist texts in order to read Sorokin's or Pelevin's prose or that, if you have not seen Piryev's film "The Tractor Drivers" (Traktoristy), then you won't understand "The Tractor Drivers-2", or that a knowledge of Soviet songs is needed if you wish to appreciate the popular television show "Old Songs About the Important Things" (Starye pesni o glavnom), which features modern stars of the Russian stage. These are just thematic and pragmatic concerns. Much more important is the derivative nature of the aesthetic, combined with history, which is the topic of this talk.

Amitav Ghosh has been extremely successful in combining narrative with history by using the time-slip fantasy technique. It is the author's ability to convince readers to "suspend disbelief". Some worry that fantasy takes time away from more important kinds of reading. Time-slip fantasy, however, is generally regarded as the most conservative of all fantasy literature. It does not deal with supernatural events, but uses a literary mechanism which allows readers to imaginatively move through time.

Over the last fifteen years, historical time-slip fantasy has become an intriguing alternative to pure historical fiction. At a time when historical novels typically do not make favourite library, time-slip fantasy can introduce readers to historical time periods and events in fascinating ways.

In order to make time-slip fantasies believable, Ghosh begins the novel by placing the protagonist in the present. The characters are typical contemporary with whom the reader can identify, whether it is Tridib, Ila or Nick and the beginning of the novel is spent in drawing the reader into the characters' world and problems. Once the authenticity of this contemporary world has been established, the protagonist experiences a time shift into either the past or the future with the help of older generation which is the grandmother in *The Shadow Lines*. Egoff (1988) reminds us, "It is time in the real world that stands still; the presence of the time traveler must be accounted for in the 'other' world" (132). Once placed into another time, the setting again becomes crucial to the believability of the fantasy, and authors expend an enormous amount of time and energy to develop 'place' in the other world. Descriptions are consistent in every detail. In fact, Norton (1989) maintains that so much detail is provided by the text that readers can create drawings that might appear on maps or in reference sources (79).

The Shadow Lines can then be seen as story of mirror-image relations between periods and between places "the contemporaneity" and "the past", "historical memory" and "the present", and "different times and places" and "one's own".

The time-slip novels have been recognized for their excellence both in critical reviews and through the various awards bestowed upon them, beyond a study of the genre itself, however, time-slip fantasy has helped the readers to develop insights into the human condition and capture the essence of their deepest emotions, dreams, hopes and fears through a journey to past and present. Time-slip fantasy has also proven itself to be a valuable vehicle for the study of the history of Indian subcontinent. It stirs emotions and adds a layer of understanding that the reader might not attain in any other way. Being able to span generations allows the reader to 'live' in two different times. Providing readers with opportunities to compare the historical context of stories with their own lives may help them to identify the "universal truths" that transcend generations and recognize that some aspects of life do indeed change over time. It would be contextual and pertinent to culminate this article with some immortal lines of poetry:

The dreamer awakes; The shadow goes by;
When I tell you a tale, The tale is a lie.
But ponder it well, Fair maiden, good youth:
The tale is a lie, what it tells is the truth.

(Carter, 2000, unpaginated)

WORKS CITED

Chouinard, Daniel, Mary, Rubio and Elizabeth, Waterston. "Editorial: Shifts in the Time-Slip Novel". *Canadian Children's Literature*, 67, p. 2, 1992.

Carter, Anne. *The Girl on Evangeline Beach*. Toronto: Stoddart Kids, 2000.

Downey, Matthew T. and Linda S. Levstik. "Teaching and Learning History: The Research Base". *Social Education*. (September): 336-42, 1988.

Egoff, Sheila A. *Worlds Within: Children's Fantasy from the Middle Ages to Today*. Chicago: American Library Association, 1988.

Ghosh, Amitav. *The Shadow Lines*. New Delhi: Oxford University Press, 1988.

Mukherjee, Meenakshi. "Maps and Mirrors: Co-ordinates of Meaning in *The Shadow Lines*". Ghosh, 255-67.

3

A Sense of Space and Time: *The Calcutta Chromosome*

Indira Nityanandam

> "We have now come to expect each new Amitav Ghosh book to be different from what has appeared before. The wistful evocation of memory to reflect on divisions of land and people in *The Shadow Lines* (1988) has nothing to do with the disjointed magic realism of his apprentice novel *The Circle of Reason* (1986). Neither however prepared any reader for the febrile frenzy of malaria research of *The Calcutta Chromosome* (1996) where the history of malaria research is spliced with this story of subaltern subversions of Western science", writes the critic Meenakshi Mukherjee. (www.indistar.com)

The Calcutta Chromosome defines a genre tag as it seems to combine all the ingredients of science fiction with that of a thriller, a subaltern text written in the post-colonial era and a whodunit of sorts. As with most of his novels, this one too has a wide sweep of both time and space and an entire gallery of characters from scientists and researchers to ordinary servants and helpers. With mosquito related research and malaria at the centre, the novel delves deep into many layers of experience. On first reading, one is left flabbergasted by the roller coaster ride but a second reading helps us understand better the artistic and thematic achievement. This paper attempts to analyse

Ghosh's use of time and space as tool of narration. John C. Hawley summarises the novelty of *The Calcutta Chromosome* when he writes:

> This novel marks something of a shift away from the exploration of personal memories and moves towards a metaphysical exploration of identity itself, suggesting at the same time that history as defined by the educated elites of the world is far less tamed than one might think. Thus, one's sense of self and of one's place in time becomes unhinged as the detective story unfolds. (156)

Every narrative needs a kind of time scheme. As E.M. Forster described it, a clock is ticking away in every piece of fiction. Writers could speed it up or slow it down or could attempt to set the hands forward or backward. In selecting a time scheme for his novel, an author can use the Aristotelian unity of time so that events of a novel occur/take place only in as much time as it takes to read the novel. On the other hand, a novelist may decide to contract or summarize time so that years may elapse between the first and last pages of the novel. The writer may choose to mix his time in a kaleidoscopic fashion so that the author aesthetically and effectively blends perception, memory and speculation. As Raban points out: "In his (a novelist's) narrative all known or expected time can be brought into focus on the immediate event, and in the process the novelist's clock is made to tell different times simultaneously" (57).

At the beginning of the twentieth century, a great change occurred in the writers' attitude towards time and space. Philosophers as well as scientists like Einstein, Bergson, Samuel Alexander, Herman Minkowsky, etc., were responsible in different degrees for initiating this change. Their enquiries and resultant theories led to a new approach among writers, especially novelists, who began to question as to whether time and space could be considered as totally separate and disparate entities. Virginia Woolf, considered to be the most brilliant of the Bloomsbury Group, rejected this division outright. She writes:

> Life is not a series of gig-lamps symmetrically arranged; life is a luminous halo, a semi-transparent envelope surrounding us from the beginning of consciousness to the end. Is it not the task of the novelist to convey this varying, this unknown and uncircumscribed spirit, whatever aberration or complexity it may display, with as little mixture of the alien and external as possible? (123)

Amitav Ghosh uses Time in a very unique and innovative way. The constant shifts between present and past events as 'time lived' and 'time remembered' in *The Shadow Lines* are further developed in *The Calcutta Chromosome*. Though it is not merely a science-fiction in the narrow sense of the term, the novel has all the ingredients of one. It is interesting to study the time and space shifts in this novel as it proves once again Ghosh's stature as a novelist willing to experiment in narrative techniques. As J.D. Soni writes, "Ghosh's *The Calcutta Chromosome* is kaleidoscope in structure, a little alteration makes a remarkable veering in pattern, uniting the past with the present with an aim to visualize the future" (196).

Ghosh has adopted the Bergsonian theory of 'duration'—not knowing past history or future progress—because to the undivided present no categorization of past, present or future is possible. *The Calcutta Chromosome* takes into its range an unspecified time in the future from the late nineteenth century. The novel opens with the present for Antar, which for us—the readers—is an unknown future date and then constantly shifts to various periods in the past, not chronologically but forwards and backwards. In remembering events, which are separated by immense patches of oblivion, man is constantly liberated from the order of time. Many of the characters often want to forget the immediate past but yearn to remember a more ancient past. From 'Mosquito Day'—August 20th—of some unspecified year in the future—we move with Ghosh's characters to years earlier when Antar was a little boy in Egypt, to a different time and place—a different continent. "Years ago" sets the tone of the novel because memory plays a vital role in the entire novel—events are often remembered to the minutest detail like the visit of the Hungarian archaeologist "with skin as brittle as a dried eucalyptus leaf" (*CC*, 5) or the "tactile nostalgia" (*CC*, 8) that he feels when "recalling the feel of those chains" (*CC*, 8). As Mukherjee says,

> If Ghosh ever drew his storyline on a blackboard he would end up with real granny's knot of a plot—each character's life intertwined with the others in some way or the other. As for direction, he proceeds in ever decreasing circles until he comes to the centre which is where he started in the first place. (38)

The naturalist writers had thought of Time and Space as separate entities as the classical physicists too had done. The Bloomsbury Group, especially Virginia Woolf first rejected this division. The time taken to recall events is very short in comparison to the time taken for the events to happen outside the mind, i.e. in space. Space, some later philosophers argued, is just a shallow foil to Time. Ghosh's novel exemplifies this dichotomy in the novelist's use of memory, "He recalled a meeting, a conversation somewhere, years ago sitting across a table. But as memory was beginning to take on an outline, it dissolved" (*CC*, 18). The blur of images helps further in dissolving the actual distances between past and present and future. This leads to a space-time continuum where myriads of impressions from different periods of one's life and experience coalesce to form sometimes even disconnected images. From Antar through Murugan we reach Sonali and Urmila and then Romen Haldar. Ghosh constantly seeks out people whose memory plays tricks. It is through Murugan again that we move backwards in time to the late nineteenth century and Ross and Lutchman, to Secunderabad and Calcutta and Austria. Gradually, 'time' or 'duration' or 'duree' as Bergson would have called it, becomes of prime import and consciousness then is only one aspect of it. We notice that throughout the novel, memories of the past, speculations about the future and worries of the present always intermingle.

As pointed out earlier, the novel begins in the future but very soon we are taken to a date in the past—21st August, 1995 and to Murugan's first day in Calcutta which happens to be 20th August, 1995. Interestingly, the novel was published in 1996. If we could look at 'time remembered' or the past in terms of 'recent past' and 'distant past', we realize that Ghosh intertwines the two masterfully. From 1995, we move, through Murugan's recapitulation of the details of Ross's research, into an earlier century—almost a hundred years ago—to 1895-98. A method often used by novelists to vary time is to vary the proportion of time allocated to particular incidents. Hence, an important single event and hence time span may be described in great detail while an entire century may be dismissed off in a single paragraph. By this handling of 'pace of time' Ghosh is able to draw the readers' attention to the relative importance or non-importance of events. Hence, Farley's visit to Cunningham's laboratory and his unexpected experiences there (though lasting only a couple of days) are dealt with in great detail. This could be also because the sweeper woman Mangala and the yet-to-named assistant are to play a major role in Ghosh's theory of science and counter-science. At this juncture in the novel, however, there is no hint of all that is to follow! Specific dates seem to appeal to Ghosh—maybe it is used by him as proof of his scrupulosity as a researcher. This could even be interpreted as a personal foible rather than an artistic or even technical necessity. Raban has called historical dates the "documentary decor" (59) of a novel.

In any analysis of a novel, usually place or location receives less importance in comparison to plot, theme, character, style, language, technique, etc. This may be slightly different when it comes to the Wessex of Hardy's novels or the Malgudi of R.K. Narayan's novels. Eudora Welty argues that it is place, "the named, identified, concrete, exact and exacting...gathering spot of all that has been felt" (57) that constitute the real essence of a story. Place concretises experience and helps the author see day-to-day experiences from a distinct point of view. This seems to give the entire work a sense of direction. This is in no way to take an extreme stand that every novel should be regional. Instead, by being rooted in a place, the novel gets an explicit, direct location where events and characters are firmly and directly rooted. In Ghosh, this place is not a single one but is a constantly shifting one—as much in place as it does in time. In most of Ghosh's novels, the sweep is not of towns and countries but of continents. Hence, we see that *The Calcutta Chromosome* begins in New York but moves with equal ease to Antar's childhood in Egypt, or to Murugan's "global childhood spent wandering between the world's capitals with his technocrat father...old American serials—the only constant—as for so many, in a peripatetic, internationalized coming-of-age" (30).

In this constant shifting to different parts of the world, Ghosh never forgets to provide a listing of places—whether known or unknown. With a traveller's penchant for the new or the untrodden, Ghosh writes of "...all the vast Unknown: Africa, Asia, Australia, the Americas, even uncolonised parts of herself" (Europe) (47). Occasionally, it could even be the oft-trodden like "the swamps around Rome, or in Algeria...in France, in Italy and the U.S...." (47-48). Later we are in "...South Africa, Malaysia, Singapore, Kenya" (75)—a virtual world-tour that this novel takes the reader on. With Ava being the best repository of memory, space and time blend superbly in cyberspace as Ava searches for Murugan's mail posted to Antar: "It was simply a question of matching the electronic fingerprints of Murugan's e-mail to every electronic signal that was still alive in the ionosphere" (107).

Places keep coming back in the novel—with different people having visited the same place in different periods. The best example of this is the remote town of Renupur: Elijah Farley disembarked there and disappeared without a trace, Mangala brought Cunningham's young assistant (later—Lakhan) from there, Phulboni had his eerie experience there and it is this that makes him believe that the villagers have their heads full of fantasies and superstitions. It is again here in Renupur that Lakhan "had drifted in from somewhere up the line" (232) and from where he later went to Sealdah. Calcutta, of course, is present all through the novel. *The Calcutta Chromosome* of the title is, according to Murugan, an artificially induced malarial parasite, which could cure or at least mitigate the dreaded 'syphilitic paresis'. Ghosh shows a keen sense of observation of the shapes, sounds and smells of places. Each place thus gets invested with a local flavour—be it war-ravaged London in *The Shadow Lines* or the crowded streets of Calcutta in *The Calcutta Chromosome*. The fresh fish which is the delight of every Bengali and scenes of the early morning fish-market, the crowded streets and stations, the shops in new market, the mosquito-ridden areas, the traffic build-up in Loudon Road—Ghosh exhibits a penchant and an excellent eye for detail.

The continuous time and place shifts provide an extra dimension to the novel. The blurring of past, present and future provides an innovative, experimental touch to the novel.

WORKS CITED

Ghosh, Amitav. *The Calcutta Chromosome*. New Delhi: Ravi Dayal, 1996.

Hawley, John C. *Amitav Ghosh*. New Delhi: Foundation, 2005.

Kumar, Shiv K. and Keith, Mckean. Ed. *Critical Approach to Fiction*. New York: Mcgraw Hill, 1968.

Mukherjee, Meenakshi. Review in *India Today*. May 15, 1996.

Raban, Raban. *The Technique of Modern Fiction*. London: Edward Arnold, 1968.

Subramanyam, N.S. *Movements in Modern English Novel*. Gwalior: Kitab Ghar, 1967.

Soni, J.D. "The Calcutta Chromosome: A Miracle of Rare Device", in *The Fiction of Amitav Ghosh*, Ed. Indira Bhatt and Indira Nityanandam. New Delhi: Creative Books, 2001.

Welty, Eudora. "Place in Fiction" in *The South Atlantic Quarterly*, Vol. LV, No. 1 (Jan. 1956), 57-72.

Woolf, Virginia. *The Common Reader I Series*.

4

Legitimacy of Subaltern in *In an Antique Land*: A Discourse on Indivisibility of the World

Deepak Thakur

The issues that figure most prominently in Ghosh's writings are: the creation of nation-states and the concept of nationalism which is deeply ingrained in the psyche of modern man and arouses myriads of doubts in Ghosh regarding its authenticity. Nationalism creates artificial lines across the globe. Despite the tightly drawn lines, borders remain porous that indicate their failure and justify the view of the author about the basic undivided and unified nature of the world. He delves into history and retrieves instances from it that prove the fundamentally unified character of the world. He also attempts to highlight the negative aspect of nationalism and nation-states, their artificial and imagined nature especially in the contemporary times, and points towards a *priori* indivisible character of the world. It is this worldview that perceives the world in an indivisible unity and makes him approach the study of history and historiography from an entirely different angle. This approach to history is characterized by the thrust on the subaltern thereby perceiving the world in its fundamental unity.

The mainstream history, in fact, concentrates on the dominant groups. The subaltern historians, on the contrary deal directly with the "autonomous domain" peopled by the average commoners. Their deductions, based on the exploration of history of ordinary people, acquire a divergent point of view that negates the conclusions of official historians. Amitav Ghosh is one among such writers who reroutes his historical attention to focus on those who, on account of their inconsequential role in the history of the world, fail even to merit a footnote in the history. This occupation of Ghosh has been noticed by Alok Kumar and Madhusudan Prasad thus:

> And history it is, in a way—a history of the micro-structures of tradition or history of Little Tradition as opposed the Great Tradition, concepts first used by Robert Redfield. The Little Tradition comprises the study of the folks or unlettered peasants as opposed to that of the elite, and *In an Antique Land* is the history of the "fellah", the common peasant of Egypt. It is properly speaking "subaltern" history. (184)

In unearthing the stories of these subaltern people he is in a way expressing his worldview that envisages a cosmopolitan world—undivided and undemarcated—that postulates a mutual co-existence among the divergent communities. It is this phenomenon that has become an anomaly in the present day world, which is divided on the grounds of nationalities.

In an Antique Land is an extraordinarily superb effort in the direction of delving into an unexplored region of history. The objective is to claim a legitimate space to the subaltern consciousness that represents an ethos of unity and wholeness. The seed of the book lies in a significantly ordinary event when the author, a graduate student in anthropology at Oxford, chances upon a letter written in 1139 A.D. by a merchant from Aden named Khalaf ibn Ishaq. The letter was addressed to Abraham Ben Yiju, a merchant from Tunisia living at that point of time in Mangalore, India. The writer of the letter and the addressee were no more significant and distinguished than thousands of traders who unobtrusively carried the business in the Indian Ocean across the continents without altering and directing the course of history and events of the time. The letter by Khalaf ibn Ishaq and another one written in 1148 catch the attention of the author on account of mention in both letters of Ben Yiju's slave (*IAAL,* 16). It is in search of the identity of the slave that leads Ghosh to Egypt and exploration of the documents of the time. The question about the identity is not less important in view of the recent developments in the historiography that intends to deviate from the "The Great Man Theory of History" (Lal, 9) and treads the subaltern grounds that becomes an important tool in perceiving the world as an undivided single whole.

The letters that finds mention of the slave launches the author on the journey of discovery of the true identity of the man and the quest takes him to Egypt in 1980. Ben Yiju's letters and other documents of the period were written in the language known as Judaeo-Arabic. This dialect in which Ben Yiju and his trader colleagues were conversant, the scholar-writer Ghosh comes to know, bore a close resemblance to the dialect spoken in villages called Lataifa and Nashawy. That is the reason that the writer decides to install himself there.

As the search for the name of the slave and his antecedents intensifies, he experiences two divergent worlds—the cosmopolitan world of the medieval times and the modern world divided into nation-states. The past supports the worldview of the author and takes "a form of commentary that uses the past to speak indirectly about the present" (Dixon, 21). In these two timeframes, the journeys of two individuals belonging to different civilizations are presented with a view to contrast the medieval and the modern world. One is that of Ben Yiju, a Jewish merchant from Tunisia who came to India via Egypt and Aden in 1132 A.D. and lived in India for almost seventeen years. The other is that of the author who visits Egypt in 1980, 1988 and 1990. The motive behind the said narrative technique is to probe subaltern terrain in human life and present an alternative view of history that brings out a borderless world. The author's regret at the loss of this world reflects his worldview. Ghosh manages to assemble the lost world of syncretism. The search for the slave unfolds a world characterized by catholicity where the people of different regions and religions across the globe co-existed peacefully, blissfully indifferent to their cultural and religious disparities. It is in retrieval of this lost world that stands in sharp contrast to the modern world that the worldview of the author gets reflected.

We come to know that Ben Yiju, the master of the slave, belonged to "Ifriqiya—in the Mediterranean port of Mahdia, now a large town in Tunisia" (*IAAL,* 153). Born in the last years of eleventh century or in the beginning of the 12th in a Jew family, he chose the career of trading in the Indian Ocean. The Jew community had already attained a professional specialization in the said trade. Having decided upon the career, it was inevitable that he would follow the most accepted path of travelling from Tunisia to Fustat, from there to Aden and sailing the sea-routes to India. In Aden, Ben Yiju had many friends. Khalaf ibn Ishaq, the writer of the letter of MS H.6, was probably his closest friend. The traders whose fortune depended on this business that was carried between India and the Middle East travelled frequently in the Indian Ocean. Abu Said Halfon, one of the traders who was a rich merchant, scholar and patron of literature and whose papers were preserved in the Geniza "was resident in different countries and continents, travelling frequently between Egypt, India, East Africa, Syria, Morocco and Spain" and his "writing bear witness to a pattern of movement so fluent and far-ranging that they make the journeys of later medieval travellers, such as Marco Polo and Ibn Battuta, seem unremarkable in comparison" (*IAAL,* 157).

It was a unique and unparalleled world where borders were non-existent. In 1132, for instance, Ghosh records, Ben Yiju moved to Malabar Coast in Mangalore and for almost two decades made India his home. Ben Yiju, during this time, married an Indian girl, Ashu. It was the marriage that reveals the world that dissolved differences of religion, culture and region, the factors that became the potent bases of nationality and nation-hood eighteenth century onwards.

The subaltern sources in *In an Antique Land* divulge extraordinary facts of the medieval time. The Malabar Coast and Calicut which was a few miles to the south were the places where the expatriate merchant community traded and settled without any sense of alienation or foreignness. Quoting Duarte

Barbosa, a Portuguese sailor, Ghosh says, the "merchants included 'Arabs, Persians, Guzarates, Khorasanys and Decaynys'" and it was Middle Eastern travellers who gave this part of the coast the Arabic name 'Malabar' (*IAAL,* 243).

The question that baffles is as to how Ben Yiju and number of expatriate merchants conducted their business with the Indians who came from varied linguistic regions. How Ben Yiju communicated with his slave who, as far as the writer knows from the documents, was not conversant with Arabic and "what language did Ben Yiju speak with Ashu, for instance?" (*IAAL,* 280). This language was a convenient mixture of Perso-Arabic and many north Indian dialects. The device of this hybrid language facilitated the existence and sustenance of the multiculturalism which was the hallmark of the time. It stands in direct contrast with the contemporary time in which nations are being divided on account of the issue of language.

The relationship between Bomma and Ben Yiju, thus, is another instance that reflects Ghosh's worldview which, in fact, is a means through which an artist perceives and interprets the world thereby deriving meaning out of it. Ghosh retrieves the subaltern from the history and interprets it in cosmopolitan light.

In an Antique Land, as mentioned earlier, moves between two time frames: the past, the medieval world of Ben Yiju and his slave and the present in which Ghosh stays in Egypt in pursuance of his research. The choice of the time frames are intentional on the part of the author to highlight the difference between the cosmopolitan nature of the world inhabited by Ben Yiju and Bomma and the modern world that creates divisions on the basis of religion, culture and nationality.

Lataifa and Nashawy are the two Nile Delta villages in Egypt where the author "installs" himself. They are Muslim villages and Ghosh, a "Hindu by default" (*IAAL,* 47), finds him surrounded by the people of different cultures. Their understanding of his culture is so inadequate that wherever he goes he is invaded with questions regarding the practices of Hinduism. They are invariably amazed and shocked at the customs and practices of the Hinduism. Once, for instance, in Lataifa he is asked by Ustaz Mustafa whether it is not a part of his religious belief to worship cows. The reaction that is evoked among the listeners is that of blasphemous scandal. "There was", the writer notices, "a sharp, collective intake of breath as Jabir and the other boys recoiled, calling upon God, in whispers, to protect them from the Devil" (*IAAL*, 47). In these villages where people judge and relate on the basis of their religious and cultural conditionings, Ghosh is an anomaly since the country he comes from seems to follow bizarre customs and beliefs—they worship cows, burn their dead and the most appalling of all, they are not circumscribed. The beliefs of the other culture somehow do not fit in their framework of thought/conditionings. Their non-acceptance and intolerance of them reflects the division that runs deep into the minds to the point of unbridgeable exclusivity. Khameez the Rat once asks him whether it is true that in his country they burn their dead. The reaction of Busaina, one among the group, that his countrymen should mend their ways and should do the thing in proper manner, reveals the extent of lack of acceptability of another culture. During the Ramadan when almost everyone in the village is fasting, the writer wants to join in the fast. He is reminded in a categorical statement that he cannot do so. "No, you can't fast; you're not Muslim—only Muslims fast at Ramadan" (*IAAL*, 75). While visiting "mowlid" dedicated to the memory of a saintly man known as Sidi Abu-Hasira, Ghosh writes about his encounter with the official with an object of bringing out the contrast between the two worlds and times:

> He was not trying to intimidate me; I could tell he was genuinely puzzled. He seemed so reasonable and intelligent, that for an instant I even thought of telling him the story of Bomma and Ben Yiju. But then it struck me, suddenly, that there was nothing I could point to within his world that might give credence to my story—the remains of those small, indistinguishable, intertwined histories, Indian and Egyptian, Muslim and Jewish, Hindu and Muslim, had been partitioned long ago [...].

> I had been caught straddling a border [...]. (*IAAL*, 339-40)

Ghosh, as has been argued, takes up the cause of the subaltern from history, and presents a world without borders. In contrast to the "multicultural bazaar" of the past, the present is shown as fragmented.

Nevertheless, despite all the perceptible divisions, his worldview perceives an inherent unity that runs deep and transcends all differences. A few flashes of the underlying unity, however, never fail to reappear and catch attention of the author. It is through his worldview that Ghosh discerns "a world of accommodations" despite its conspicuous extermination which, the writer feels, is "still alive, and, in some tiny measure, still retrievable" (*IAAL*, 237). Thus, he interprets the world primarily on cosmopolitan lines. There is presence of borders but they remain for him artificial and false.

That is precisely why during his stay in Egypt, he never fails to notice those common threads that run through mankind despite their differences in creed, culture and religion. When it comes to the basic human emotions, instincts and needs, people's response is alike. In Lataifa, for instance, where his presence caused an awkward unease on account of the difference in beliefs and religious practices, it was quite normal to see some of the inhabitants giving him discourse on relative superiority of the Islam. It was in one of such encounters that one day the author met Ustaz Mustafa who, after discourse on the incomparability of his religion, advised him that he should convert and become a Muslim. He was sure that if his father had read the holy books of Islam he would surely have converted himself. While Ustaz Mustafa was arguing thus, a sudden thought struck his mind and he asked if it would upset his father if the writer changed his religion. When Ghosh replied that it might, he suddenly stopped and said, "Well, it would not be right for you to upset your father. That is true" (*IAAL*, 52). Ghosh observes:

> After that the heart went out of his efforts to convert me: he had a son himself and it went against his deepest instincts to urge a man to turn against his father. And

> so, as the rival moralities of religion and kinship gradually played themselves to a standstill within him, Ustaz Mustafa and I came to an understanding. (*IAAL*, 52)

The "understanding", Ghosh intends to imply, relates to the domains of those basic human emotions that are commonly shared by mankind. On this level the differences of belief simply melt and give way to the collective experience that unites human beings.

This is the reason why Ghosh has been able to strike a lasting relationship of genuine friendship with many of them. They may be living with their own beliefs and creed, but when it comes to human relatedness the said beliefs and creed are relegated to the background. Shaikh Musa, a devout and staunch Muslim, is one of those whose friendship with the writer comprises one of the poignant aspects of the book. It is for him that Ghosh brings a pocket Quran as a gift when he goes to Cairo. Shaikh Musa keeps the Quran with loving cherish. When Ghosh revisits him after a long span of eight years, Shaikh Musa shows the Quran to him that he has treasured with love as a tender gift from a dear friend. On learning that Shaikh Musa'a younger son has passed away, the writer's sorrow at the news and his sharing of grief with his friend is an instance that touches the human chord. Ghosh illustrates a rare human bonding that transcends narrow nationalistic considerations. His friendship with Nabeel is yet another instance that transcends the restrictive borders of culture.

It is not only in human relations that Ghosh notices the concurrence that rises above the differences of petty ethnicity; he also discerns the characteristic similarity in the nature of beliefs, legends and stories that are associated with religious faith. Folklores and myths that are generally linked with the saintly figures may have different names, situations and locales, but the similitude that they exhibit in respect of spirit of religious faith is an evidence of fundamental unity of the world. Ghosh came to Mangalore, the place Bomma belonged to. He came there hoping to solve the mystery of name and identity of the slave named Bomma. During the stay, the writer came across many Bhuta shrines. The shrines were the places of worship for those who were the followers of the Bhuta-cult. The writer wanted to visit one of these shrines but every time he planned, it did not materialize. One day, he got an opportunity to visit the shrine with a taxi driver who happened to be a devotee of the Bhutta cult. He struck a conversation with the Pujari who told him that many stories and legend about the shrine. When the port of Mangalore was completed, he told, it was decided to connect it with the city. It was soon discovered that if the work were to go ahead according to the plan, it would directly cut through the shrine. The people protested but the engineers ignored them. One day the engineers arrived with their bulldozers to demolish the shrine. To their utter consternation, as they proceeded, the machines and bulldozers got immobilized. Despite their concerted effort, the work got stalled. Finally the road was diverted by skirting around the shrine. The story had now entered the folklore of the people. The driver turning to the writer asked if Ghosh had heard anything like that. The author suddenly recalled that once he had heard a similar story in Egypt (*IAAL, 265-66*).

As a matter of fact, the story was told by Zaghloul to the writer in Nashawy. Sidi Abu-Kanaka was a saintly figure who lived long time before the birth of Zaghloul. He was a well-known figure and when he died the villagers made him a special grave in their cemetery. It was a sacred tomb for the villagers and they believed that the Sidi was their protector. It so happened that the government came out with the plan of building a canal for the area to serve the farmers. The work proceeded well till it reached the cemetery. The villagers were shocked and offended that the work of the canal would disturb their dead—a sacrilege as per their belief. They appealed to the authorities who turned deaf ears to their request.

The villagers watched with mute anger as the workers dug and ploughed the graves of their ancestors. But one day something unusual happened. One grave refused to yield to spades. Repeated efforts came to a sheer naught. The officials were baffled. They consulted the elders of the village who told them that the grave belonged to Sidi Abu-Kanaka. "And so it happened that the canal was made to take a slight diversion there, and on that plot of land the people of the village built a maqam for the Sidi" (*IAAL*, 138-40).

The similarity between the two stories is striking. The places are different: one is Mangalore in India and the other a small village in Egypt; the people belonging to these places follow different religious beliefs: one follows Bhuta cult and the other Islam. As such, there seems not even the remotest possibility of any kind of relationship between the two. While listening to one story, the writer is reminded spontaneously of the other as if his mind has struck upon something common between these two divergent religions.

Others may limit their sight to the differences among cultural groups but for Ghosh, they are merely varied shades while the light, the source, is identical. His worldview sees beyond differences and recognizes that component of mankind that has survived and sustained a constant onslaught of divisions. That is why he is aware of survival of Bamma's world that has continued "in defiance of the enforcers of history" (*IAAL*, 342).

WORKS CITED

1. Dixon, Robert. "Travelling in the West: The Writings of Amitav Ghosh", *The Journal of Commonwealth Literature,* 31, (1996): 3-24.
2. Ghosh, Amitav. *In an Antique Land.* New Delhi: Ravi Dayal, 1992. All citations are from this edition and marked *IAAL.*
3. Kumar, Alok, and Madhusudan, Prasad. "The Novels of Amitav Ghosh: A Study in the Sociology of the Symbol". *Symbolism in Indian Fiction in English.* Ed. Ramesh K. Srivastava. Bombay: ABS Publications, 1997.
4. Lal, Vinay. "A Meditation on History", *Social Scientist,* 21, (1993): 8-98.

5

Feminine Consciousness in Amitav Ghosh's Novels

Anju Bala Agrawal

Amitav Ghosh's novels claim a unique position in the postcolonial literature. Portrayals of women in his fiction is neither overt radical feminists nor the stereotypical images of Sita and Savitri. In his novels he shows the cultural complexities and feminine consciousness through family relationships. Her women are mostly independent women earning their livelihood and sometimes engaged in social work also. To some extent, her women are empowered and need no help of male to survive. Ghosh's women characters are central to his narrative. They function as signs rather than as subjects with a will and consciousness. This paper throws a light on female characters of Ghosh.

In *The Circle of Reason*, we find many male and female characters as passengers of the rickty boat Mariamma which is taking them to al-Ghazira as migrant labourers. Incidentally, 'Mariam' is the south Indian name for Mary, and Mariamma means for Mother Mary, which means 'amma' (mother in Tamil). Apart from male characters Alu, Balram, village landlord Bhudeb, Rakesh, Professor Samuel, there are several female characters travelling on the same boat. Among them, main figure is Zindi, a 'madam' who runs a house of prostitution in al-Ghazira after she was banished from her matrimonial home on account of her barrenness. Karthamma and Kulfi have been picked up by Zindi to be prostitutes. These women's condition is the most illustrative of revolt and oppression, betterment and loss. When Professor Samuel sees the Indian women who are going to al-Ghazira to be prostitutes in Zindi's house as enslaved and exploited: "She's a madam...if she wasn't, why would she be herding these poor prisoners in the cabin? I tell you, she's going to sell them into slavery in al-Ghazira. Something like that. Or worse" (*CR*, 173). On the other hand, Zindi's perspective is different. She not only sees herself as being of help to the women, but she also insists that the relations between them are not of 'business' but of 'family':

> And, as for women, why, when I get to India I don't have to do anything. These women find me and come running. Take me, Zindi-no, me, Zindi-didi—don't take her, she's got lice. They go on like that. But I don't take them all. I take only the good girls—clean, polite, hardworking. That's why I have to go to India myself to look...the whole of al-Ghazira knows that Zindi's girls are reliable and hardworking...and so I get a little extra, too, not much. It's not a business; it's my family, my aila, my own house, and I look after them, all the boys and girls, and no one's unhappy and they all love me. (*CR*, 181)

Zindi and Samuel's conversation expresses the situation of the migrant women as commodity ("I take only the good girls", "she's going to sell them"), a labourer ("Zindi's girls are hardworking and reliable"), a daughter ("my family.... I look after them"), as a "prisoner", and a "slave". Actually at *Mariamma*, migrant women are both enslaved as well as "free". They are speaking agents and abject subjects. To quote, "they don't look like prisoners.... They seemed quite happy to come onto the boat" (*CR*, 173).

Karthamma is pregnant. Her labour has started and she should deliver the baby there on the boat but she refuses to give birth to a child. If we take her desire for a house and a car and everything else for her child literally, we may interpret it as a general desire for material comfort for her unborn child and the forms as the instrumental means to go about attaining it. Figuratively, forms are marked by a desire for 'home': home as a place of comfort, as a sense of rootedness and belonging, as a future time of a secure life. For Karthamma, 'home' is not just the domestic space of a house, but also to a community (national or otherwise) in which one has a place. Her fixation on the forms whose names she doesn't even know demonstrates the extent of power that those disempowered imagine as held by bureaucracy and the law. The forms indicate not only a bureaucratized, regulated experience of life and Karthamma's faith in it, but also hold out the promises of a middle-class lifestyle in a capitalist nation state. Karthamma imagines a new life for her child.

In *The Shadow Lines*, the narrator has close relationship with the three major women characters—Tha'mma, Ila and May. The narrator's grandmother is called Tha'mma in the family and that is how we know her throughout the novel. She grows up in the tumultuous days of the Indian freedom struggle in Dhaka and is fiercely nationalist. She reveals to the narrator that she had once dreamed of joining the Bengali revolutionaries who struggled to overthrow the mantle of colonial oppression and she would have readily killed a British officer but for husband's work, she migrates to Calcutta in the thirties when he suddenly dies. A relative arranges a job for her to teach in a school. There she singlehandedly raises her children proudly refusing all help from family and friends. Fervently patriotic, she has embraced the anti-colonial nationalism in whose revolutionary activities she could not participate directly because she was a woman.

Ila occupies a central position in the novel in relation to the narrator's exploration of self-identity. Ila represents a post-colonial female perspective. Out of the reach of the conservative, restrictive, patriarchal society of Calcutta, she leads an independent life in London and makes her own rules, but she is inextricably trapped between the two cultures in rejecting one and being rejected by the other in turn. Ila is the privileged daughter of a diplomat and attempts to articulate a cosmopolitanism. She has grown up in different parts of the world. She visits India in the summer holidays but she decides to study and live in England. The reason behind this decision is that Ila can't tolerate Indian patriarchal oppression. An incident clears this notion. There is a confrontation between Ila and her cousin Robi at a discotheque in Calcutta. Robi denies Ila to dance with any man but she defiantly begins to dance on the dance floor with a stranger. Robi hits the stranger and drags Ila out of the disco, saying that "girls don't behave like that here...it's our culture" (*SL*, 87). Ila, furious and crying, shouts at the narrator, "Do you see why I've chosen to live in London? Do you see? It's only because I want to be free.... Free in your bloody culture and free of all of you" (*Ibid.*).

She marries to Nick Price to incorporate herself into the dominant Western culture, but it only serves to perpetuate her marginalization. When the narrator, commenting on Nick's sleeping with other women after his marriage to Ila, she tells her that her sins have finally come home to roost.... "I'm about as chaste, in my own way, as any woman you'll ever meet" (*SL*, 190). Ila is the only cosmopolitan woman in the novel, but her cosmopolitanism is constructed as suspect as she is not rooted in any one culture, like the inherent Indianness of Robi or the Englishness of Nick. Both of them share Ila's globetrotting background. Ila reveals herself as having shaped her values on the conservative, Indian norm even as she outwardly struggled against them. She maintained her 'chastity' in spite of trying to be free of the bloody Indian culture, and rebelling against the suppression of female sexuality.

The grandmother also desires freedom from British subjection but she doesn't like Ila's desire of freedom. "It's not freedom she wants...she wants to be left alone to do what she pleases; that's all any whore would want. She'll find it easily enough over there; that's what those laces have to offer. But that is not what it means to be free" (*SL*, 88). In fact, the grandmother's notion of freedom as liberty from colonial subjection refuses Ila's notion of personal freedom, but for both, the source of freedom is either the nation or a migrant, metropolitan cosmopolitanism.

May price emerges as the only woman whose movement towards freedom is posited as real and endorsed by the narrator, unlike the illusions of Tha'mma and Ila. May is Tridib's love across the sea. Tridib starts writing to May at the age of twenty-seven, when she's nineteen. He knew May since he was eight and she was a baby. Some five years after he starts writing to her, May visits India, and a visit to Dhaka, which includes Tha'mma and Tridib, is also planned. In the course of retrieving Tha'mma's geriatric uncle from their ancestral house in Dhaka, the old uncle, Tridib and Khalil, the Rickshaw puller are killed. The actual manner of their death is recounted by May many years later to the narrator, who sees in the manner of Tridib's death the falsity of many notions. May has since moved on to activities and interests related to a global humanitarianism. As we see, when she gets out of the car to save the oldman, "your grandmother...said...I'd get everyone killed. I didn't listen; I was a heroine" (*SL*, 250). May's path to freedom lies in her realization that she is not guilty of causing Tridib's death. She leads a guilt-ridden tortuous path for many years; lives out a self-abnegating and ascetic existence, but is finally able to hold out a glimpse of the last redemptive mystery (*SL*, 252).

In *The Glass Palace*, women act as independent entities, growing and developing according to their own inclinations and finding social acceptance, defining their own space, determining their own lives, fighting their own follies, enjoying the fruits of victory and never fearing to taste the bitterness of defeat. Most of the women characters are shown as determining the major decisions of their own lives. Besides it, they are invested with national consciousness. In *The Glass Palace*, the strength and sanity of the woman is shown in the case of Ma Cho. Raj Kumar, who works as a keeper to Ma Cho, views her at nights and learns about female anatomy and even gets his first physical sensations through her. But Ma Cho resists herself and refrains from getting into any physical intimacy with him. This shows her thinking process, quite sane and normal, and this seems to be a regular pattern, in Ghosh's novels, where woman stands as a preserver of cultural and spiritual essence.

Similarly, when the English force Burmese king Theban and queen Supayalat to exile, Dolly, a young girl looking after the princess, becomes physically intimate with one of the local servants, Sawant. But Sawant is snatched from her by the princess, who herself is in need of a man. She is hurt, emotionally confused and yet when Uma coaxed her to marry Raj Kumar, she agrees to do so because she thinks that marriage being a sacrament in the Hindu context, is the only suitable career open to a woman. But even though Dolly nurses her child Dinu, perceiving her role as a mother more important, yet a feeling of emptiness spreads within her and she feels: "I couldn't go back to the life I've led before" (*GP*, 235).

Dolly gracefully accepts the pain and suffering and even though she has a strong desire for renunciation after her visit to a Buddhist nunnery, yet stops herself as she is deeply committed to her responsibilities. But later on, she proves her indomitable spirit and strength of convictions in ultimately entering the monastery and withdrawing from the world. Dolly is an emblem of the endurance and acceptance. She stands for courage, honour, hope, compassion and sacrifice. Her tenacity of spirit lifts the other characters. There is a feeling that feminine virtues such as obedience, humility and patience encourage woman to give in to oppression. But it is important to remember that obedience is not the same as subservience, humility not the same as masochism, and patience not the same as impotence. Women possessing these qualities are to be treated as persons on equal footing with men. Dolly shows that a woman can fulfill herself in a loving and harmonious relationship with others. What governs her is the act of giving, a deep concern for the other, which is a point of profound significance.

Uma is a woman of substance. After her husband's sudden and tragic death, she travels abroad. She is quite the equal of many respectable and cultured Western women in similar circumstances. She does not like to spend time in leisured ease. She later joins Indian Nationalistic Movement and is part of the intelligentsia of the subcontinent in a peculiarly displaced way. She is imbued in a culture that gives her what Said terms an almost "aggressive sense of nation, home, community and belonging" and she is, like most of Ghosh's other protagonists, "a citizen of the world" (Said, 12). Uma Dey who leads the conservative, sheltered life of an early twentieth century Bengali lady has no difficulty in adjusting to life in America and Europe. In fact, Ghosh's women have a cosmopolitan outlook, so essential in this era of globalization.

Ghosh's *The Hungry Tide* creates a sustainable ecology where human life is as changeable as the ebb and flood of water. The novel presents women's distinct experiences through Nilima and Kusum on one hand and Piyali Roy and Moyana Mandal on the other. While Nilima and Kusum represent the yesteryears, Piyali and Moyana belong to the current time. Kusum, a tribal woman, felt as an outsider and she, with self-assertion returns to the tide country-Bhatir Desh, the tide country in the Sunderbans. She asks for Nilima's help to safeguard her people but Nilima refuses, as she could not go against the government. Kusum, in the novel, reveals that women neither are naturally submissive nor uncomplaining, nor incapable of protest at the structures of the society. Though Horen wishes to marry Kusum and provide security, she never felt the need. She chose Horen at the last hour of her life as a tribute to his life-long concern. Ghosh points out that women like Kusum are capable of turning social norms to suit themselves. Kusum represents nature as a woman, with a hint of eco-feminism, and reshapes the culture with the help of her male counterparts. Kusum is the most inspiring character for she voices the innate tragic bewilderment of human civilization—the eternal tangle between progress and poverty; fauna and food; conservation and sustenance. On hearing the policeman's announcements that the island had to be saved for its trees, that it belonged to a project to save tigers, Kusum ruminates: "Who are these people, I wondered, who love animals so much that they are willing to kill us for them?" (*HT*, 262).

Nilima Mashima belonged to an aristocratic family with a good educational background and based on the reforms of

Raja Ram Mohan Roy, prepared a suitable ground for women to play active roles outside their limited family circle. The empowering elite section was in the process of converting the traditional past to modernity that percolated as a new sensibility about women's duties and responsibilities. Nilima is no exception and she remains well within possible and practicable limits. She, against the wishes of her family, marries Nirmal, a political radical and leftist. After marriage, they come to Lusibari Island to settle and start their respective missions. Nirmal teaches in a local school and gets distracted in the settlers' intrinsic problems of living and existence. Nilima has made a trust. She raises funds for building a hospital and school in 'Lusibari' for reforming and civilizing the settlers' life. Both of them are satisfied in their own way. Nirmal, a little before his retirement, somehow reaches an island of this region named 'Morichjhapi' and there during some struggle, he becomes mentally disturbed and dies after some time. Nilima has a deep love for him, but she faces his loss with bravery and remains engaged in her NGO's activities.

Piya Roy is the daughter of Bangla parents who had immigrated to Seattle. She's a woman used to the solitude and rigors of the life of a scientist working in the field. Piya often works in areas where she knows neither the customs nor the language, and can survive for days on just energy bars and Ovaltine as she studies river dolphins. She's come to the Sundarbans to find more of these rare creatures and live with Nilima. Piyali Roy belongs to the present generation, a cytologist researching marine mammals, a rare profession for women. Her tenacious spirit to explore the penetrating secrets of nature, extends her stay in India. Piyali is aware of her vulnerable conditions as a scientist and has abandoned emotional language for the pure objective discourse of science. She is highly ambitious and the basic difference between her and Nilima is their definition of home. To Piyali, her career is her life, "home is where the Oracella are". Nilima, in spite of all her social work, remains a traditional lady and for her "home is where I can brew a pot of good tea" (*HT*, 400). Moyna, another woman character in the novel, is a woman with soaring aspirations, unlikely for a tribal group. Fokir, a local fisherman is her husband, but she works in the hospital and brings up her little boy. Fokir's personality becomes dim before her. But altogether, all the women characters share a commonality of experience. It was their desire for continuous reaffirmation that made them strong. They never lose their faith in the essential grandeur of their existence.

Amitav Ghosh's *Sea of Poppies* is the first volume in a projected trilogy. The novel is a vehicle for what Ghosh hopes, will be a completely new way of understanding the origin and dispersal of the Indian diaspora around the world today and the role of the British empire in that process. The story begins with Deeti, a simple, pious lady, caring mother and an efficient housewife. Deeti is a young mother living by the Ganges some 50 miles east of Benares. She grows poppies because she must (the destruction of the rural economy is of no concern to the British), but though she is not in any conventional sense a user, opium has infiltrated deep into her family life.

Married to Hukam Singh, a crippled worker in the Ghazipur Opium Factory, the unfortunate Deeti figures out that on her wedding night, she was drugged with opium by her mother-in-law, so that her brother-in-law could consummate the marriage in place of her infertile husband. This brother-in-law is the real father of Deeti's daughter Kabutri. When her husband dies, Deeti sends Kabutri to stay with relatives. Deeti looks almost certain to meet her doom when she chooses to go through with the *sati* ritual (immolation on her husband's funeral pyre), but then Kalua, the ox man from the neighbouring village, comes to her rescue. The couple flees and unites but this is not acceptable to their fellow villagers. In order to escape Deeti's in-laws, she and Kalua become indentured servants on the Ibis. Many of the women who fled India as coolies were indeed upper-caste widows, but there were no brawny heroes to snatch them from their fates. They simply left, alone—an act dramatic enough for that time and place.

She is completely ordinary in every way, except for her ability to see "visions". With this character development, it might seem as though the book is taking a typical turn into the exotic world of rural India, with its spirits and spooky romance, but this is far from the case. Deeti's journey is the most real experience that can be written about, a journey where she leaves home, finds love, becomes a leader, fights evil, and as a village woman, rises to the most extraordinary heights in a novel that also includes a dashing and good-hearted American sailor, a caring oxcart rider, various sketchy seamen, a dorky young French orphan, a Chinese opium addict, and an Indian raja. Deeti has a mystical quality that nags. Wading in the Ganges at the novel's start, she envisions a ship "like a great bird, with sails like wings and a long beak" (8). The novel opens with the vision of a ship which Deeti sees:

> The vision of a tall-masted ship, at sail on the ocean, came to Deeti on an otherwise ordinary day, but she knew apparition was a sign of destiny for she had never seen such a vessel before, not even in a dream: how could she have, living as she did in northern Bihar, four hundred miles from the coast? (*SP*, 3)

Though she has never before laid eyes on a schooner like the Ibis, she somehow knows that it is coming for her. At the— novel's close, lying one night on the deck of this same vessel, she holds a poppy seed between her fingers. "Here", she tells her lover. "Taste it. It is the star that took us from our homes and put us on this ship. It is the planet that rules our destiny" (*SP*, 462). On the Ibis, she acts as a leader among other ladies.

Thus, Ghosh portrays women as life givers, sustainers and continuers of the race as well as women in search of an identity. The women in Amitav Ghosh's novels negotiate with her milieu to arrive at justifiable resolutions and each attempt is an accomplishment in itself. In continuity of the tradition developed by Tagore, Narayan and Sahgal, Ghosh develops women who are strong and can express themselves and come to their decisions. They are out of the purposive control of men and make their own way. Zindi, Karthamma, Tha'mma, Ila, Dolly, Uma, Piyali, Nilima, Moyana, Kusum, Deeti are makers of their fate. Nowhere we have found them dependent on men. They have their own identity and carry on whatever they want to do in their life. They are symbols of growth, progress and movement. His women characters break the pattern of sexuality and sensuality and take their place as whole human beings freely and equally along with men.

WORKS CITED

Ghosh, Amitav. *The Circle of Reason*, New York: Viking, 1986. Here referred as *CR*.

——. *The Shadow Lines*, New York: Penguin, 1988. Here referred as *SL*.

——. *The Glass Palace*, New Delhi: Ravi Dayal and Permanent Black, 2000. Here referred as *GP*.

——. *The Hungry Tide,* New Delhi: Harper Collins Publishers, 2004. Here referred as *HT*.

——. *Sea of Poppies*, India: Penguin Books, 2008. Here referred as *SP*.

Said, Edward. *The World, the Text and the Critic*, New York: Vintage, 1991.

6

Across the Cultural Borders: Journeys, Mobility and Migration in Amitav Ghosh's *The Hungry Tide*

Dinesh Kumar

Amitav Ghosh's novels are marked with journeys, visits and human movements across time and space. They also capture the problematic of the issues such as nationality and gender. *The Hungry Tide* is one such novel which emphasizes not only crossing the land but also crossing of water bodies at different places.

The Hungry Tide begins with a focus on Kanai Dutt, who supervises an office of translators in New Delhi. He stands on a railway platform looking at Piyali Roy and subsequently they end up in the same compartment. They begin the conversation and Dutt understands that both are in a journey—from Calcutta to Canning in the Sundarbans. Railway station, train and journey placed at the beginning of the novel impart it metaphors of movement and they promise human movement across many boundaries. Further, Dutt's role as a translator implies an interlingual, cross-cultural theme of the novel.

Kanai Dutt recollects how he had spent some time in the Sundarbans when he was a young school boy. His current trip is a return visit to the Sundarbans and the reason for his journey is that his aunt Nilima has informed him that his uncle Nirmal had left a journal, specially, for Kanai. Though this journal had been written before 1979, it had only recently been discovered in some corner of the house. Thus, the journal promises a journey into the past—Kanai's prospective migration into a different time and into different experiences, guided by someone else's perspective.

Kanai finds out that Piya was born in Calcutta though she had been shifted to the United States when she was just one year old. He also understands that she does not know Bengali and that she is a student of Cytology at the Scripps Institution of Oceanography in California. She is currently on a trip to study marine mammals which are found exclusively in the Sundarbans. She is heading to Canning whereas Kanai wants to go to Lusibari where his aunt runs a charitable institution. Amitav Ghosh marks the Sundarbans, the train journey and Oceanography as metaphors of migration as they indicate the spirit of human exploration into the world of new experiences.

When Piya comes to Canning, she is almost harassed by a guide whom she hires and a guard who is imposed upon her by the government is also of no real use. They distract her from her study of dolphins. She even falls into the river and she is saved by a fisherman, Fokir. From that moment she finds Fokir a better guide and she sends away her handymen. Though Fokir doesn't know English, he and Piya manage to communicate. This connection between Fokir and Piya is also a border crossing as it transcends the limits of cultures and languages.

Readers also get to know that the trust and the school run by Nilima Ghose are built over the site established by a British idealist, Sir Daniel Hamilton. The house is called Lusibari which means Lucy's house. Lucy was Hamilton's wife who had died on her way from England to join him in the days of British Raj. Hamilton was a visionary who had bought ten thousand acres of the Sundarbans to rehabilitate the poor people. He had laid down one condition that the inhabitants would have no caste system and no tribal identity. He had also urged them all live as fishermen though some of them were farmers. These people moved in three migratory waves—in the 1920s, in 1947 after partition and in 1971 after the Bangladesh War. Thus, Hamilton in his life and vision embodies the spirit of borderless life. The human settlement that he develops is a semi-communist region where people transcend the boundaries of caste, religion and nationalism.

Nirmal and Nilima reach Lusibari in 1950. They reach the Sundarbans after their hurried marriage against wishes of Nilima's father. Subsequently, Nirmal plans to take over the management of Hamilton's estate. When they reach Lusibari, they understand that Hamilton Estate is caught in by a number of legal hassles. Nilima establishes the women's union and she forms the Badabon Trust in the 1980's. Nirmal and Nilima stand for a journey together in life—the conjugal journey.

Kanai learns that his childhood friend Kusum had been abandoned by her mother and she was subsequently taken care of by the Women's Union. He also learns that she subsequently married Rajen who had become handicapped in a bus accident in Calcutta. Kanai comes to know that Kusum had given birth to a son, Fokir though Rajen commits suicide, run over by a train. Kusum tells Fokir the story of Bon Bibi, a good spirit which fights the evil spirit Dokkhin Rai for the control of forests and waterways. The story illustrates the life of Dhona who is seduced by the evil spirit into offering a young boy, Dukhey as food to Dokkhin Rai, who can assume the shape of tiger. However, Bon Bibi saves Dhukhey at the right moment. This story is a part of the local myth that Kusum represents and it also brings alive her childhood memory. It also indicates how fiction and fact crossover in the lives of local people. This story also has had a lasting effect on Kusum's family as her father had built a temple in Bon Bibi's honour which is visited subsequently by Fokir and Fokir's son Tutul. Unfortunately soon after transferring the story to Fokir, Kusum abandons him.

Nirmal starts writing his journal in the village of Morichjhapi after his retirement from his job as a headmaster. Though he lives into the image of a writer, the journal is the only written work that he has to his credit. The journal is an account of his life—an assessment of his failures, marriage and his idealism. It is also a marker of the entire journey of his life. Besides, it records the experiences of Nirmal's visit to Morichjhapi to find Kusum. It also indicates the dangers of the

Bangladeshi refugees who had gone to Morichjhapi from the refugee camp in Central India. Thus, Nirmal's account reflects the plight of Bangladeshi refugees and their migration to Morichjhapi and Ghosh uses a journal as a record of alternative history that documents the border-crossing of refugees.

Nirmal meets Kusum and she takes him to Garjontola, the place where Bon Bibi temple is located. Nirmal knows that Horen has fallen in love with Kusum and they are expected to get married. However, she is killed in a massacre sponsored by the government against the refugees. Thus, Nirmal's account records the subaltern experiences of the migrant refugees.

In the present time of the narrative, Fokir is an adult and is married to Moyna, an educated woman. She is forced to marry Fokir though she wants to go for nursing. Kanai admires Moyna for her determination and ambition. She represents the human urge to cross the boundaries of one's class with the help of ambition and education.

Horen and Kanai accompany Piya and Fokir in their journey to observe dolphins. However, Kanai senses an approaching cyclone and he learns that Piya and Fokir have gone out in a small boat. As the storm breaks out Horen and Kanai are forced to return to Lusibari. Meanwhile Fokir takes the boat to Garjantola in anticipation of the help from Bon Bibi. Fokir and Piya climb a mangrove tree and tie themselves to the trunk. They are thrashed by a heavy storm and enormous tidal waves. When the storm subsides, Piya realises that Fokir had died in protecting her from lashing tidal waves. Fokir body is later cremated and Kanai returns to New Delhi. His return is a return to life from the face of death. Piya too has come back to life from the world of death. Kanai hands over Piya a complete translation of Bon Bibi legend to make her understand the full depth of Fokir's spirituality. This translation makes Piya understand the values of a different culture. She also understands that she was loved by both Fokir and Kanai. She also redefines human relation. For her, it is like the boundless mixing of fresh water and salt water of Sundarbans. Thus, Sundarbans becomes a metaphor of seamless life—a life beyond the boundaries of conventions, constructed gender, caste and nationality.

Piya returns, later, to the Sundarbans to work at the Badabon Trust. She plans to raise money to realise Nilima's dreams. She becomes the agency for financing a house for Moyna and higher education for her son, Tutul. She also decides to work for the conservation of endangered dolphins. Furthermore, she identifies Nilima's house as her home suggesting that she doesn't want to wander any more. Kanai plans to return to Sundarbans of what he remembers from the reading of journal of Nirmal. Thus the novel ends on a happy note though the spirit of Fokir continues to haunt the survivals. Piya's decision to work for the dolphins is a pronouncement of her new eco-spiritualism which she has learnt from Fokir and local fishermen. She crosses the corporeal boundary of human shape to connect to the spirits of other lives such as that of dolphins and trees. Kanai uses translation and writing as modes of migration. He uses these literary devices for a transcultural understanding of the lives and spirituality of the people of Sundarbans.

Language is one of the boundaries between people. *The Hungry Tide* punctures this linguistic divide. Though Piya and Fokir are kept apart by language, they are able to communicate effectively. Their relationship crosses all the traditional barriers between people. Piya contemplates on this relationship, comparing it with the relationship of her parents:

> ...the two of them, Fokir and herself, they could have been boulders or trees for all they knew of each other: and wasn't it better in a way, more honest, that they could not speak? For if you compared it to the ways in which dolphins' echoes mirrored the world, speech was only a bag of tricks that fooled you into believing that you could see through the eyes of another being. (Ghosh, 2004: 159)

Piya subsequently learns to love without language. Kanai, the translator of cultures gives up his urban mask when he comes to live near a swamp. Fokir, the unlettered fisherman, falls in love with Piya who is an embodiment of science and modern civilization.

The Goddess, Bon Bibi, is also a symbol of transcendence and mobility as the deity of the tide country. She is the embodiment of a plural syncretic local cult: she presides over the flood; she is the goddess of hope and also of vengeance.

The Hungry Tide also marks a constant re-figuration of the land-mass. John Hawley explains how this geographical reshaping by the tidal water implies border crossing and its symbolic significance:

> The tide comes in twice daily, resulting in a constant reshaping of the land and an uprooting of anything permanent. Such a setting makes an apt symbol for the ebb and flow of history and the uprooting of populations, both of which have come to be seen as "Ghosh-ian" themes. Furthermore, just as the natural tides of the area tend to obliterate the sense of permanent division between land and sea, Ghosh's characters gradually learn to recognize the transient nature of the divisions between individuals—of whatever social class. (Hawley, 2005: 132)

Piyali's project in the Sundarbans offers her a kind of life-style that crosses all boundaries. She is drawn to biology because it allows her to be on her without a fixed address and to go beyond the familiar community. Thus, her research is a manifestation of human soul's interest in distant places. Further, characters cross water in this novel many times. Kusum and Nirmal cross the water on their way to the shrine and Kusum tells Nirmal that they have just crossed the border between the realm of human beings and the realm of the evil dominated by Dokkhin Rai. Nirmal suddenly recognizes how borders are largely imaginary:

> I realised, with a sense of shock, that this chimerical line was, to her and to Horen, as real as a barbed-wire fence might be to me.... To me, a townsman, the tide country's jungle was an emptiness, a place where time stood still: I saw now that this was an illusion, that exactly the opposite was true. (Ghosh, 2004: 224)

Another migratory experience captured in *The Hungry Tide* is that of refugees. Nirmal identifies himself with the Bangladeshi refugees who are dispossessed. Refugees also indicate the state of eternal mobility as they are homeless. Ghosh records this vision of homeless, ever-migrating group of people:

> How strange it was to hear this plaintive cry wafting across the water. It seemed at that moment, not to be a shout of defiance, but rather a question being addressed to the very heavens, not just for themselves, but on behalf of bewildered humankind. Who, indeed, are we? Where do we belong? (Ghosh, 2004: 254)

Nirmal also becomes aware of his own borderless location. He starts seeing the world through the eyes of poor refugees:

> It was as if I were hearing the deepest uncertainties of my heart being spoken to the rivers and the tides. Who was I? Where did I belong? In Kolkata or in the tide country? In India or across the border? In prose or in poetry?... Where else could you belong, except in the place you refused to leave. I joined my feeble voice to theirs. (*Ibid.*)

The novel begins with the point of view of a visitor. Kanai presents himself as a visitor and examines Piya and notices the differences in her. His initial impression of Piya presents her as a foreigner:

> It occurred to him suddenly that perhaps, despite her silver nose-stud and the tint of her skin, she was not Indian, except by descent. And the moment the thought occurred to him, he was convinced of it: she was a foreigner; it was stamped in her posture, in the way she stood, balancing on her heels like a flyweight boxer, with her feet planted apart. (Ghosh, 2004: 3)

Kanai also reads from a Bengali script. This script speaks about rivers and islands. However, this description yet again emphasizes that there are no clear boundaries between terrains:

> The rivers' channels are spread across the land like a fine-mesh net, creating a terrain where the boundaries

> between land and water are always mutating, always unpredictable. Some of these channels are mighty waterways, so wide across that one shore is invisible from the other; others are no more than two or three kilometres long and only a few hundred metres across. Yet, each of these channels is a 'river' in its own right, each possessed of its own strangely evocative name. (Ghosh, 2004: 7)

The script also explains how land is constantly reshaped by the currents. It speaks about the state of flux which even concrete land-masses are subjected to. This description also touches upon the borderless nature of locations:

> There are no borders here to divide fresh water from salt, river from sea. The tides reach as far as three hundred kilometres inland and every day thousands of acres of forest disappear underwater only to re-emerge hours later. The currents are so powerful as to reshape the islands almost daily—some days the water tears away entire promontories and peninsulas; at other times it throws up new shelves and sandbanks where there were none before. (Ghosh, 2004: 7)

Characters also use thoughts to effect mental migration in *The Hungry Tide*. Piya, for instance, though travels physically across Bengal, goes back to America mentally. Memories and sensations bring the continents together in her thoughts:

> Looking over her shoulder, Piya spotted a tea-seller patrolling the platform. Reaching through the bars, she summoned him with a wave. She had never cared for the kind of *chai* on offer in Seattle, her hometown, but somehow, in the ten days she had spent in India she had developed an unexpected affinity for milky, overboiled tea served in earthenware cups. There were no spices in it for one thing, and this was more to her taste than the *chai* at home. (Ghosh, 2004: 9)

Kanai's profession as a translator is also a kind of journey. He moves through languages and communities. Ghosh explains the transnational significance of Kanai's job:

> He ran a bureau of translators and interpreters that specialized in serving the expatriate communities of New Delhi; foreign diplomats, aid workers, charitable organizations, multinational companies and the like. (Ghosh, 2004: 20)

The Hungry Tide, in contrast to other novels of Amitav Ghosh, has a narrow geographical setting. It is confined to the Sundarbans estuary in the Bay of Bengal. Though the novel presents limited border-crossing as far as the geographical locations are concerned, it moves across a wide range of conceptual questions related to human beings and their sharing of a complex and delicate ecosystem with animals. The novel touches upon the conservation issues of dolphins and tigers along with its interest in the history of human settlement in the Sundarbans.

Amitav Ghosh also brings into picture in *The Hungry Tide* the inter-locking relation of various lives. He indicates how the life of one species depends on the life of another. He shows how tiger preservation threatens human life and how tigers regularly attack and kill islanders. The state remains passive in this war between two species and it allows the death to be a perpetual drama. Amitav Ghosh indicates that with some amount of will and planning, both the tigers and human beings can be protected. This vision also indicates that the boundaries of lives between species have to be overlooked to develop a healthy ecosystem.

The Hungry Tide also critiques the official version of history and nationality with the help of local myths. Local beliefs subvert the religious and national versions of human history. The novel presents a local reality of the Sundarbans which straddles between West Bengal and Bangladesh. Geographically too, the Sundarbans is a point of connection between the boundaries of two countries. The Sundarbans also has local religion—the belief in the goddess called Bon Bibi. However, the epic of Bon Bibi is strongly inflected by Islamic influences. It also reveals strong rootedness to Hindu tradition. This kind of syncretism is common in Ghosh's novels. It echoes cross-cultural interest in history and anthropology. It also indicates a kind of migration, mobility across the boundaries of religions.

The tide country also has a specific geographical identity in *The Hungry Tide*. Though it is a part of Bengal, it can also be seen as a separate region. By placing the locale of the novel away from the main land and yet connected to it, Ghosh ensures a regular movement of characters in and out of the Sundarbans. Kanai, while reading the note books of his uncle, comes across the following passage which explicates the uniqueness of the tide country:

> There is no prettiness here to invite the stranger in: yet to the world at large this archipelago is known as "the Sundarbans" which means, "the beautiful forest." There are some who believe the word to be derived from the name of a common species of mangrove—the *sundari* tree, *Heriteriaminor*. But the word's origin is no easier to account for than is its presence prevalence, for in the record books of the Mughal emperors this region is named not in reference to a tree but to a tide—bhati. And to the inhabitants of the islands this land is known as bhatirdesh—the tide country—except that bhati is not just the "tide" but one tide in particular the ebb-tide: it is only in falling that the water gives birth to the forest. To look upon this strange parturition midwived by the moon, is to know why the name "tide country" is not just right but necessary. (Ghosh, 2004: 8)

The Hungry Tide also crosses the edges of key concepts such as nationality and identity. It shows the ephemerality of ideas such as nation and ethnic identity. For instance, the multiplicity of names for the Sundarbans creates a metaphor for its ephemerality. The metaphor of inconstant land is another statement on its ephemeral identity. The Sundarbans is subject to radical alterations as a result of summer storms. The islands are often washed away by the cyclones which also generate huge tidal waves. These disasters also bring into question the issue of survival. In Sundarbans, left to the mercy of elements, the line between life and death is very porous.

Amitav Ghosh also interrogates the conventional divide between the predator and the prey in *The Hungry Tide*. The dense mangrove forest, from a human point of view, is as barren as a desert. However, it also has a terrible beauty—it is a place teeming with crocodiles, snakes, sharks and man-eating tigers. Thus, it becomes a place where man is more often a prey than a predator.

The Hungry Tide also marks an overlap of fantasy and reality. Like the Sundarbans which are immersed and re-immersed with the tide, the narrative is also an overlap of fantasy and reality. Amitav Ghosh captures the strangeness of the reality of the Sundarbans which touches upon the realm of a nightmare:

> At no moment can human beings have any doubt of the terrain's utter hostility to their presence, of its cunning and resourcefulness, of its determination to destroy or expel them. Every year dozens of people perish in the embrace of that dense foliage, killed by tigers, snakes and crocodiles. (Ghosh, 2004: 8)

The style of novel also marks hybridity—a cultural border crossing. Amitav Ghosh combines Bengali localism with the Standard English, marking a migration and movement across the dialects and cultures. He sprinkles Bengali colloquialisms throughout, creating a 'chutneyfied' English which makes the readers understand the life and culture of the Sundarbans through a global language. The novel also crosses the boundaries literary traditions. The most interesting of Ghosh's formal experiments in the novel is his attempt to compose an English version of the Bengali metre *dwipadi poyar*: a rhymed couplet of about 12 syllables with a caesura. This effectively captures the nuances of oral folk poetry in English.

Like his other novels, Ghosh's *The Hungry Tide* is also concerned with many issues of migration such as the geographical enigma, travel, exploration, encounter and memory. Memory in Ghosh's novel has a cartographic significance and it is a place-making device. In gradual sedimentation of memory, places emerge like photographs from dark plates. A place which is remembered in Ghosh's novel is also lived in Amitav Ghosh. The narrative in *The Hungry Tide* and the memories of Nirmal and Kanai are involved in a place-making enterprise.

Piya, in coming to the Sundarbans from her Western habitat, experiences a cultural difference. Though she is relatively alien to the place, she uses sensory perceptions and memories to build familiarity with the space around her. Ghosh describes how Piya mixes her memories with space-making, acculturation strategies:

> There was a time when those were the smells of home; she would sniff them on her mother, on the way back from school; they would fill the lift on its journey up to their floors. When she stepped inside they had greeted her, like domesticated animals, creatures with lives of their own...her response was to fight back, with a quietly ferocious tenacity, against them and against her mother, shutting them away with closed doors.... But here the ghosts of these creatures seemed to be quieted by their surroundings. The spell of Fokir's fingers was broken only when a breeze carried the acrid odour of burning chillies directly into her face. And then suddenly the phantoms came alive again, clawing at her throat and her eyes, attacking her as though she were an enemy who had crossed over undetected. (Ghosh, 2004: 96-97)

The Hungry Tide also marks Amitav Ghosh's movement across the boundaries of genres and disciplines. It weaves together fiction, autobiography and history. In his interview with the U.N. Chronicle, Amitav Ghosh's explains the interdisciplinary project that he has handled in the novel:

> My previous novel, *The Glass Palace,* was very much about my father's history. *The Hungry Tide* is again closely related to my family. This is my first book that is completely located and situated in Bengal and it was very important to me for exactly that reason. It was also very exciting to explore the deep layering of Bengal. I feel in some mental and emotional way I'm in a process of returning, which will take me a long, long time, and it is currently underway. Typically, it takes me between

> three and four years, but sometimes more, to conceive the idea of a novel and actually execute it. *The Glass Palace* took me five years; *The Hungry Tide*—took four. I spent a long time in the Sundarbans—living in a village, meeting people, learning how to catch crabs. (Ghosh, 2008)

Amitav Ghosh's words not only explain how the personal experiences overlap with historical details but also imply how *The Hungry Tide* is a blend of fiction, autobiography and history.

Thus, *The Hungry Tide* offers many overt, subtle and symbolic modes of border crossings. Memory is a prime mode of mobility in the novel. Ghosh also projects Sundarbans as a borderless locale wherein the identity of the individuals is constantly reshaped. One can aptly evoke John C. Hawley's observation about the novel that Ghosh uses imagination as an agency of border crossing:

> Ghosh is interested in what might be called imaginary geographies—his preoccupation in *The Shadow Lines* comes to the fore again here—when Piya remarks that she "could tell that the world Kanai inhabited was as distant from the India of her father's memories as it was from Lusibari and the tide country". (p. 200) (Hawley, 2005: 142)

In *The Hungry Tide*, the modes of migration are thus more subtle. Piyali Roy moves between America and India whereas Sundarbans holds a history of human migration from the colonial days to the present. The people of Sundarbans have reached the archipelago in search of labour and better social life. Kanai uses translation as a mode of travel. He crosses over cultures and languages in his translation assignments. *The Hungry Tide* also, captures a vision of cross-cultural understanding. Fokir who represents the native culture and Piyali who represents Western nationalism meet at the magical and myth-ridden Sundarbans. Their meeting and their subsequent journey together in search of dolphins mark a movement across linguistic barriers and cultural walls.

WORKS CITED

Ghosh, Amitav. *The Hungry Tide*. New Delhi: Ravi Dayal, 2004.

Hawley, John. *Amitav Ghosh: An Introduction*. New Delhi: Foundation Books, 2005.

"The Chronicle Interview: Amitav Ghosh".

From http://www.un.org/pubs/chronicle/2005/issue4/0405, p. 48 html, 22 Feb. 2008.

7

Dominant Imageries in Amitav Ghosh's *River of Smoke*

Vivekanand Jha

The second of the ambitious Ibis trilogy based on the historical narrative about the opium trading, trafficking and addiction, the novel, *River of Smoke,* is yet another milestone and epoch-making historical novel in the history of Indian fiction which makes the readers reminisce the bruised and pleasant past and their perpetuating repercussion even in the present. The extraordinary scholarship and erudition of Amitav Ghosh comes into display in narrating and storytelling of the novel. *The New York Times* vehemently and vociferously writes in the book review of Amitav Ghosh's *River of Smoke*: "No writer in modern India has held a novelistic lamp to the subcontinent's densely thicketed past as vividly and acutely as Amitav Ghosh" (www.amitavghosh.com). In another review and critical appraisal, *Literary Review* writes: "For those who like to see history bought alive through the deployment of wave upon wave of plausible detail, *River of Smoke* should prove a marvellous read" (http://www.amitavghosh.com/riverofsmoke_r.html#gpm1_19).

The present article would focus its attention on working of imageries, metaphors and other figure of speech in the novel, *River of Smoke*. Before we delve deep into this aspect let us refresh our basics and fundamentals pertaining to working of imageries in the novel in general. There's more to novel than catches the physical eye. Imagery is the ornaments and garments in a literary genre employed to evoke mental images, not only of the visual sense but of sensation and emotion as well. Images ingeniously and artistically stir up mental picture and appeal to the senses. Image is employed in literary genre to give a concrete and vivid portrait of idea to be conveyed with a conviction that a picture is worth a thousand words. The images are nothing but feelings, emotions or ideas that may have denotative as well as connotative meanings.

Imagery by virtue of sensory perceptions is broadly divided as visual, auditory, olfactory, gustatory, tactile, organic and kinesthetic imageries. Something that can be depicted and described through sight is known as visual imagery. Similarly auditory imagery delineates sound; olfactory imagery represents smell; gustatory imagery demonstrates taste; tactile imagery refers to touching that has feeling of hardness, softness, wetness, heat and cold; organic imagery signifies internal sensation, hunger, thirst, fatigue and nausea and kinesthetic imagery talks of movement and physical tension.

The imagery of a literary work is a word or a set of words that may appeal to senses rather than what one sees with his naked eyes. Figurative language is the language that uses imagery, and metaphors and similes are two trustworthy representatives of the imagery. Images symptomatic of complementary meanings and associations in ways that walk off beyond the reasonably straightforward identifications of metaphor and simile are often called symbols. Imagery involves one or more of five senses and the novelist employ a word or phrase to kindle reader's memory of those senses. These memories can be positive or negative that decides the fate or the mood of the novel. The imagery is a contrivance by virtue of which the novelist makes his meaning emphatic, impulsive, passionate, strong, comprehensible and persuaded. The use of images in the novel is equally significant for both the novelist and the reader. The novelist makes his objective emerge to the reader exactly as it appears to him and to the reader it provides his imagination with some doable meanings to grip upon.

Amitav Ghosh's novel, *River of Smoke* is stuffed, suffused and swollen with imageries, symbols and metaphors. Besides application of pertinent metaphors and other figure of speech, the utilization and materialization of simile is all pervasive and predominant in the novel, *River of Smoke*. He uses perpetual and frequent use of similes to present vivid details of the plot and narration of the novel to the readers. He is coiner of words and mesmerizes the readers with apt and apposite uses, appeals and inspirations of ideas and thoughts. The language, dialogue and description of his novel are potentially charged with sublimity of thought, contemplation and deliberation. He has different approaches, style, techniques, choice of words and diction for different characters and he pick them in proportion to the rank and file of the characters, situations and settings of the novel. On the comprehensive and elaborate linguistic and lexicographic versatility of the novel, *River of Smoke*, *The Canberra Times* writes in a luminous and gleaming review:

> Language is clearly a glorious obsession for the author, considered by many to be one of the top Indian writers of the day. River of Smoke is the second volume of his *Ibis Trilogy*, following the successful *Sea of Poppies*, short-listed for the Man Booker Prize in 2008. His highly successful historical fiction combines an exciting plot, historical accuracy and marvellous local colour. Delving into the Anglo-Indian dictionaries one discovers that the pidgin English spoken in Canton and other Chinese trading ports, contains many words that both emanated from, or later entered, Indian languages. Portuguese phrases and the French Creole spoken in Mauritius add to the salmagundi. As well as linguistic or philological observations, the author puts wry remarks into the mouths of his characters, such as, "Really there is no language like English for turning lies into legalisms". (http://www.amitavghosh.com/riverofsmoke_r.html#gpm 1_3)

Anhita, an opium carrying ship is struck by storm and almost ten per cent of total opium is destroyed by it. The visual imagery is noticed when owner of opium and Anhita, "Bahram could see crates crashing against the bulkheads like rafts against a reef" (29). He struggles against onslaught of storm and tactile imagery is used "when Bahram stepped off the ladder his feet shot out from under him, throwing him face-forward into a heap of dung like sludge" (30). And "there was opium in his eyes, his ears, his nose, his windpipe—it was as if he were drowning" (31). The storm has created a horror into the psyche of Bahram and which appositely expressed through auditory imageries: "and then, above the roar of the storm, he heard a breaking, tearing, splintering sound, as if the ship were being torn apart" (31). The assistant and confidante of Bahram, Vico was too affected by this hazardous storm and his predicament is revealed through visual imagery where "he looked like he'd seen a ghost" (32). Because of storm Bahram is inadvertently administered by opium and in its intoxication he remembers his extramarital lover, Chi-mei through optical imagery: "everywhere he looked, his eyes conjured up her face. Like a Chinese lantern the image seemed to hang before him" (33).

Bahram couldn't enjoy real love and warmth from his lawful wife, Shireenbai due to unequal and asymmetrical marriage between them. But it was mere a marriage of convenience and despite rigid opposition offered by his mother, Bahram had to remain as a house-husband in the family of Seth because of deplorable and dejected economic condition of his family. The living standard of Bahram was bucolic and inappropriate in comparison with that of the Seth's family and it was a cause of clumsiness and embarrassment for him. Even his in-laws were deeming him with an eye of contempt and derision which is expressed through an apt imagery: "it was as though a bumptious and somewhat uncouth poor relative had insinuated himself into their home with an eye to dispossessing them of it" (49). And "in the shipyard he had proved worse than useless; at home he seemed unable to get along with most of the family—if he carried on like this he would soon become a burden on the family" (51).

Bahram is besides himself while describing the beauty of extramarital darling Chi-mei and she is depicted through visual imagery where "her face was pert and lively, with glinting black eyes, and cheeks that glowed like polished apples" (67). The use of sensual imagery is amply clear while depicting the characterization of Allow who works as a mediator and messenger in furthering the extra marital love-making between Bahram and Chi-mei and "he looked like any of the urchins who wandered around the foreign enclave, begging for coins and offering to run errands" (70-71). The beauty of Chi-mei's boat is described through animal imagery: "it was a brightly painted vessel, with two decks and a stern shaped like an upcurved fishtail" (195). Another animal imagery of similar nature is noticed while describing the boat of Allow: "its stern was carved to look like a gigantic fishtail, rising out of water in an elegant curve" (295). The boat of Allow is further exemplified by auditory imagery when Bahram heard "a distant tinkling, like the sound of a boat's bell" (295). The setting of ambient condition under which Allow's boat carry Bahram is depicted through visual imagery: "The boat had begun to move now and as its prow parted the fog the ripples of the bow wave went lapping through the water like misty shadows" (298).

None has control over Time and Chi-mei is not any special to be unaffected by it. Her beauty is plagued by the worm of age which is narrated through domestic imagery and "over the years she had grown a little portly, and her face had become plumber, but her clothes were still sack-like in cut and severe in colour" (107).

On board of this very boat Bahram is offered by Allow to inhale opium and intoxicating effects of opium on Bahram is described through some of apt imageries: "it was as if he were a ship that was steadying itself after being battered by a furious gale" (299). And "that marvelous god-like lightness in which the body and the spirit were freed from gravity, of all kinds" (299). In the intoxication of opium, Bahram is in sensual dream and is shown to be indulged in love-making with some girl who is described through olfactory imagery: "she smelled like the river, of woodsmoke and silted water" (300). When he woke up from opium-fuelled dream he found no girl in his vicinity and distance and his amazement is expressed through sensual imagery: "that was all it was—an opium-fuelled dream, conjured up by the pipe. That would explain why he hadn't seen her face, and also why it had seemed so perfect-like the imaginary night-time couplings of adolescence" (302).

Besides *Anhita* and *Ibis*, *Redruth* is another ship which was notably talked about in the novel for transporting plants across the seas and it is owned by a Scottish Botanist, Frederick Fitcher Penrose. The ship was named after the birth place of Penrose's wife and permeated with the greenery of outstanding and curious plants and they were suitably placed into sliding boxes of glass which were like miniature greenhouses. The ship was loaded and renovated with all the extraordinary and bizarre facilities and conveniences. The plants were representing every part of the earth and they were methodically arranged by no less than the possessor of the ship, Mr. Penrose himself. *Redruth* was the unique creation of Mr. Penrose who had infused his heart and soul into her creation and its beauty is portrayed through series of some sumptuous similes and auditory imageries:

> If ships could be built in the image of their owners, then there would be no question about whom this one belonged to—she was like an extension of Fitcher's very being. Like Fitcher, the *Redruth* was lean and angular, with sharply upcurved lines—her bowsprit even had a way of 'twitchering and shaking' that was strangely reminiscent of her owner's brow. Even the sound of the wind, blowing through the *Redruth's* rigging, seemed different from that of any other vessel: if ship could speak, then *Redruth*, Paulette imagined, would express herself in a voice that recalled Fitcher's broad accent and whistling vowels. (75-76)

The statue of Fitcher Penrose, a botanist and owner of yet another ship *Redruth,* is depicted through animal imagery where his "eyebrows jutted out like a ferret's whiskers" (35), domestic imagery where his "chin that curved upwards like the blade of a scythe" (35). And visual imagery where "his eyes fixed on the ground, as if he were cataloguing the greenery on which he was about to tread" (35). Fitcher in search of rare plant ambles through the bush and the setting of bush is described through visual imagery: "On either side were towering talipots, arranged in straight lines, as if to flank an avenue" (40). The interaction between Penrose and Miss Paulette is expressed through kinetic imagery wherein "Fitcher tried to stay close, but the fellow was going like a mail coach and there was no keeping up with him" (42). The room where Miss Paulette used to stay is described and depicted through domestic imagery: "At the centre of the room lay a pile of sheets and curtains, heaped up like after-grass to form a pallet" (43).

Fitcher Penrose, in his first meeting with Miss Paulette, offers her a gardening job on his ship, *Redruth*, to pay off the obligation that he owed to her father but this offer infuriates Miss Paulette and she declines his proposal deeming it nothing more than a charity. The word 'charity' uttered by Miss Paulette took Fitcher Penrose by bewilderment and he was not such a man who broke into tears easily but a layer of moist began to float over his eyes. The morose and despondent mood of Fitcher Penrose is revealed through imagery of nature and: "he looked at the wet ends of his fingers as though they had metamorphosed into something inexplicable—like tendrils sprouting on the ends of thorns" (60).

Fitcher Penrose prefers to live peculiar and bizarre world and he is a character of resolute determination and diligence which is revealed through imagery of nature and "like a gnarled old tree, growing upon a stony slope, Fitcher was unshakeable in his determination to extract a living from the world" (79). He was never after money rather money was after him to see his perfection of professionalism. The wealth for him was not a source of luxuries and materialism rather "it was a burden, like the sacks of cabbages that had to be hoarded in the cellar for seasons of scarcity" (79). Penrose has restless engagement in the form of tending plants on board of the ship, *Redruth* and his carefulness for plants is displayed through animal imagery: "it was like caring for a garden that was tethered to the back of a large and extremely energetic animal" (95). Penrose was mesmerized by the inadvertent appearance of plump porpoise on the deck of his ship whose enchanting beauty is described through domestic imagery: "he was delighted to see the creature on the Redruth's deck 'threshing about like a pilcher in a pan-crock'" (98).

The foreign or European women are not allowed to enter into Canton and when this fact is revealed to her by Penrose she was simply open mouthed and in utter disappointment which is expressed through visual imagery and "it was as if a flaming sword had descended from heaven to shut her out of Eden, forever depriving her of the chance to inscribe her name in the annals of botanical exploration" (104). This is the prime reason of Canton being overcrowded with bubbling bachelors and this fact is expressed through animal imagery when Mr. Robert Chinnery explains to Miss Paulette: "I am told that at certain times of year bachelors flock there like birds to a wintering hole" (167).

In a letter to Miss Paulette, Mr. Robert Chinnery describes the shape and form of the boat in which he travelled to Canton through the animal imagery: "I came in a passage-boat—a most curios vessel, shaped like a caterpillar and just as slow" (179). The nautical imagery is employed to describe the rush and crowd of foreigners in Fanqui-town, the foreign enclave in Canton, and Mr. Robert Chinnery writes to Miss Paulette that: "in a way Fanqui-town is like a ship at sea, with hundreds-no, thousands-of men living crammed together in a little sliver of a space. I do believe there is no place like it on earth, so small and yet so varied, where people from the far corners of the earth must live, elbow to elbow, for six months of the year" (185). The old China Street in Canton is enchanted to the view due to its cleanliness and quietness which is narrated through visual imagery: "The gap overhead is covered with a kind of matting, which is laid down so artfully that below, at the level of street, it is always cool and shady, like a pathway in a forest" (209).

Mr. Robert Chinnery portrays characterization of Jacqua with contrasting and captivating visual imagery: "Jacqua is not tall and nor is he athletic in build, but there is in his face a luminous quality, in his eyes a glitter of calm and directed intelligence that no paintbrush could ever capture" (255). Mr. Robert Chinnery in another letter to Miss Paulette provides miniature presentation of Canton city with the help of imagery from the world of game: “The public places and monuments stand out like the tallest pieces on a chessboard, their positions being marked with cascading roofs and soaring spires” (376).

Neel reads out to Bahram an article published in the journal, *Repository* which elucidates ill effects of opium on its addicts and is expressed through imagery of death: “in the sequel the poison takes effect, the habit becomes fi xed, and the sleeping smokers are like corpses—lean and haggard as demons” (133). Both Bahram and Zadig had opportunity to come across and communicate face to face with Napoleon Bonaparte. Before they could see him, the news of his being held captive on St Helena caused a sense of astonishment to Zadig and his amazement is expressed through optical and auditory imageries: “for Zadig it was as if a bolt of lightning had struck the timbers beneath his feet” (151). The manifestation and personality of Napoleon Bonaparte is portrayed through some awful imagery of science: “it was his gaze, most of all, that Bahram was not to remember, for it was as penetrating as a surgeon’s knife, and it cut into him as if to lay bare the flimsy nakedness of his bones” (169). The working culture of office of Bahram on Anhita is described through science imagery where extended metaphor of watch mechanism comes into play: “Bahram’s employees—with the possible exception of Vico—knew only as much as they needed to and no more. Bahram’s daftardars were like the parts of a watch, each doing what was required of him but unaware of the functioning of the whole: only the Seth himself knew how the ensemble was put together, and for what purpose” (224). The Journal, *Register* is run by Compton in Canton and the worthiness and comprehensiveness of the news it provides is projected by Vico to Neel in the manner of exaggeration: “I’ll take you to meet Compton, said Vico. His shop is like a bazaar for the news” (266).

The new governor of Canton, Mr. Lin is hell bent to set free Canton and other parts of China from ill and fatal addiction of opium and to curb this trade he issues written order after order for opium trader as a sign of caution, warning and wake up call. The sudden change in the stance of Chinese authority on the trading of opium in China takes Bahram by surprise and he is found conspicuously under pressure and stress. While Neel reads to him one of such orders, he finds Bahram at his wit's end. Such bewilderment of Bahram is depicted through auditory imagery: "here Neel was interrupted by a curious grinding noise, like the gnashing of teeth" (315). The Chinese soldiers raid the suspect of opium trader and the fearful and appalling appearance of soldiers is expressed through visual imagery: "half a dozen soldiers, silhouetted against the light: with their pointed plumes they looked unnaturally tall, like giants" (331).

Though the upheaval caused by Chinese soldiers in Canton as a cautioning sign to curb trading of opium by foreigners, has ceased for time being but its after effects in term of annihilation and obliteration can be still noticed through some of visual imageries: "Yet, evidence of the recent Upheavel was littered around us; shards of glistened in the dust; fence posts lay scattered about, like twigs after a storm, having been uprooted and hurled against the factory walls; and the gates of some of factories were so badly battered it seemed a miracle their hinges had not given way" (370). Describing through animal imagery Zadig Bey eulogizes Captain Elliott: "The most important thing to know about Captain Elliott, he said, is that he is a Pucka Sahib: the colonies are to him what water is to a fish—his element, his breath, his being" (371). Mr. Charles King tries to convince Bahram to surrender the opium on board of Anhita but his ploys to hoodwink on the name of faith, belief and religion "struck Bahram like a thunderbolt" (470).

The animal imagery is used by Mr. Robert Chinnery to describe himself "curled up like a kitten" (501). The ground before the residence of Bahram in Canton has transformed into cantonment and "it was as if a carnival-site had been transformed overnight into a parade-ground" (507). The sentence replete with onomatopoetic utterances is used for storm struck Bahram "when he was neither speaking nor moving, the effort of self-containment would often result in a small storm of toe tapping, tongue-clicking and knuckle-cracking" (30). When first time Neel visits to Bahram the latter asks "why are you standing like a tree? Come closer na?" (128).

The use of climax is conspicuous when it is told in the novel that Vico "liked nothing better than to spend his days in bed, eating, drinking, farting and fornicating" (226). The use of hyperbola and exaggeration are noticeable when Vico "heard a breaking, tearing, splintering sound, as if the ship were being torn apart" (31) and Penrose received "a shock that almost toppled him from his mount" (37).

The visual imagery is employed to describe how a boat-woman is managing and keeping living chicken on the cooking boat: "The woman reached up and picked a chicken off the roof, plucking it from its covey as though it were a fruit on a vine" (86). Ah Fatt looks attentively towards Anhita, the ship owned by his father, Bahram and when Neel asked Ah Fatt the reason for watching the ship so keenly "Ah Fatt shook his head as though he had been woken from a trance" (86). Bombay and India is haunting into the psyche of Ah Fatt due to his spiritual and filial relation with these places and these are so favourite spots to Ah Fatt that he wants to "fly there Like Monkey King" (90). Visual imagery is employed to reveal the personal experience of Mr. Robert Chinnery "was walking by, a sailor disappeared into the shadows of Hog Lane with a creature that looked like a painted hag" (208).

Amitav Ghosh peerlessly employs his repository of words in portraying characters, settings, plots, conflict, climax, anticlimax, etcetera of the novel. The novel, *River of Smoke*, is replete, pervaded and permeated with epigrammatic, riveting and mesmerizing words, phrases and sentences and they make an outsized list: Kalua being sentenced to death for a simple act of self-defence (13)/ on the return leg of his first voyage (36)/ pallyvouzing idiom (41)/ the rudiments of an education (46)/ her prospects were sure to be contaminated by the stain of misfortune (47)/ potentially astronomical (77)/ spasms of embarrassment (82)/ weather-eye (83)/ a target of mockery (89)/ in the annals of botanical exploration (104)/ still sack-like in cut and severe in colour (107)/ miracle-monger (109)/ no matter how diminished their circumstances (160)/ listening in rapt attention (206)/ time-hallowed canons (221)/ braided torrents of speech (221)/ pampered sons of fortune (227)/ a snort of disbelief (229)/ in the last light of day (231)/ chest swell in proprietorial pride (231)/ the fear inspired by his acid tongue and scathing pen (233)/ a lady who is fat, fair and forty (236)/ attractions of the marital bed (236)/ thunderous peroration (238)/ groan under the yoke of tyranny (238)/ a crisis of unprecedented magnitude (240)/ an inveterate trouble maker (244)/ out of the earshot of spies and informers (284)/ hermit-like solitude (293)/ wreathed in wisps of fog (295)/ the splash of the oars (298)/ as if the river itself had turned into a surging torrent of smoke (301)/ nerves were fraying ever thinner under the strain (313)/ toying with his breakfast (314)/ a single person must not be allowed to slip through the net of the law (314)/ a vomit-inducing stench (318)/ one of them tugged at his elbow and whispered (358)/ in a matter of minutes (360)/ I was greeted with sullen stares and peevish frowns (372)/a long-yearned-for desire (374)/ inordinately glad (375)/ our words have filled your ears as the empty wind (390)/ Bahram took the glass from him and drained it at a gulp (394)/ dinner took on a defiant exuberance (399)/ with one excellent course following after another (404)/ a storm of applause now swept through the hall, drowning out the rest of Jardine's speech (405)/ ripple of excitement (418)/ received with exclamations of disbelief (418)/ cries of amazement (419)/ swelteringly hot (423)/ ominous deliberations (427)/ the boat was moving quite fast, with scores of oars dipping rhythmically in the water (426)/ miles of densely packed habitations (428)/ a brief flurry of anxiety (429)/ a stroke of genius (437)/ Mr. Wetmore would emerge from his self-imposed seclusion in time for his accustomed glass of negus (448)/ a fumigatory round of his house (449)/ Vico had climbed the stairs so fast he had to stop and catch his breath (454)/ to retrieve one small victory from the ashes of the day (458)/ in a state of extraordinary perturbation (461)/ a murmur of disbelief (462)/ this is not time for theological debate (463)/ a bald-faced lie

(467)/ spasms of rheumatism (471)/ in transports of delight (535)/ the people of the humblest hamlets (537)/ his knotted muscles began to relax (545).

The novelist, Amitav Ghosh pushes the readers into the flashback of sense, sensibility and psychology of nineteenth century world when opium was moot point of debate, discussion, deliberation, dispute and debacle. The novel, *River of Smoke* is not only a source of enjoyments and endearments for the readers but it is also a fountain of inspiration, perspiration, learning and vocabulary building classes through distant education that fasten and hypnotize them with its incessant splendor, exquisiteness and gorgeousness. We should have no doubt in proclaiming and predicting that the ambitious ibis trilogy of Amitav Ghosh is advancing towards making a record in the literary history.

WORK CITED

Ghosh, Amitav. *River of Smoke*. New Delhi: Penguin Books India, 2011. All the textual references with page number(s) that are cited in the article are from this edition of the book only.

8

Opium, History and Narration in *River of Smoke*

Rajnish Mishra

The present paper attempts to present *River of Smoke* as an example of fiction that highlights how history of opium trade has been skillfully narrated in the novel by carefully interweaving it with the lives of the characters in the novel. It attempts to explore the various thematic strands of postcolonial responses to the shared past of the peoples of the imperial colonies like India, and those under the shadows of the Empire, like China. Amitav Ghosh's *River of Smoke* was chosen because it is a critique of the imperialist expansionism and exploitation of the peoples of Asia by the white races and focuses on the mechanism of domination and exploitation and the way in which they were written out of the discourses of power.

Ibis trilogy, of which *Sea of Poppies* and *River of Smoke* are parts, is a postcolonial critique of the imperial exploitation of the peoples of Asia. History is revisited and judgment is passed over the power misused to exploit the imperial subjects in the past. The imperial mission did not end with the independence of the colonies. Neocolonialism came to the fore:

> Histories...take the form of narratives, and the ways in which the events described are portrayed, linked and made sense of are themselves susceptible to critical interrogation...historical events do not mean things in themselves but, rather, their meanings are generated by

> the ways in which they are described and linked together to form a historical narrative, and the resonances produced by that narrative depend on the recognition by its audience of the familiar story-telling devices it employs. (Malpas, 98)

River of Smoke is woven on the warps of history with woofs of individual lives. It is the tale of a city—the city that is called Canton—in the years that led to the first opium war that shocked China and caused its awakening. It became one of the main causal factors behind China getting exposed to the Western ideas and practices and to its modernization. The imperial mission of civilizing the natives in the colonies, teaching them the gospel—of Jesus and of the free trade, and of making the world a better place (for themselves) was the central factor that shaped the world from sixteenth century onwards. It is seen at work in Amitav Ghosh's *River of Smoke*.

The imperial colonizing power had created its allies in their colonies but they had also created powerful and persistent antagonists. In *River of Smoke* Seth Bahram can be seen as an ally and Commissioner Lin as an antagonist of the imperial powers. Bahram, a very convincingly Janus like character can tell Napoleon very honestly and philosophically: "Opium is like the wind or the tides: it is outside my power to affect its course. A man is neither good nor evil because he sails his ship upon the wind. It is his conduct towards those around him—his friends, his family, his servants—by which he must be judged. This is the creed I live by" (*River of Smoke*, 105). Thus, he tries to cover a clear trail of greed with a thick layer of specious rationalization. He is a colonial subject whose profit was allied with that of his masters, so he allied himself with them. It is the same trait that the postcolonial theory sees as the main reason behind the success of the imperial powers in colonizing and exploiting a large part of the world for a long time.

The Indian merchant was not duped into trading opium, nor was he coerced in any way. He chose his path with the sole motive of profit with the independence to take action. He wasn't naïve or innocent but he was fully aware of what he was doing. The tenets of his religion, which he had explained to Napoleon, very clearly showed how the forces of light (Ahura Mazda or the Creator) and the forces of darkness (Ahirman or the Devil) are in an eternal struggle. Like any other Zoroastrian whose aim was to "embrace the good and to banish evil", his path was clearly chalked out (102). Yet all he did was to embrace evil and to carry it to millions of Chinese every year, year after year, in the form of opium.

His power and part he played in the drama of evil on the stage of china was negligible when compared to that of the East India Company, the white merchants and the Government of Britain. They deserved most of the blame. Their role in China's enfeeblement is very clearly brought forth in Commissioner Lin's public dispatch to Queen Victoria. The facts mentioned and claims made in it are both historically verifiable and morally just. He blamed the foreign merchants of seducing the people of China into using opium for their profit and then flooding the country with illegally brought opium. It was the Dutch who had introduced non-medicinal use of opium to China. In the beginning, the menace was primarily for the leisured upper classes and the masses of China were comparatively free of any danger. When the Englishmen adopted opium as a commercial enterprise, they converted it into the hand of death and destruction. The foreign trade deficit England was facing because it needed the Chinese products, especially tea, but China did not need anything from them. Thus was created an immense foreign trade imbalance. It prompted them to "invent" opium's addiction for the common man of China.

Opium, the powerful economic force, was a very potent drug. It controlled human brains and lead to addiction. Those who controlled the production and supply of opium also controlled its slaves. As Bahram very shrewdly explained to his sasarji: "Opium is just like that. It is completely useless unless you're sick, but still people want it. And it is such a thing that once people start using it they can't stop; the market just gets larger and larger" (*River of Smoke,* 90). Opium became the medium of strengthening and expanding the Empire, as it was behind the generation of huge revenues that went into the Empire building.

In the beginning of their interactions with China, the west was totally at a loss because the Chinese wanted none of their products, whereas, they needed a lot from there. Thus a kind of trade originated that was in favour of the Chinese. It was totally according to the diktats of Free Trade, yet it was unprofitable. So it had to change. Opium became the medium of change when it was insidiously inserted into the Chinese market, legally, and later, against the law of the land. The "trafficking in opium tilted the balance of global trade to benefit the west" (Brook, 3). The edicts of the Chinese emperor against opium were proven to be powerless because of the "deadly combination of expanding Chinese demand and skyrocketing British supply. ...Lin Zexu was appointed imperial maritime commissioner in 1838 to stop the opium trade" (Brook, 6). His tough measures culminated into the opium war (1839-42), that ended with a shameful defeat for the Chinese.

It was this defeat, some historians claim, that opened China to the Western influence and resulted into its modernization. Just like some claim that India benefited largely through its colonization by the British because they gave it the foundation of modern nationalism and all the basic institutions required to run a state effectively. As if India was a wilderness, sans any system, before 1757 and it would never have modernized itself had it not been shamefully and deleteriously exploited by its colonizers. The other side of the same coin of exploitation was the havoc wreaked on the Indian farmers. This devastation of the economy of two prosperous Asian nations was whitewashed by the white people and even some native historians is shocking. The course of Chinese history was changed in the brief span of less than three generations and they did it so effectively, efficiently and insidiously that the world started to believe that China had always been a heavy consumer of opium since time immemorial. The long lasting image of the Chinese opium dens and addicts spread throughout the world and stuck with those of Chinese origin well up to mid-twentieth century. This wholesale whitewashing of history and silencing of all parallel versions prompted Ghosh to begin his Ibis trilogy of which *River of Smoke* is the second part.

Ghosh had stated in an interview with *BBC* that he had started the Ibis trilogy with its first part, *Sea of Poppies*, as the story of indentured immigrants from Bihar. The indentured immigration had started in the 1830's, at the end of the decade came the opium war with China and the firm establishment of the opium based trade of the Raj. It was no coincidence, pointed out Ghosh in the same interview, that they had to leave merely twenty years after the opium trade stopped. Thus is ended the cycle that had started with Warren Hastings' coming up with the idea of balancing the trade deficit of the East India Company with China. The other side of the same coin of exploitation was the havoc wreaked on the Indian farmers. That this devastation of the economy of two prosperous Asian nations was whitewashed by the White and even some native historians was shocking to him. His being a postcolonial thinker-writer made his position strong when he decided to create a series of novels on the imperial exploitation of a large part of his mother continent, i.e. Asia. The narrator and the characters with whom his sympathy lies at any point of time, have a voice that is strong and exposes incisively the exploitative nature and the double standards of the concept of free trade and those who used it for their sole benefit—the biggest imperial power of all the times—England.

Free trade was the excuse that the English merchants gave to explain away their unforgivable conduct. In fact, there was nothing "free" about their trade practices for others. Theirs was the side that had all the freedom. They had the license to exploit under the banner of free trade. It was not only the conservatives who favoured this legalized and systemic exploitation of the millions. Even the liberals were on its side. The British Parliament and queen were in league with the merchants whose actions brought the much needed revenues and many other things from all over the world. Mr. Charles King, the only honest man amongst all the merchants who had never tried to exploit the Chinese or trade in opium, and whose uprightness and goodwill were recognized by a personage as great as the Commissioner Lin himself, was universally disliked amongst white merchants. His refusal to deal in opium had resulted into his being thrown out of the clique of the merchants whose profit came from it.

The institutionalized and vicious cycle of the exploitation of the non-white peoples was because of the Empire over which the sun never set. The Chinese wanted no English products. Therefore, they were seduced to use opium. To adequately supply the demand thus created, they forced another of their colonies—India—to produce more and more of it by bringing a vast area of land under its cultivation belt. The Indian farmer was forced to stop growing other crops and to cultivate opium only. The sea of poppies inundated large areas of India and broke the age-old crop cycles and also damaged irreparably and irreversibly the sustainable way of land use and life. Patna and Malwa opium were the varieties that were exported. England had monopoly over opium trade in most parts of India. Even if a native entrepreneur like Seth Bahram had not entered the trade, it would have gone on unhampered and unaltered.

It was because of the champions of free trade that opium became the foundation of the whole economic system of the Empire. It financed the Empire and the surplus that was generated, went into the expansion of the Empire. The whole opium centric economy was, as Bahram told his father-in-law, very strange in nature. Opium was totally useless for an average healthy man. It became Important and useful only for its addicts. It was this fact that finally got the Englishmen's success in opening deep inroads into China. The English merchants used all means, from rhetoric to brute force, in order to convince those who opposed their line of thinking. They perpetuated their ideology in various garbs. Religion, politics, economics, ethics all ingredients went into the making of the pot-pourri used to convince all races all over the world. Burnham, Jardine, Dent, etc. are few of the most prominent voices that philosophy of a white exploiter. They are the forces of darkness to which Bahram sells his soul. He is betrayed at the end and regrets it later. Zadig Bey summed it all up very neatly when he warned his friend that the Chamber would fain yielding him up to the Chinese just to save Dent, as there was no gunboat behind him.

Bahramji's probable treatment in the hands of the English merchants would not at all be shocking, as it would be keeping with their treatment of his country and his fellow countrymen. The apostles of free trade increased the volume of trade with India in the seventeenth century, but when at the end of that century "great quantities of cheap and graceful Indian calicos, muslin and chintzes were imported in England, and they found such favour that the woolen and silk manufacturers were seriously alarmed...[they forced passing of Acts of] the Parliament...prohibiting...the use of any printed or dyed goods of which cotton formed any part" (Lecky qtd. in Raychoudhary, 63). Later they flooded the Indian market with cheap factory made cloth and damaged the system of production completely. The East India Company converted India from the workshop of the world to the producer of raw materials for English factories and the consumer of their products, and "about £100 million was drained in Britain from India between 1757 and 1815" (Raychoudhary, 68).

When India's manufacturing industries tried to survive even after this exploitation, *laissez-faire*, or free competition among the unequals played the role of dealing the fatal and final coup de grace. "Political domination was the basic factor in bringing Industrial Revolution in Britain" (Raychoudhary, 83) and the same modus operandi were used on China. "In 1830, the auditor-general of the East India Company declared that every year at least £4,000,000 had to be carried back from India to England" (Fairbank, 173). The Cambridge History further explains that this money was used to buy opium that was exported to China, to be sold in Canton and the sale yielded another £3,300,000. Thus, West had finally found a way to address the huge deficit it was facing in its trade with China. By 1830's it had finally found something that it could supply to China in return of many valuable things. Yet, no foreigners were allowed inside the walls of the city of Canton itself. They were not allowed to sell their goods anywhere else either. Opium, that was the mainstay of their trade equation, was soon to be removed from it through an imperial edict that banned its trade all over China. This edict was the final deciding factor that made the Western merchants' need to get unrestricted access to the Chinese market clear and pressing. What they wanted was possible only when all the Chinese restrictions on trade and movement of the westerners were lifted.

Whig liberalist policies found their compatible partner in the form of the Manchester lobby. Together, they adopted and modified from China itself the government's policy of non-intervention in trade policies and practices of the Chinese merchants. Ironically, guilds and a controlled market were the European way of trade and the exposure to new culture and system had brought in the novel idea of *laissez-faire* to Europe. *Laissez-faire*, a French word that literally means "to leave (somebody) to do (something)" took the form of the slogan of Free-Trade and it was used against the colonies to exploit them. It was the same ploy used against the Chinese too but there they found resistance to their looting. Commissioner Lin stood against their plan, and he seemed to be succeeding.

In response to the Captain's steps, the Commissioner blockaded the factories and ordered all the Chinese people working there out of the enclave. The enclave was effectively sealed from all the sides. Even its riverfront was blockaded. The Chinese servants who were removed in the morning returned as a corps of militia and were posted in the Maidan. Their whole manner had changed with the change in their role. They had left their old clothes and manners behind and had donned new uniform and pride that was previously never thought of. Captain Elliott's letter to the Commissioner that demanded travel permits for all, elicited a reply that underscored the true nature of opium trade. The letter stated that the white barbarian had:

> brought opium—that pervading poison—to this land, thus profiting themselves to the injury of others. As High Commissioner I issued an edict promising not to delve into the past but only requiring that the opium already

> here should be entirely delivered up and that further shipments should be effectually stopped from coming. Three days were prescribed within which to give a reply but none was received. As High Commissioner I had ascertained that the opium brought by Dent was comparatively in large quantity and summoned him to be examined. He too procrastinated for three days and the order was not obeyed. In consequence a temporary embargo was placed on the trade and the issuing of permits to go to Macau was stayed. In reading the letter of the English Superintendent I see no recognition of these circumstances, but only a demand for permits. I would ask: While my commands remain unanswered and my summonses unattended, how can permits be granted? Elliott has come into the territory of the Celestial Court as the English Superintendent. But his country, while itself interdicting the use of opium, has yet permitted the seduction and enticement of the Chinese people. (*River of Smoke,* 304)

The Commissioner demanded the surrender of the whole lot of opium and of all the foreigners signing a bond of obedience to his orders. They could then carry on with their trade, if it was legitimate. He knew that they could not seize the cargoes on the British ships as their naval forces were far superior. So, he took hostage all that were in the enclave. By his ploy he made them surrender all the opium. The merchants called it robbery and complained of being forced to betray their investors. They were totally at loss in understanding how "subjects of the world's most powerful nation" were made to do so against their wish (*River of Smoke,* 306). Mr. Slade offered them another perspective: that it'd give Lord Palmerstone a *casus belli* and it would then be possible to declare war. He presented his case with force and clarity and with precedents.

There was a heated debate in the British Parliament. Thomas Babbington Macaulay, the eloquent Whig parliamentarian, roared that the Englishmen belonged to a country unaccustomed to defeat, to submission or to shame; to a country which had exacted such reparation for the wrongs to her children as had made the ears of all who heard it to tingle...to a country which had not degenerated since the great Protector vowed that he would make the name of Englishman as much respected as ever had been the name of Roman citizen. (qtd. in Fairbank, 195). To this eloquent appeal to public emotions the Tory Gladstone responded with an appeal to reason and to the sense of justice and honour of the Englishmen. He declared the proposed war unjust and disgraceful. He openly condemned the act of his countrymen and also spoke against Captain Elliott's protecting a dealer in contraband goods. He called the war unjust and was in support of the anti-war resolution. He had mentioned the British flag hoisted in Canton to support and protect drug trafficking. Lord Palmerstone convinced the Parliament that the issue at hand was not opium trade, but all future trade between China and England. He reminded them that they had been insulted and war was the only reply. Both Elliott and Lin were removed disgracefully from their positions. Elliott's replacement, Sir Henry Pottinger, had explicit instructions from Palmerstone to get huge sums of compensation, "opening of 4 new ports, retention of Hong Kong and the cession of more islands where goods could be landed free of duty" (Fairbank, 201).

It wasn't about the specific instance of the East India Company or opium trade. It was all about imperialism as an exploitative system. Lenin was to call it the most corrupt form of exploitation later. In his famous essay "Imperialism, the Highest Stage of Capitalism", Lenin pronounced: "The enormous growth of industry and the remarkably rapid process of concentration of production in ever-larger enterprises are one of the most characteristic features of capitalism". Capitalism had its own tendencies and forces that grew in the nineteenth and twentieth centuries into their most shameless and exploitative form—imperialism. *Laissez-faire* demanded for a barrier free market for the home country on one hand. On the other hand, it gave rise to monopoly and its variations. "England became a capitalist country before any other, and by the middle of the nineteenth century, having adopted free trade, claimed to be the 'workshop of the world'" (Lenin).

India was the workshop of the world in sixteenth and seventeenth centuries. It was slowly converted into a producer of raw materials through a planned process that was to be replicated in all the colonies and even in China. The mechanism of converting a workshop into a producer of raw materials and consumer of finished English products was perfected in India. The gradual and definite destruction of all native production and manufacturing industries, the molding of the nature of native economy and crop production cycles and the closing and opening game of domestic markets was something in which the English merchants and Parliament were adept at. They had ruined Indian industries and the capital looted from there and through the continued revenue generated from there, they sponsored industrial revolution and the expansion of the Empire. Their next cycle of capitalist expansion was to be funded by using the hitherto gained capital in cycles like that based on opium in China. They wanted tea and gave opium in exchange. They had a surplus which was endangered. They reacted to that with barbaric and decisive force. The Chinese had always looked upon the British merchants as barbarians and time proved them right. The British and French gunships bombarded Canton and left only the factories unharmed. As Neel would tell Deeti, the angry mob set fire to the factories and they were never rebuilt. Later on, there was:

> a typical 'White Town' of the kind the British made everywhere they went—it was cut off from the rest of the city, and very few Chinese were allowed inside, only servants. The streets were clean and leafy, and the buildings were as staid and dull as the people inside them. But behind that façade of bland respectability the foreigners were importing more opium than ever from India—after winning the war the British had quickly put an end to Chinese efforts to prohibit the drug. (*River of Smoke,* 329)

Things had changed as the foreigners had forced the Chinese to open up so that they could bring more opium than they did before. Neel hated the enclave of Shamian and looked at it with disgust as "the new enclave was like a monument built by the forces of evil to celebrate their triumphal march through history" (*River of Smoke,* 324).

WORKS CITED

Brook, Timothy and Bob Tadashi Wakabayashi. "Opium's History in China". *Opium Regimes: China, Britain and Japan, 1839-1952.* Ed. Timothy Brook and Bob Tadashi Wakabayashi. University of California Press: Los Angeles, 2000.

Fairbank, John K. Ed. *The Cambridge History of China.* Vol. 10. *Late Ch'ing, 1800-1911, Part 1.* Cambridge University Press: Cambridge, 1978.

Ghosh, Amitav. "Opium financed British Rule in India". *BBC News.* 23 June 2008.

———. *River of Smoke.* 2011. n.d. Web. PDF. 27 November 2011.

Lenin, Vladimir Illyich. "Imperialism, the Highest Stage of Capitalism". Fordham.edu. n.d. Web. 24 December 2011.

Malpas, Simon. *The Postmodern.* New York: Routledge, 2005.

Raychoudhary, S.C. *Social, Cultural and Economic History of India.* Surjeet: Delhi, 1998.

9

Postcolonial Reading of Boundaries in Amitav Ghosh's *In an Antique Land*

Vishwanath Bite

Amitav Ghosh's *In an Antique Land* (1992) incorporates two narrative strands: a medieval narrative and a contemporary one. In the medieval narrative, Ghosh attempts to reconstruct the lives of a medieval slave named Bomma and his patron, Ben Yiju, a Tunisian Jewish merchant who lived in the twelfth century and moved between different parts of the Orient. His journey took him to Egypt and Aden then Mangalore before he finally settled in Egypt. As Ghosh reconstructs the lives of these two medieval characters, he conjures up a medieval, cosmopolitan world where people moved between different parts of the region without the troublesome procedures of visas and checkpoints. The region was not yet divided by borders that were later carved by colonialism. Also, people interacted regardless of cultural, religious, linguistic or class differences. For his historical research, Ghosh relies on translations of medieval letters and documents by the prominent medievalist scholar S.D. Goitein as well as his own decipherment of some manuscripts that are written in Judeo-Arabic. These documents were housed at the Cairo Geniza and later transferred to libraries in the West where Ghosh gains access to them.

The medieval narrative runs parallel to a contemporary narrative based on Ghosh's anthropological fieldwork (for his

PhD research) in two Egyptian villages, Lataifa and Nashawy back in the early 1980s. His journey leads to a world that is different from that of Ben Yiju—a postcolonial world fraught with boundaries that run across national, cultural, linguistic, religious and class differences. Unlike Ben Yiju, Ghosh feels out of place in Egypt as the *fellaheen* (villagers) constantly ask him questions that reflect a monolithic, stereotyped notion of India and Indians. These boundaries are contested in the light of the heterogeneity and tolerance of the medieval world. During Ghosh's second visit to Egypt in 1988, there is a reference to the Iran-Iraq War (1980-88) and the travel of many villagers to work in Iraq. The narrative ends prior to the outbreak of the Gulf War (1991) during his next visit to Egypt in 1990. This is a world torn by war and strife that divide people and nations yet one that still holds a possibility for cross-cultural communications; affinities and bonds develop between Ghosh and the Egyptians despite their national, religious and cultural differences.

Geopolitical and historical forces may drive people and nations apart—people who used to co-exist on the same land. However, there are moments in history that recover affinities and bonds, challenging these separating forces. One contemporary example can be found in Palestine which used to embrace people of different ethnicities and religions including Jews. With the rise of Israel as a state for Jews, conflict has replaced co-existence and led to a rift that confounds national with religious identities. This rigid framework, adopted by Israel—where the law of return privileges Jewish immigration to historical Palestine while denying the Right of Return for Palestinians (as UN resolution 194 upholds)—is contested even by Jews. Rabbi Michael Lerner underscores the support of many Jews for the 25th January Egyptian Revolution (2011) thereby undermining the view of the conflict as Arab versus Jewish: "We hope that Egyptians will hear the news that they have the strong support from many in the Jewish world" (n.pag). Earlier in the article, Rabbi Lerner employs history to compare the plight of the Jewish people in the past to that of Egyptians in the present:

> Yet it is impossible for Jews to forget our heritage as victims of another Egyptian tyrant—the Pharaoh whose reliance on brute force was overthrown when the Israelite slaves managed to escape from Egypt some 3,000 years ago. That story of freedom retold each year at our Passover "Seder" celebration, and read in synagogues in the past month, has often predisposed the majority of Jews to side with those struggling for freedom around the world (un paginated).

This "story" stands as a counter-narrative to official narratives. The identities of Jews in the previous citation are shaped by their resistance to tyranny and it is not only a matter of race and ethnicity. Thus, it is a story where continuities between the past of one group and the present of the other are joined, affinities are highlighted, boundaries are contested, stereotypes are deconstructed and eventually "mental maps" (to borrow Migdal's term) are redrawn.

Seeking affinities and continuities between the past and the present is at the heart of Amitav Ghosh's *In an Antique Land.* Inderpal Grewal writes: "[i]nstead of the break with the past that diaspora theories suggest, Ghosh's text produced continuities of many kinds, especially of the precolonial past with the transnational present" (184). The medieval, precolonial world Ghosh conjures up—through reconstructing the lives of the medieval Ben Yiju and Bomma—is one where travel was smooth and where people intermingled with one another regardless of differences. As this world comes to life in the text, the postcolonial world is subverted—a world where common grounds and mutual understandings hardly exist. Cross-cultural understandings of the past are replaced with barriers that separate people and create stereotypes of the other.

Ghosh's text constitutes an important intervention in so far as it incorporates histories that challenge contemporary geopolitical boundaries. The work of subaltern scholars highlight subalterns' central role in shaping history and politics. Their work critiques official mainstream narratives for leaving them out, Guha writes:

> What clearly is left out of this unhistorical historiography is the *politics of the people*. For parallel to the domain of elite politics there existed throughout the colonial period another domain of Indian politics in which the principal actors were not the dominant groups of the indigenous society or the colonial authorities but the subaltern classes and groups constituting the mass of labouring population and the intermediate strata in town—that is, the people. (Italics in original 40)

Unlike mainstream historiography, Ghosh's text represents subalterns as active agents in shaping their world and gives them a voice. In the opening pages of his book, Ghosh inverts the structure of official history—first introducing the medieval subalterns, the slave and his patron, who become the protagonists of his narrative and then moves on to give an account of figures and events that would usually form the subject matter of mainstream historiography (*Antique Land*, 13-15). Here and throughout the text, they merely serve as a backdrop to the history of the medieval subalterns.

Nationalism, as Edward Said notes, entails boundaries that are not unlike those embedded within the colonial enterprise: "to accept nativism is to accept the consequences of Imperialism, the racial, religious, and political divisions imposed by Imperialism itself" (*Culture and Imperialism*, 276). In other words, boundaries within the nationalist context are constructed between members of postcolonial nation-states. In order to examine how peoples' histories in Ghosh's text subvert these boundaries, it is important to understand the spatial and temporal configurations associated with postcolonial geopolitical boundaries in the contemporary era. These boundaries—initially constructed by Western colonial powers—do not only entail spatial divisions but also a Eurocentric conception of history where the East as a "geographical space" "temporally" lags behind in relation to the more modern and advanced West.

Histories in Ghosh's text present an alternative configuration of space and time to that embedded within contemporary boundaries. His travel in time conjures up a pre-colonial world that is more progressive and advanced than the postcolonial contemporary world that he visits. Contemporary boundaries are subverted through Ghosh's juxtaposition of past and present. However, a reading that stops at interpreting the text as mere juxtaposition between both worlds risks simplification. The contemporary narrative depicts a postcolonial world where boundaries separate people; however, there are numerous stories in this narrative that uncover bonds and affinities forged beyond national borders. Moreover, the past and the present in the text are not confined within separate realms. Ghosh's journeys through space and time converge as he discovers traces of the medieval "time" in the contemporary 'space'. Thus, histories in the text question divisions produced by boundaries through uncovering affinities and continuities across space and time.

The contemporary world in the narrative reveals spatial and temporal configurations that separate people. Any place is a potential checkpoint; Ghosh is stopped by an officer on his visit to a shrine during his stay in Egypt and his passport is checked. Earlier, he is asked for his identity card by one the villagers who suspect him. The contemporary map of the region is best encapsulated in his reference to an incident when one of the *fellaheen* asks him whether he can reach India on a donkey:

> Thinking of all the reasons why it would not be possible to travel from Egypt to India on a donkey, something caught fire in my imagination and I began to talk as I had never before, in Lataifa and Nashawy, of *visas* and *quarantines*, of the *ribbon of war* that stretched from Iraq to Afghanistan, of the heat of Dasht-e-kebir and the height of the Hindu Kush, of the foraging of snow leopards and the hairiness of yaks. (Emphasis mine, 173)

The above description uncovers a geopolitical map that is far removed from that of Ben Yiju's world—a world where different parts of the region were interconnected: "to the young Ben Yiju, journeying eastwards would have appeared as the simplest and most natural means of availing himself of the most rewarding possibilities his world had to offer" (Ghosh,

IAAL, 153). In Ben Yiju's time, travel was neither contingent upon *visas* nor was the region yet distorted by *quarantines* and *ribbons of war*. Paradoxically, means of communications are much faster and advanced today yet mobility in the past was much easier. In this respect, Hind Wassef writes: "No national boundaries, in the sense we have today, restricted such movement. And when he Ben Yiju went to live in Aden and Mangalore, there too no question of nationality arose that made him an outsider or refugee in the modern sense" (87). In the light of Wassef's words, the non-existence of borders has borne on Ben Yiju's status as he traveled, for borders are intertwined with the notion of citizenship.

In fact, Ben Yiju's experience was a collective one in the same way Ghosh's experience in Egypt represents the experience of many in the contemporary world. Territorial divisions in the contemporary post-colonial world have not only problematized travel and movement between different parts of the region but they have also precluded mutual understanding between people. In a 1993 interview published in *Newsweek*, Ghosh says: "Today nationalism, once conceived as a form of freedom, is really destroying our world.... The nation-state prevents the development of free exchange between peoples" (52). Unlike Ben Yiju, the Hindu/Indian Ghosh is made to feel different in Egypt as the Muslim/Egyptian *fellaheen* consistently ask him questions that reflect contemporary intolerance towards difference. Their questions also reveal stereotypes born out of these boundaries. Their questions about whether he worships cows, whether he is circumcised and whether Indians burn their dead derive from a stereotyped, monolithic conception of India.

Boundaries are not only confined to Ghosh's experience in Egypt. He recalls stories from his part of the world which reflect hostilities and intolerance on the basis of religious difference. He recalls an early childhood experience when he used to live with his family in Dhaka (in East Pakistan which later became Bangladesh) and the threat which a minority group of Hindu refugees were subjected to in this Muslim majority area. Many of these Hindu refugees would seek protection in the house of Ghosh's Hindu family who used to take them in and have them settle in the garden of their house. Ghosh recounts a particular incident when they were all besieged by a crowd that wanted to get in and the painful experience they all went through. He also refers to parallel stories in Calcutta where the Hindu majority committed acts of violence against the Muslim minority though in both cases he refers the benevolence on the part of other Muslims and Hindus which saved many lives (*Antique Land,* 204-10). Towards the end of the text, there are also references to the Iran-Iraq War and Ghosh's last visit to Egypt takes place in 1990 during the interval between Iraq's invasion of Kuwait (1990) and the Gulf War (1991). This is a world torn by violence and struggle over constructed borders.

The medieval narrative conjures up a different geopolitical map. Unlike Ghosh who feels out of place in Egypt, Ben Yiju was part of a harmonious community of merchants based on "understandings that clearly presuppose free and direct communications between the participants, despite their cultural, religious and linguistic differences" (Ghosh, *Antique Land,* 280). In fact, Ghosh goes a step further in reconstructing the story of the Jewish Ben Yiju and Bomma—who was familiar (Ghosh believes) with unorthodox beliefs and traditions that are subversive of Hinduism (*Antique Land,* 263). Their relationship was not only established beyond religious differences but one that was based—Ghosh would like to think—on seeking common grounds. Ghosh would like to imagine that both of them shared an interest in unorthodox practices that "eventually became a small patch of level ground between them" (*Antique Land,* 263).

In addition, class differences did not constitute a problem in marriage in medieval times, in contrast to the present. In the contemporary narrative, Ghosh refers to one of the *fellaheen* who marries the girl he loves after he travels to the Gulf and makes sufficient money—that is after he moves up in the material scale. Unlike the contemporary subaltern, class difference was not problematic; Ben Yiju marries his slave Ashu. In pre-colonial times, "'slavery' was...often a kind of career opening" and "a means of creating fictive ties of kinship between people who were otherwise unrelated" (Ghosh, *Antique Land,* 260). There is a difference—Ghosh points out—between past and present connotations of slavery.

These examples subvert the time configuration modeled on dominant Eurocentric views about the linear forward movement of history. Ghosh's narrative presents an alternative time configuration; it presents a reversed model where the past is shown to be more progressive and liberal than the present as Padmini Mongia writes: "Bomma's mediaeval society is richly seen by Ghosh as a vital, cosmopolitan one that put to shame our current notions of cosmopolitanism" (159).

Not only does the text present an alternative temporal configuration but also an alternative spatial configuration that subverts the one produced through colonial territorial divisions of the region in the early part of the twentieth century. Retrieving stories of the past play a central role in subverting boundaries constructed in the present. However, it is important to note that Ghosh's text does not produce an essential model of past and present. Stories in the contemporary narrative challenge contemporary borders and boundaries by uncovering contemporary affinities and continuities across space. In Nashawy, Ustaz Sabry warmly introduces Ghosh to the villagers referring to their countries' parallel histories, socio-economic conditions, mutual support and the collaboration of their leaders during colonial and postcolonial rule (134). These stories challenge the borders of nation-states and mainstream narratives that highlight differences and divisions between them.

Ghosh demonstrates in an article how the Third World has not merely been a recipient of nationalism but has shaped and redefined its meaning so that it has become associated not—as Ghosh notes—with Western conception of it as "an ideology of xenophobia and parochialism" but with "xenophilia, the love of the other, the affinity for strangers—a feeling that lives very deep in the human heart but whose existence is rarely acknowledged" ("Confessions of a Xenophile" unpaginated). For Ghosh, the institutionalized partnership in the form of the

Non-Aligned Movement had cultural roots and origins; he believes it is a movement whereby cross-cultural dialogues between nations were resumed after they were disrupted for some time by colonialism. Conversely, he believes in the integral role of such an institutionalized structure for cross-cultural interface: "no matter how sincere an individual's desire for cultural communication might be, it is impossible for such exchanges to occur in the absence of an institutional framework" ("Confessions of a Xenophile" unpaginated). Continuities are integral to Ghosh's vision not only spatially and temporally; he views continuities between partnerships established on top (the institutional) and affinities forged from below (the cultural).

Several stories in the narrative uncover affinities and bonds across space and challenge the spatial configuration created by national borders—configurations constructed and maintained by power structures. Stories of the people incorporated in the narrative produce a spatial configuration that conjures up an alternative map—a map where people in the postcolonial Third World are not wholly trapped within national borders of the state. The text represents affinities that are products of cross-cultural communication and lived experiences forged beyond national and cultural boundaries. Ghosh refers to a conversation with the father of one of the villagers who once joined the Second World War as a worker—an experience which brought him into contact with Indian soldiers. Ghosh narrates: "they [Indian soldiers] had made a deep impression on his memory and at our first meeting he had greeted me as though he was resuming an interrupted friendship" (231). In fact the entire narrative is based on resuming "an interrupted friendship" between people of the region which according to Ghosh was disrupted with colonial intervention in the region. Cross-cultural encounters bear on the villagers' empathetic feelings towards Ghosh making Ustaz Sabry's mother tell him at one point: "Just the other day he [Sabry] said to me, the people of Egypt and India have been like brothers for centuries. You must consider yourself one of our family" (186). Such moments foreground what Migdal refers to as "people's mental maps"—maps that contest national state borders.

The text also exhibits another kind of affinity—one that develops not on the basis of common grounds between nations but on the basis of human empathy. This empathy is revealed during Nabeel's (one of the villagers) visit to Ghosh's place and the former's reflection on his homesickness. Their encounter represents a moment of human understanding that transcends difference. In retrospect, Ghosh comments: "Nabeel's comment stayed in my mind; I was never able to forget it, for it was the first time anyone in Lataifa or Nashawy had attempted an enterprise similar to mine—to enter my imagination and look at my situation as it might appear to me" (152).

Through Ghosh's personal experience, the reader is not only exposed to affinities between people but also to parallel stories across national borders. Ghosh hears a story about governmental attempts to build a canal and people's opposition to the idea on the basis that the canal will pass through the shrine of Sidi Abu-Kanaka (138-40). Eventually a miracle forces officials to change the route of the canal. When they fail to dig at the site of the tomb, they open it and find out that that the body is still intact (Ghosh, *Antique Land,* 139). This story stands parallel to another story Ghosh hears in India about a Bhuta shrine though in this story it is a road instead of a canal (265-66). Here again people resist the construction of the road but officials proceed in their plan until the bulldozers were fixed in place and eventually the route was changed (265). Usually nations construct stories about themselves that distinguish them from another. Ghosh's text foregrounds stories that reveal similarities between people.

Boundaries in Ghosh's narrative are not only subverted through juxtaposing past and present or revealing affinities across space but also through uncovering continuities between the past and the present. Ghosh demonstrates how moments from the past which do not fit within contemporary world views are severed by "History". In other words, mainstream historiography configures a certain relationship between the past and the present and omits what does not fit. Said notes "how memories of the past are shaped in accordance with a certain notion of what 'we' or, for that matter, 'they' really are" ("Invention, Memory and Place", 177). Unlike mainstream history where stories of the past are constructed to serve the present, in Ghosh's text the present is shaped by the past. Ghosh goes through an experience during his attempt to visit the shrine of Sidi Abu-Hasira which reveals to him the suppressive force of official history. Sidi Abu-Hasira, a man of saintly qualities, is of North African Jewish origin and after his move to Egypt converts from Judaism to Islam (Ghosh, *Antique Land*, 329).

On his way to visit the shrine, Ghosh is stopped and sent for interrogation to an officer who cannot understand the rationale behind an Indian's interest in visiting the tomb of a Jewish figure. Ghosh links this to the role of official history in forgetting or leaving out past stories and thereby severing links that once existed between people in the past. In reference to his inability to provide contemporary evidence to the officer about past "intertwined histories", he writes: "I had been caught straddling a border unaware that the writing of History had predicated its own self-fulfillment" (*Antique Land*, 339-40). Later in his research about Sidi Abu-Hasira, he discovers that the site of the shrine brought together members of religious groups (not only Jews) thereby revealing to him the diversity which characterizes the site of the shrine. Ghosh reflects: "It seemed uncanny that I had never known all those years that in defiance of the enforcers of History, a small remnant of Bomma's world had survived, not far from where I had been living" (342). Traces of the cosmopolitan past outlive the suppressive force of official history. The latter is embedded in the worldview of the officer (the text suggests) who interrogates him and also in the intimidating questions he is subjected to during his stay in the villages of Lataifa and Nashawy.

Ghosh blames "the West" for bringing this harmonious, heterogeneous, tolerant world to an end. In the text, the "West" manifests itself in different forms. Colonial intervention in the sixteenth century brought an end to "a culture of accommodation and compromise" (Ghosh, *Antique Land,* 260). Ghosh also links the process whereby the Geniza was divested of its documents to the Imperial enterprise. He also notes an "irony" in the transfer of these documents—many of which belong to the Egyptian Jewish community—to the West since "for the most part they went to countries which would have long since destroyed the Geniza had it been part of their own history" whereas "Masr...was left with no traces of its riches: not a single scrap to remind her of that aspect of her past" (95).

The role of the West in constructing contemporary boundaries is best couched in a statement where he says: "It was as though the borders that were to divide Palestine several decades later had already been drawn, through time rather than territory, to allocate a choice of Histories" (95). The "West" still maintains its foothold even after the end of colonialism; the movement of history within the postcolonial context is conceived of in Eurocentric terms. This Eurocentric model comes out in the heated conversation between Ghosh and Imam Ibrahim when each of them argues about the superiority and progress of his postcolonial country and the inferiority of the other using a "Western" yardstick (to what extent the country of each is closer to the West). Ghosh comments: "We were both travelling, he and I: we were travelling in the West" (236). The result of their "travel in the West" entails the construction of barriers between them: "it seemed to me that the Imam and I [Ghosh] had participated in our final defeat, in the dissolution of the centuries that had linked us..." (Ghosh, *Antique Land,* 236). "Travel in the West" leads not to progress but to a setback. Mongia writes:

> By offering a glimpse into the cosmopolitan, humane circuit of relations prevalent in mediaeval India up to the moment when European dominance via colonialism enters its history, Ghosh poses a postcolonial challenge via the pre-colonial. In Ghosh's telling of this history, an alternative picture emerges, one that is tantalizing and heartbreaking because it offers a picture of the world and of relations between peoples which might have

> unfolded had the rupture introduced by colonialism not occurred. (161)

By uncovering continuities across space and time, subaltern histories in the text contest boundaries and reveal their constructed nature. Robert Dixon notes that Ghosh neither relies on Western languages nor on theoretical models in retrieving the subaltern. For his purpose, Ghosh makes use—Dixon notes—of the Arabic language and empirical research in both history and anthropology. The latter approach "is a challenging model to literary critics in the Western academy whose critical practice involves the applications of high theory to third world texts—we might call *that* 'travelling in the East'" (Dixon, 22). In the light of Dixon's words, the movement in Ghosh shifts from East to West; stories and lived experiences in the third world deconstruct boundaries initially constructed by the West. Also, contemporary boundaries are challenged through a movement from present to past; the text reverses the relationship so that it is not the present that controls what is to be remembered but it is the present moment that is shaped by the past.

WORKS CITED

Gandhi, Leela. "'A Choice of Histories': Ghosh vs. Hegel *In An Antique Land*". *New Literature Review,* 40 (2003): 17-32.

Ghosh, Amitav. "Confessions of a Xenophile". *Outlook Magazine,* 22 Dec. 2008: n. pag. Web. 29 Dec. 2011.

———. *In an Antique Land.* London, Granta Books. 1992.

———. Interview with Claire Chambers. "'The Absolute Essentialness of Conversations': A Discussion with Amitav Ghosh". *Journal of Postcolonial Writing,* 41.1 (May 2005): 26- 39. *Informaworld.* Web. 29 Dec. 2011.

———. Interview with Gretchen Luchsinger. "Lessons from the 12th Century". *Newsweek,* 13 Dec. 1993: 52.

———. Interview with T. Vijay Kumar. "'Postcolonial' Describes You as Negative': An Interview with Amitav Ghosh". *Interventions*, 9.1 (2007): 99-105. *Informaworld.* Web. 29 Dec. 2011.

Shammas, Anton. "The Once and Future Egypt". Rev. of *In an Antique Land*, by Amitav Ghosh. *New York Times Book*

Review 1 Aug. 1993: 26. *Academic Search Complete*. Web. 29 Dec. 2011. Soueif, Ahdaf. "Intimately Egyptian". Rev. of *In an Antique Land*, by Amitav Ghosh. *Times Literary Supplement* 15 Jan. 1993: 7.

Srivastava, Neelam. "Amitav Ghosh's Ethnographic Fictions: Intertextual Links between *In an Antique Land* and His Doctoral Thesis". *The Journal of Commonwealth Literature,* 36.2 (2001): 45-64. *SAGE Premier*. Web. 29 Dec. 2011.

Wassef, Hind, "Beyond the Divide: History and National Boundaries in the Work of Amitav Ghosh". *Alif: Journal of Comparative Poetics,* 18 (1998): 75-95. *JSTOR*. Web. 29 Dec. 2011.

10

Socio-politico-historical Documentation: A Study of Amitav Ghosh's *Sea of Poppies*

Ch. Swathi

Perhaps it would not be an exaggeration to ascertain what has already been said—Ghosh's writings are a true reflection of society. And the novel in question *Sea of Poppies* (2008) is an epitome of realistic depiction set in the period of Opium wars, where history forms the backdrop against which the lives of unfortunates are depicted quite realistically. The novel accommodates people from multifarious backgrounds drawn towards a common destiny. The blend of people from different backgrounds is such that one gets a glance at varied cultural backgrounds—Zachary is an offspring of a white man and a black woman which makes him a mulatto; the lascars and girmitiyas are again chosen from different castes and classes with their own rituals and cultures, and there are a host of other 'English' characters like Mr. Burnham and Paulette. The characters that picture in the book mostly consist of people from the margins who become the representatives of unfortunate people across the globe. It is quite interesting to note that the lives of many characters are re-fashioned by sweep of socio-political and historical events they have no control on.

A common notion among many scholars, that oppression and resistance co-exist resulting in certain level of subversion in many instances, proves right in the novel. In the book subversion takes place in the beginning itself where Deeti feels an odd inclination to include the Ibis and its crew in her shrine: "I just know it must be there; and not just the ship, but also many of those who are in it; they too must be on the walls of our puja room" (9). The accommodation of people from various backgrounds into Deeti's shrine is an act of refashioning the identities and creating a whole new set of people who are rendered by fate as 'jahaj bhais' and 'jahaj bhens'. This ship brotherhood that crops between girmitiyas from a shared destination is a proof of formation of new relationships that stand at odds against the set rules and norms of society. And sharing life between such a multifarious group of people on sea provides an opportunity to defy norms that rule the land. And the journey motif is clear as the passengers on board the 'Ibis' fashion new identities. And Deeti's shrine is a new place where people—who do not count in the lives of rich landlords—are remembered forever as new-born.

At this juncture it is useful to understand the word 'girmitiya' as it carries a lot of history to it. When Deeti hears the word she realizes the implications of being a girmitiya. She understands that they are so called because "in exchange for money, their names were entered on 'girmits'—agreements written on pieces of paper. The silver that was paid for them went to their families, and they vanished, as if into the netherworld" (72). The issue of immigration, a recurring theme in Ghosh, finds place in this context. The atrocities meted out to the indentured labour are depicted quite vividly through the experiences of the 'coolies' aboard the Ibis as they are shipped to an unknown territory. It is useful here to focus on the issue of indentured labour, a favourite theme with Amitav Ghosh. The system of transporting indentured labour to far-off places facilitated the rulers with ample hands to labour throughout their lives. This system indirectly meant slavery with an altered name where the lives of the 'girmityas' were bound to the whims and fancies of their lords and their lives are at the disposal of their owners to whom they had bargained not only their bodies but also their souls. However, as the book is just the first of the trilogy it is premature to comment on this issue.

Journey motif stands clear and loud through the book and the ship 'Ibis' becomes a platform for many unfortunates to come together as a family and their brotherhood surpasses all boundaries of discrimination. They are a proof to unity that could stand as a solution to merge all 'imaginary boundaries' irrespective of cast and creed. The vessel that carries a multifarious sect of people at once becomes a vehicle to realize dreams and to earn money (for the rulers) and an illusionary vehicle of transport to the coolies. Fear of the unknown is evident in the passengers of Ibis as their destiny is unknown, they do not know what inhabits the land they are being taken to. This is depicted through the reflections of Deeti, who compares Mauritius with Lanka—an island infested with demons:

> She tried to imagine what it would be like to be in their place, to know that you were forever an outcast; to know that you would never again enter your father's house, that you would never throw your arms around your mother; never eat a meal with your sisters and brothers; never feel the cleansing touch of the Ganga. And to know also that for the rest of your days you would eke out a living on some wild, demon-plagued island? (72)

The fear of being uprooted and dislocated forever is evident in such anticipation. The characters act as agents who mirror the lives of indentured labour—coolies—who were driven by their fates to far off places in order to survive. Again there are many reasons stated for the displacement of people throughout—for instance Deeti is forced by circumstances, where in order to save herself from immolation elopes with an untouchable, in whom she finds true love; Munia is forced by her family circumstances where she is rendered an outcast. As is in the interest of Ghosh these characters become the voice through which marginal issues are streamlined. By doing so Ghosh confers agency to the powerless.

The ship also symbolizes corruption and slavery as it was built to serve as a 'blackbirder', a vessel to transport slaves. The formal abolition of slavery transforms the vessel into a carrier of girmitiyas', indentured labour. And the description of the ship—first through the eyes of Deeti who feels its presence in mind, without even setting her eyes on it, renders eeriness and uncertainty to it. Her description of it as an apparition deepens the inhibitions. At once the ship asserts itself as an apparition to Deeti; to sahibs it is a means of covering up losses in opium trade with China by transportation of coolies; and for the Halder family the winds from the ship are 'suqlat', a colour representing sudden reversals of fortune. And there surely is a turn in Neel's fortune but in a negative manner.

It is a relevant undertaking to highlight the issue of power here. There are various manifestations of power and in this novel the issue of power is a major theme, introduced mainly through the story of the royal family's encounter with the British. The shift in power relations can be studied closely by using the concept of power defined by French philosopher Michel Foucault. The issue of exploitation of power can be introduced here where Neel is wrongly accused of forgery and is sent to prison as an ordinary person. Their family is completely ripped off of power and forced to live on consideration of their employee. Not content with this the British arrange for deportation of Neel to Mauritius for completion of his sentence as a prisoner. One cannot but draw parallels between Neel and the Burmese king Thebaw and his family, mentioned in Ghosh's *The Glass Palace* (2000), exiled to a remote place, Ratnagiri, in India. This system of exile can be understood clearly through the notion of power proposed by French philosopher Michael Foucault. According to Foucault,

> Power is something that a group of people or an institution possesses and it is concerned with oppression and constraint. He states that power is often conceptualised as the capacity of powerful agents to realise their will over the will of powerless people, and the ability to force them to do things which they do not wish to do. Power is also often seen as a possession, something which is held onto by those in power and

which those who are powerless try to wrest from their control. (Mills, 33-35)

The Royal descendant is rendered powerless and exiled to a place and thus pushed to the periphery from center, from power to powerlessness. Foucault's *Discipline and Punish* (1977) discusses how the exercise of power and domination has been conceptualised within society as a constructive feature of social life. Discipline, according to him, is a way of controlling the movement and operations of the body in a constant way. It is a type of power that coerces the body by regulating and dividing up its movement and the space and time in which it moves. It is a technique of power which provides procedures for training individuals where its practice is shifted from the body to the psyche as the primary target of punishment, such as deprival of wealth and rights or liberation (138).

Foucault's work illustrates that when a group of people are separated from society it is not a random affair. They are discerningly divided off from the population, through discursive and exclusionary exercises of sovereign power, and subjected to disciplinary ways that control them through strategic power relations. This is evident in the case of Neel as he is exiled to a distant place from his homeland and monitored closely by the rulers. Through this pathetic situation, Ghosh projects the peak of suppression, domination and colonialism of the British Empire.

The notion of 'Delinquency' as proposed by Foucault can be used to understand the operations of power. This is part of the discipline and punishable theory that is evident in Neel's case. A 'delinquent', according to Foucault, is created by the operation of the carceral system and the human sciences, and strictly separated from other popular illegal activities. He is part of a small, hardened group of criminals, identified with the lower social classes. Most importantly, he is defined as abnormal, and analysed and controlled by the mechanisms that Foucault describes. There are several advantages in replacing the criminal by the delinquent: delinquents are clearly set apart from the rest of society, and therefore easy to supervise and control. Foucault argues that the figure of the delinquent was a response to the danger presented by the lower orders in the nineteenth century. It is a common practice in rural areas to brand the tribal and other lower community groups as born criminals who are then used as scapegoats by the powerful for their own convenience (266).

Neel becomes a scapegoat and is gradually deprived of the basic traditional necessities like food from home. In the beginning he is allowed to receive visitors and to receive food from his home as the culture persists. But gradually his treatment alters and he is treated with utmost carelessness and neglect that the prison-in-charge and others insult him beyond words. He is ripped off his honour and pride. As he is driven out of his place Neel's thoughts are dragged towards his wife whom he faces stripped of all pride and shame: "Neel stumbled and lowered his eyes; he could not bear for her to look at him; it was as if the uncovering of her face had stripped the veil from his own manhood, leaving him naked and exposed to the gloating pity of the world, to a shame that could never be overcome" (174). He is dishonoured in front of his people and deported to a far-off place like any ordinary convict and is beaten and treated very grossly.

The issue of power relations is starkly evident in the book where most of the characters become victims in the power game. The plight of those royal families who have assisted the British in establishing a strong hold on Indian soil is evident through the story of Halder family that is ultimately cheated off its dignity and zamindary by the deceptive white sahibs. The need to integrate themselves with the powerful rulers as a survival tactics is evident from the following lines:

> In the era of the Mughals, they had ingratiated themselves with the dynasty's representatives; at the time of the East India Company's arrival, they had extended a wary welcome to the newcomers; when the British went to war against the Muslim rulers of Bengal, they had lent money to one side and sepoys to the other, waiting to see which would prevail. After the British proved victorious, they had proved as adept at the learning of

> English as they had previously been in the acquisition of Persian and Urdu. When it was to their advantage, they were glad to shape their lives to the world of the English. (84)

One cannot but draw parallels between the Halders, and Parsis mentioned in Bapsi Sidhwa's *Ice-Candy Man (*1988) where the plight of the minority community is such that they must manage to hunt with the tiger and run with the hare simultaneously. The habit of the whites to use people around them to meet their own ends is evident in case of Neel Halder who meets a very impolite and rude behaviour from Mr. Burnham who does not find any scope for profits possible with Neel. Neel's father's insistence to familiarize with the ways of the English is an attempt at identification with the ruling race which ironically proves a source of indignation of whites for Neel, as it is a known fact that the whites tried to produce a sect of natives who would inculcate their ways of life and represent them when necessary to rule over the other natives. But this westernization was supposed to be restricted where the new breed of natives should not try to integrate themselves so completely into the English ways and view themselves as equals to the Whites. This division was guarded closely:

> The Raja had hired a British tutor for his son, to make sure that he had a thorough schooling in English. But far from putting him at ease in the society of Calcutta's Englishmen, Neel's education had served exactly the opposite end...by both temperament and education, Neel was little fitted for the company of such men as Mr. Burnham, and they in turn tended to regard him with dislike that bordered on contempt. (88)

Such a man of refined behaviour and of royal background is dragged out of his house and degraded to such an extent that he is left in tatters and treated as worse than an ordinary person. The arrogance of ordinary servants of the British empire, even while in encounter with the kings of India, is evident during a conversation between Mr. Doughty and Zachary, as Mr. Doughty comments thus on the royal lineage: "it's not as if he's real nobility, mind: the Rascallys call themselves Rogers, but they're just Ryes with an honourary title-bucksheesh for loyalty to the Crown" (48) and the resistance to nativisation is depicted through Mr. Doughty's warning to Zachary:

> The zubben, dear boy, is the flash lingo of the East. It's easy enough to jin if you put your head to it. Just a little peppering of nigger-talk mixed with a few girleys. But mind your Oordoo and Hindee doesn't sound too good: don't want the world to think you have gone native. And don't mince your words either. Mustn't be taken for a chee-chee. (49)

Mr. Burnham can be identified as a representative of the English class that has always exploited the native royal families wearing the garb of friends, but always ready to exploit the situation in times of necessity. It is just part of the game that Mr. Burnham plays with Neel, who does not dream a situation where Mr. Burnham would file a case against him claiming the offense of forgery on the part of Neel. So it strikes as a great shock when Neel defends himself and names Mr. Burnham to clarify the practice that had existed for so many years:

> his (Mr. Burnham's) gomusta had assured him that this (Rashkali's hundees carrying Mr. Burnham's name) was the time-honoured practice of the old raja, who had agreed with his partner long ago that there was no need to send every note across town for endorsement...Neel, being something of a perfectionist...insisted on doing the job himself...this was known to...Burnham. (171)

And Neel's trust in a person like Burnham leads only to misery and when, without comprehending the seriousness of the situation, he tries to explain to the officer that the real urgency of the situation dawns of him—that he has been cheated off his trust: "'But surely', Neel protested, there will be no need, if Mr. Burnham explains what happened?" and the reply from the officer renders Neel dumbstruck: "It was Mr. Burnham, sir, who alerted us to the crime" (171). These words are taken by Neel in disbelief as he comprehends the seriousness of the offense and his knowledge that there are minimal chances of escaping the trial.

The theme of Hybridity comes out through the characters Zachary and Paulette who, in the course of the story, refashion themselves. Zachary is born to a white man and a black woman rendering him a hybrid. And there are further changes that take place throughout. His reincarnation in the novel is not instantaneous as he evolves gradually towards the end of the novel. For instance, his name 'Zachary' is transformed into 'Zikri' (one who listens) and this seems as a beginning of 'indianisation' and the natives on board Ibis become agents of his transformation. He alters his language and uses pidgin to converse with the lascars. And Serang Ali's possessiveness of Zachary is an instance of his representation of the low-class lascars who take him to be 'pucca' sahib and who is perhaps the only 'white' sahib to share their food and water. This raises hopes in the lascars who force their leader Zachary to follow their biddings.

Zachary's identity becomes very crucial towards the end of the novel as it triggers a whole new transformation of Nob Kissan Babu's personality as he becomes an agent of redemption for many unfortunates on Ibis. His origin becomes a reason for his intimacy and identification with the lascars and also becomes a reason for Paulette's increasing identification with him. This indianisation is true in Paulette's case too. The birth of Putli in the hands of a native woman, her relationship with her wet nurse and her consideration of Jodu as her sibling, and the relationship shared by Jodu's mother and Paulette's father—all these reasons, along with her own inability to feel comfortable in the Western clothes and in the presence of the whites, renders her a hybrid. Her birth itself is quite a start as she loses a mother and finds a new one in Jodu's mother who breast-feeds her. The bond grows stronger as Paulette grows up learning Bengali as her first language and tastes rice-and-dal khichri as her first solid food and prefers sari to pinafores. Thus gradually her nativisation is complete.

Jodu and his family are outcasts because of their relationship with Lambert family—similarly Paulette and her father are rendered outcasts as they do not adhere to the customs and conventions of the Whites. The reason is given as a realization of Jodu who comes to understand that the reason why "Pierre Lambert had left his country was that he had been involved, in his revolt against his King; that he was shunned by respectable English society because he publicly denied the existence of God and the society of marriage" (68). The relationship between Jodu and Paulette is quite fascinating as they represent the dawn of a new world scenario where equality prevails, defying all kinds of constraints. All these people are the in-betweens who play a major role in subversion of the dominant structures. These outcasts are very important agents of change that can be realized in any society.

Internalization of master-slave concept is deeply ingrained into the minds of the natives who appreciate a 'pucka' sahib or memsahib and would not tolerate a person who speaks in native tongue. This is clear in the response of the servants of Mr. Burnham who ignore Paulette if she speaks to them in Bengali and they would disapprovingly look at her if she wore anything not 'pucka'. And so, in order not to get sneered by servants for her Indian ways, Paulette sleeps in sari during nights and quickly hides it away by morning before anyone could notice. It is this nativity that helps her in getting on well with girmitiyas on Ibis without giving away her true identity. Her transformation from Paulette to Putli to 'Pugli' is something that indicates her complete assimilation into the Indian ways of life irrespective of caste and creed.

The attempts of Burnham couple to mould her according to their culture and to reinstall her into their ways leaves them disappointed as she resists any such kind of imposition by her benefactors. Within the carefully structured family practices of Burnham, Paulette introduces her own ways of living without assimilating into the mainstream and resisting any kind of inculcations. Nobo Krishna Panda, famous with his masters as Nob Kissin Pander, is seen in the beginning as an agent responsible for the shipping of indentured labour to far off places. He is obsessed with speaking English and acting like a true gentleman who would not wish to be addressed in Bengali as he speaks only chaste English. He is the person who becomes responsible for Neel's arrest as he suggests Burnham to wrongly accuse of forgery. From such a degraded agent he transforms into an agent of redemption without his intention.

Colonization has several faces and some of those are unmasked in the novel. Through the story of Deeti the history of East India Company's trade in India is depicted. The British who had taken India under their rule compel the farmers to grow Opium against the common practice. This dearly affects the lives of people involved in Opium agriculture as they are deprived of their rights to their land. And many get addicted to the drug and drag their lives in a dream-like (drug-induced) state. The use of opium and the cruel intention of the British in indulging in forced cultivation of Poppy is quite lucidly given through the reflections of Deeti:

> ...for if a little bit of this gum could give her such power over the life, the character, the very soul of this elderly woman, then with more of it at her disposal, why should she not be able to seize kingdoms and control multitudes? (38)

Deeti's married life stands as stark evidence to such misery. Ironically the drug that enslaves the people also becomes a means of evading both physical and psychological sufferings. Deeti's marriage with an 'afeemkhor', Hukam Singh, is but one of many families who are rendered unfortunate by the opium trade forced on them by the British. Their lives are so drenched in poppies that nothing goes untouched by it directly or indirectly: "a dish of stale alu-posth, potatoes cooked in poppy-seed paste...massaging poppy-seed oil into...hair..." (7). The hunger for money and power drives the rulers to force poppy plantation on farmers who bear the unfortunate consequences of such an unhealthy and useless task. The agents would go from home to home and get the occupants to sign 'asami' contracts and force cash advances on them to cultivate poppy:

> The hut's roof was urgently in need of repairs, but in the age of flowers, thatch was not easy to come by: in the old days, the fields would be heavy with wheat in the winter, and after spring harvest, the straw would be used to repair the damage of the year before. But now, with

> the sahibs forcing everyone to grow poppy, no one had thatch to spare—it had to be bought at the market, from people who lived in faraway villages, and the expense was such that people put off their repairs as long as they possibly could. (29)

And resistance to forceful plantations often leads to being used as scapegoats to be drawn to court trials on the pretence of robbery: "It was impossible to say no to them: if you refused they would leave their silver hidden in your house.... It was no use telling the white magistrate...he earned commissions on the opium and would never let you off" (30). And the outcome of such hardship is just about enough to pay off the advances forced by the agents.

A glimpse is provided into the hierarchy within the Indian caste system where even a slight eye contact with a low-caste person would bode ill for the day. This is brought out quite vividly through the character Kalua, from a leather-worker's caste. The encounter between Kalua and the high-caste Rajput, Hukam Singh, is an interesting one as the latter avoids Kalua's eyes so as not to bode illness and hence when he climbs into Kalua's bullock cart he sits facing to the rear. Even Deeti is forbidden to look at him. But ironically fate brings them together in a situation where caste and class boundaries are blurred. There is an instance where inhumanity spreads its hood like vicious serpent as the atrocities meted out to the lower-caste people take on a new dimension altogether. And the victim is Kalua who is treated inhumanly by the village landlords as witnessed by Deeti. Here again she becomes an agent to voice the atrocities meted out to unfortunates like Kalua:

> This animal (horse) they lead towards Kalua, who was himself being held as if by a tether. Now she (Deeti) heard a whimpering, sobbing sound as Kalua fell suddenly to his knees, clutching at the Thakur's feet... This earned him volleys of kicks and curses...the men forced Kalua to his feet and pushed him stumbling towards the mare's wishing tail.... Then, while one of the held the horse steady, the others whipped Kalua's

> naked back until his groin was pressed hard against the animal's rear. (56-57)

At this juncture there is a reference to violation of Deeti's body as she is rendered unconscious by her in-laws and raped by her brother-in-law. The irony of the situation strikes hard as she realizes that to be a victim a person need not necessarily be a woman: "Ever since the night of her wedding, Deeti had been haunted by the images of her own violation: now, watching from the shelter of the poppy field, she bit the edge of her palm, to keep from crying out aloud. So it could happen to a man too? Even a powerful giant of a man could be humiliated and destroyed, in a way that far exceeded his body's capacity for pain?" (57). And Deeti's bold act after this incident is an act of subversion as she defies the social norms by crossing the invisible boundaries of caste and class and cleanses Kalua's defiled body: "she put out a hand to touch his chest, but only to snatch it back; to think of touching a naked man was bad enough and when that man was of Kalau's station, wasn't it almost a plea for retribution? ...in defiance of the world's unseen presence, she put out a finger and allowed it to fall on Kalua's chest" (58). And the coming together of these two victims of power shows a possibility of a new beginning. Here again it is relevant to introduce Zachary's recollections of his past life that reflects universality of exploitation and discrimination. His recollection of the images of a black person being killed by a group of white carpenters is just one instance that stands as a proof of racism. The incident stands as evidence to the existing conflict between the blacks and the whites:

> He saw again a face with a burst eyeball, the scalp torn open where a handspike had landed, the dark skin slick with blood. He remembered, as if it were happening again, the encirclement of Freddy Douglass, set upon by four white carpenters; he remembered the howls, "kill him, kill the damned nigger, knock his brains out"; he remembered how he and the other men of colour, all free, unlike Freddy, had held back, their hands stayed by fear. And he remembered, too, Freddy's voice

> afterwards, not reproaching them for their failure to come to defence, but urging, them to them to leave, scatter: "It's about jobs; the whites won't work with you, freeman or slave: keeping you out is their way of saving their bread." (51-52)

The issue of 'white man's burden' is evident from the conversation between Mr. Burnham and Zachary where Mr. Burnham enlightens Zachary about his intention of utilizing the Ibis for a greater purpose than trading opium—shipping human cargo. When Zachary uses the word 'slaves', Mr. Burnham clarifies that the word is 'coolies', not 'slaves'. He is all praises for God's benevolence: "when God closes one door he opens another? When the doors of freedom were closed to the African, the Lord opened them to a tribe that was yet more needful of it—the Asiatics" (79). When Zachary is startled with this prospect of human 'freedom' Mr. Burnham justifies his intentions thus:

> Freedom, yes, exactly...Isn't that what the mastery of the white man means for the lesser races? As I see it, Reid, the Africa trade was the greatest exercise in freedom since God led the children of Israel out of Egypt, Consider, Reid, the situation of a so-called slave in the Carolinas—is he not more free than his brethren in Africa, groaning under the rule of some dark tyrant? (79)

In another instance Burnham voices out his self-assigned responsibility to work towards upliftment of the 'so-called' uncivilized people of Third World: "And if we reflect on the benefits that British rule has conferred upon India, does it not follow that opium is this land's greatest blessing? Does it not follow that it is our God-given duty to confer these benefits upon others?" (115). The word freedom when uttered by people like Burnham takes on a very ironic tone as he represents the race that curbs human freedom and treats people as slaves and goes to any extent to meet its own requirements. During a conversation over dinner with Neel, Burnham refers to war with China where his words are truly ironical:

> The war, when it comes, will not be for Opium. It will be for a principle: for freedom—for the freedom of trade

> and for the freedom of the Chinese people. Free Trade is a right conferred on Man by God, and its principles apply as much to opium as to any other article of trade. More so perhaps, since in its absence many millions of natives would be denied the lasting advantages of British influence. (115)

It is ironical, and subversive, that Ghosh chooses a white man to unleash the true picture of the colonizers. Mr. Lambert chooses to be associated with the natives than with the colonizers who, according to him, are cunning people who exploit the natives passing themselves off as men of God, whose responsibility is to civilize the world. Mr. Lambert fears for his daughter's safety in his absence and his conversation with Nob Kissin Pander voices his view of the colonizers: "If she remains here, in the colonies, most particularly in a city like this, where Europe hides its shame and its greed, all that awaits her is degradation: the whites of this town will tear her apart, like vultures and foxes, fighting over a corpse. She will be an innocent thrown before the money-changers..." (137).

It would be appropriate to conclude by stating that the novel is a blend of issues related to the people who thrive on the margins. By voicing several issues through the marginalized, Ghosh bestows agency to the silenced, an opportunity to highlight the forgotten, neglected stories.

WORKS CITED

Ghosh, Amitav. *Sea of Poppies*. India: Penguin Books India, 2008.

———. *The Glass Palace*. New Delhi: Harper Collins, 2000.

Foucault, Michel. *Discipline and Punish: The Birth of the Prison*. Trans. Alan Sheridan. London: Penguin, 1977.

———. *Power and Knowledge: Selected Interviews and Other Writings 1972-77*. Ed. Colin Gordon. New York: Pantheon, 1980.

Mills, Sara. *Michel Foucault*. London: Routledge, 2003.

Sidhwa, Bapsi. *Ice-Candy-Man*. England, 1988.

11

The Zest for Life and Struggle for Existence in *The Glass Palace* by Amitav Ghosh

Vandana Rajoriya

The Glass Palace, as Amitav Ghosh puts it, not only grasps the reach and fall of empires across the twentieth century, but also maps with unerring skill the rival geography of human heart. Through the intertwining stories of Dolly and Rajkumar, the history of the twentieth century is told across three generations; spread over three interlinked parts of the British Empire: Burma, with its conflicting undercurrents of discontent; Malaya, with its vast rubber plantations, and India, amid growing opposition to British rule. But what is the most striking part of the novel is the ever evident zest for life and struggle for existence which we find in it throughout right from the beginning till the end. Like all other novels of Amitav Ghosh, *The Glass Palace* too has the capacity to transport you into its own world and make you get the feel of the fears and anxieties, pains and troubles of its characters but at the same time you cannot but marvel at the zest for life, at the kind of struggle which its characters make for ensuring their existence and wonder at the strength, the energy they endure throughout.

The feelings which naturally arise in us throughout are those of wonder and awe rather than pity and compassion. Such are the characters, their understanding, their vision that you are left with no option but to simply marvel at them. They are barely found to be unsure of themselves, rather are fully aware of their needs, aspirations, wants, and future course of action and so on and so forth even in the toughest and trying times of struggle and chaos. The narrative opens with our protagonist Rajkumar whom we find walking into the new unknown city, Mandalay, in search of a job with someone, Ma Cho merely at the age of eleven. But to our surprise he is not worried and shows no signs of fear or anxiety rather he is lost observing the beauty of Mandalay fort:

> The citadel was a miracle to behold, with its mile long walls and its immense moat. The crenellated ramparts were almost three storeys high, but of a soaring lightness, red in colour and topped by ornamented getaways with seven-tiered roofs...so intriguing was the ordered pattern of these streets that Rajkumar wandered far afield, exploring. It was almost dark by the time he remembered he'd been sent to the city. (*The Glass Palace*, 5)

The boat on which he used to work needed to be repaired and as the boat owner came to know that the repair work may take almost a month's time or even longer; he had told Rajkumar along with some others to find a new job as he was unable to feed the crew for that length of time. So we come to know that Rajkumar has to go to Mandalay and find a job with some Ma Cho who used to run a food stall there. Ma Cho was a half-Indian woman who often provided work to the stray Indians like Rajkumar who needed a job in Mandalay. Like most of Amitav's characters in the novel Ma Cho is the women who is fighting and doing her bit of struggle for her existence. When Rajkumar reaches to her she is not in her best moods. A harried-looking small woman in her mid-thirties with spirals of wiry hair hanging over her forehead, like a fringed awning; we find her busy frying vegetables, squinting at the smoking oil from the shelter of an upthrust arm. She glares at Rajkumar suspiciously asking him about what he wants. When Rajkumar tells her that he is there in search of a job she bursts out at the top of her voice:

> What do you think—I have jobs under my armpits, to pluck out and hand to you? Last week a boy ran away

> with two of my pots. Who's to tell me you won't do the same? And so on. (*The Glass Palace*, 5)

But much mature for his age Rajkumar understands that her outburst is not directly aimed at him rather has more to do with other worries of life and he waits till she is done. She after enquiring about Rajkumar's parents who we come to know are dead, offers him the job of carrying the bowls of soup and noodles to the customers, washing-up utensils, etc., warning him that he won't get anything more than three meals and a place to sleep. He happily accepts that as he knows that that is all he needs.

The characters in the novel are all struggling in their respective states of life but we find that they are not passive and fetch whatever little opportunities of enjoyment life provides them with in those trying times of struggle and war. So we find another man, Saya John who is a contractor in teak camps, who has lost his wife. He comes to otherwise lonely Ma Cho in his free hours to share his burden of grief with her. Although he cannot marry Ma Cho due to various reasons known to her but they readily take whatever bit life has to provide them with. Saya John we come to know is an orphan like Rajkumar who was brought up by Catholic priests, in a town called Malacca, who were from different places and spoke various languages. Saya John learnt a bit of Hindustani from them along with other languages and we find him laughing off his state when Rajkumar enquires about it:

> The soldiers there were mainly Indians and they asked me this very question: how is it that you, who look Chinese and carry a Christian name, can speak our language? When I told them how this had come about, they would laugh and say, you are a dhobi ka kutta—a washerman's dog—na ghar ka nag hat ka—you don't belong anywhere, either by the water or on land, and I'd say, yes, that is exactly what I am. He laughed, with an infectious hilarity.... (*The Glass Palace*, 10)

But as Rajkumar's life was not meant to be easy with much struggle lying ahead and therefore we find troubles pouring in. The British wage a war against Thebaw, the king of Burma, in the name of teak wood defeating him with their advanced fleet, powerful cannons and guns.

The realities of life, ably manifested in the course of novel by Ghosh, which change in minutes often baffle us and make us think about them twice in details. We wonder at the changing face of life and it's so-called seeming realities when those people who could not have even dared to stand in front of queen, who could have never even dared to think of entering the Mandalay fort, loot the place and taking with them whatever they can get hand at, when the soldiers responsible for the safety of the fort themselves start looting it along with others. When colonel Sladen announced that the Royal family was being sent into exile, and that they are to be provided with an escort of attendants and advisors and asked for volunteers; his appeal went unanswered and there were no volunteers:

> The king's gaze, that mark of favour once so eagerly sought, passed unchecked over the heads of his courtiers.... This is how power is eclipsed: in a moment of vivid realism, between the waning of one fantasy of governance and its replacement by the next; in an instant when the world springs free of its mooring of dreams and reveals itself to be gridled in the pathways of survival and self-preservation. (*The Glass Palace*, 42)

Then we come across Dolly, the heroine of the novel, Evelyn and Augusta and a few other girls who were orphans brought up by queen in the palace and who had nowhere else to go, except with the king and queen. In the due course of novel one by one all of them leave barring Dolly our heroine who stands by the queen in her hours of need.

The story of Uma Dey, Dolly, Rajkumar and their children, nieces, and nephews—and their children's children, nieces and nephews—takes us from the rubber boom of the industrial age to the front lines of Second World War, from India's struggle for independence to Burma's fall and its transformation into Myanmar under a military dictatorship. *The Glass Palace* is at once a gigantic history, a family saga and an adventure story. It is so richly and compassionately rendered that at times you are baffled at its immensity and at others you come to feel you are somehow a part of its vast extended family whose story finds its humble origins in two orphans Rajkumar and Dolly standing innocently on the threshold of the twentieth century who are uprooted from their roots not once but twice by the life but at both times they endure their share of struggles with endurance and survive heroically.

The characters of Ghosh impress us by the marked differences in their conduct. They are not the innocent characters made heroic by chance and destiny but are fully conscious characters ready for their share of various struggles as when they come to them. They act with full knowledge of what their actions will call upon themselves. The way the characters are sure of themselves at times make us look at them with utter disbelief, at times to wonder at their endurance but they are so true to life that we feel their living presence throughout. The characters have the courage of hoping, of looking forward to life, even in their most difficult and trying times. For instance let us see the following conversation between Arjun and Dinu:

> 'But, Arjun...' Dinu's voice was still gentle. 'You must see that you don't have a hope....'
>
> 'Did we ever have a hope?' he (Arjun) said. We rebelled against an Empire that has shaped everything in our lives; coloured every-thing in the world as we know it. It is a huge, indelible stain which has tainted all of us. We cannot destroy it without destroying ourselves. And that, I suppose, is where I am....
>
> Dinu put his arms round Arjun again. He could feel tears welling up in his eyes, yet there was nothing he could say; there was nothing to be said.... For Arjun, now, he felt not pity but compassion: what must it be like to visualise defeat so accurately, so completely? There was a sort of triumph in this—a courage—the value of which he did not wish to diminish by arguing. (*The Glass Palace*, 518-19)

And, when Dinu tells him to be careful while climbing a vine-swathed ladder; although fully aware of his evident defeat and possible death Arjun replies smiling that 'I'll be all right.'

And 'one day we will laugh about this' we feel like saluting his spirit.

The treatment of women characters in Amitav Ghosh is too different from the traditional notions of female characters and their existences in fiction. They are not sleeping beauties but living creatures which rather than being a burden on their counter parts or anybody else are always ready with their struggle or their share of fight as and when needed. In the series we first have Ma Cho, the lonely woman, struggling with her lot, who runs a food stall and offers job to many stray Indian boys like Rajkumar when in need of job form time to time. Then we meet the Queen Supayalat, the ruthless but courageous lady whom we find standing erect even in her defeat. Queen Supayalat in the due course of novel, we come to know, is a wilful woman of adamant determination and strong disposition who can go at any length to ensure safety and well being of her husband and family:

> She ordered the killing of every member of the Royal Family who might ever be considered a threat to her husband. Seventy-nine princes were slaughtered on her orders, some of them new-born infants, and some too old to walk. To prevent the spillage of royal blood she had had them wrapped in carpets and bludgeoned to death. (*The Glass Palace*, 38-39)

The war too was largely of Supayalat's making. It was she who challenged Kinwun Mingyi, for his peace appeals and said that: "Why grandfather. It is you who should wear a skirt and own a stone for grinding face powder" (*The Glass Palace*, 39).

In the due course of novel we find her struggling to maintain the standard of her vanished court even in exile in the small district town of Ratnagiri when the king Thebaw has given his hopes and accepted his lot. We often wonder at her eccentricity and particularity about royal code of conducts like *shiko* and all but we are left with no option but to marvel when instead of blaming her daughter for her conduct she justifies her stand and deals with her pregnancy with almost all heroic courage and strength while in other cases we would have surly found women of her status to be brooding and blaming the destiny and time and the conducts of their children in the name of society, culture, name, reputation and so on and so forth. And it is only when she rebukes the collector for pleading to hide first princess's pregnancy in the name of name, reputation and so on calling it a scandal that we realize her practicality:

> There is no scandal in what my daughter has done. The scandal lies in what you have done to us; in the circumstances to which you have reduced us; in our very presence here. What did my daughters ever do, Collector-sahib, that they should have to spend their lives in this prison? Did they commit a crime? Where they tried or sentenced?...'shame on you, Collector-sahib, that you should presume to judge the conduct of my children; shame on you that you should have the effrontery to come into this house and speak to me of scandal. (*The Glass Palace*, 151)

Be it queen Supaiat or Dolly, or Uma, or Alison, or Ma Thin Thin Aye or the Princesses we find that whenever the times are tough and test them they don't give up rather they remain ready with their share of struggle and fight back and stand by. Uma after suicide by her husband is not shattered rather finds her way to life by becoming active in politics and moving from place to place dealing with political affairs worldwide. Alison after death of her parents takes the responsibility of her grandfather and the estate of Morningside on herself and carries it on well as is also observed by Dinu:

> He knew his father wanted Alison to sell Morningside—it would be too much for her to manage on her own, he'd said; the estate would lose money. But as far as he could tell Morningside was running smoothly enough and Alison seemed to be very much in control. He couldn't see that she had any need for his advice. (*The Glass Palace*, 333-34)

When the Japanese soldiers catch hold of Alison's grandfather and one of them points a rifle towards him, without even thinking for a while Alison pulls out her revolver and fights back almost heroically:

> She took aim at the man with the bayonet, hoping to drop him. But at exactly that moment another soldier stepped across her line of fire; the bullet hit him in the ribs and he fell screaming to the ground. (*The Glass Palace*, 333-34)

Although she fails to save her grandfather but spiritedly fights back till her last breath impressing us with her courage. And when she is hit by a bullet and becomes sure of her approaching death; instead of being sad she is rather glad to know that she did not submitted herself at any others disposal, that she fought back and will die in her familiar surroundings and not some alien far off place:

> She was glad that it would end like this; with her eyes resting on something familiar. She remembered what Dinu had said about his mother and the sweets she had shared with her captors. The memory made her smile; that wouldn't have suited her at all. She was glad that she'd made them pay; that she hadn't gone without striking back.
>
> She could hear their footsteps now and knew that they were running towards her. She raised the gun to her temple and shut her eyes. (*The Glass Palace*, 456)

And we as readers marvel at her heroism. Ma Thin Thin Aye, the Burmese Research Scholar is another women character to impress us with her beauty and brain and courage in due course of the novel. When Dinu is filled with admiration and awe for her stories; we as readers realise her skill well enough for the refined taste of Dinu. And when one day sickened by the acts of imperialists of Burma Dinu complains to her, who is now his wife, about the way these frauds, themselves the worst colonialists, use past to justify the present while taking away even to freedom to read and write from its people. Her calm, smiling and intelligent reply arrests us with its beauty, logic and truth:

> Daw Thin Thin Aye smiled and shook her head in reproof. She said: "To use the past to justify the present is bad enough—but it's just as bad to use the present to justify the past. And you can be sure that there are plenty of people to do that too; it's just that we don't have to put up with them." (*The Glass Palace*, 537)

But it is not long that she remains silent against injustice and soon we find her writing and striking back. Then there is another beautiful woman Aung San Suu Kyi. She too like Amitav's most of the other female characters is not a sleeping beauty but an active original thinker and a powerful speaker who even in her house arrest remains the center of city's political life and addresses the people gathered outside her house from her house. And such is her charisma that even Jaya who could not understand a word of her speech is not left unimpressed and observes:

> The laughter is her charisma, Jaya thought. She could hear echoes of Aung San Suu Kyi's laughter everywhere around her in the crowd. Despite the swarning intelligence agents, the atmosphere was not heavy of fear-filled. There was a good-humouredness that seemed very much at odds with the deadened city beyond. Jaya understood why so many people had pinned their hopes on Aung San Suu Kyi; she knew that she herself would have been willing to do anything that was asked of her at that moment: it was impossible to behold this woman and not be half in love. (*The Glass Palace*, 542)

The realisation of the majestic power a women and her speech can exercise over a nations power holders make us wonder and appreciate her whole heartedly. And when Jaya hesitates about the surety of success of a politician like her we are filled with awe and cannot help marvelling at Dinu's reply about her already having succeeded:

> But she has already succeeded...don't you see? She has torn the masks from the generals' faces...she has robbed them of words, of discourse. They have no defence against her but to call her an imperialist...which is

> laughable...when in fact, it is they who invoke the old imperial laws and statues to keep themselves in power. The truth is that they have lost and they know this...this is what makes them so desperate...the knowledge that soon they will have nowhere to hide...that it is just a matter of time before they are made to answer for all that they have done. (*The Glass Palace*, 542)

At times we are taken aback at the frank admissions of Ghosh's characters of their mature understandings of their deeds and the way they are sure of themselves. We hardly find them brooding over ifs' and buts' of their respective lives. It is as if only that was the way they could have acted and hence they acted upon like that and their frank openness to reality, their full knowledge and awareness of the stark realities of life impress us time and again. For instance let us look at the following response from Alison to Dinu for his proposal of marriage after developing of physical intimacies with her:

> Why marriage? Isn't this good enough?.... 'You don't know me, Dinnu.'.... 'I'm not like you. I'm wilful, I'm spoilt: Timmy used to call me wayward. You'd hate me in a week if you were married to me.'

When Dinu insists saying that he wants to marry her and questions that 'what if there's a child? Her reply although very practical shocks us but at the same time we see in her the birth of a new women, a modern women, who can be stopped by nothing, who can manage business, take decisions, fight for herself and others, take care of elders, shoulder household and other responsibilities but at the same time seeks pleasures at her disposal and is content with whatever life has provided her with: 'We'll see then. For now—let's just be content with what we have' (*The Glass Palace*, 358-59).

After having lost their son and hard earned money and estate, Dolly and Rajkumar decide of moving to India along with their daughter in law Manju and her little breastfed baby. Unlike Dolly and others Manju was of weaker sort and finds it difficult to keep pace with them. Her agony makes us feel pity when she prefers carrying wood to her baby crying with hunger. At times Manju works a bit of rice into a paste and tucks it into a corner of the child's mouth who seems to relish the taste. She feels her to be 'a hungry girl, greedy for life' but this seems to us true for the most of the characters in the novel. When exhausted and unwilling Manju shouts at Rajkumar, her father in law, in contempt calling him *buro* he loses his inner strength and bursts out crying like a stricken child but strong and enduring Dolly intervenes in time and taking his arm pushes him to keep going:

> 'You can't stop now, Rajkumar—you have to go on'. At the sound of her voice, some inner instinct seemed to take hold of him. He slung the bundle of firewood over his shoulders and walked on. (*The Glass Palace*, 472)

At this we as readers feel like saluting her never giving or never say die spirit which seems so alien to us when compared to the other lot of female characters which we normally come across in conventional novels.

It is also so very strange to note the way in which Amitav's novel is created much above and in a totally different way than the fabrics of the so-called conventional novels. Unlike the conventional novels we don't have the traditional models of heroes and heroines and villains who are responsible for the whole tragedy rather we find here who are all heroic, impressive, very sure of themselves and their conducts and you keep realizing that they could not have acted otherwise in the circumstances in which they were put to by the fate and the destiny. That in any other way, there were no other deeds which would have made them stand in a better position in front of us. It is always as if there was no other way as if it was only thing which could have been done and therefore was so done.

In such tough and trying times as those of war, life keeps on moving, people marry, have children and make living and when Amitav by way of Dinu comments on this progressiveness of life you are left with no option but to marvel at his understanding and insight of human nature and history and the way of life. The novel is very true to life and in it encompasses all the various shades of life in their varying magnitudes.

Novels of Amitav Ghosh are always a result of social, cultural and political research brought together in the novel passionately, philosophically and thoughtfully and *The Glass Palace* is no exception to it. And when he tells us about the amount of effort he had put in to build up the fabric of this novel and its story, we cannot but marvel at the time and effort which is behind the making of the vast panorama of the sea of life and its various never giving struggles for life and existences which is lying in front of us in the form of this novel:

> In the five years it took me to write *The Glass Palace* I read hundreds of books, memoirs, travelogues, gazetteers, articles and notebooks, published and unpublished; I travelled thousands of miles, visiting and re-visiting, so far as possible, all the settings and locations that figure in this novel; I sought out scores of people in India, Malaysia, Myanmar and Thailand. (*The Glass Palace*, 549)

Amitav Ghosh's one of the greatest gifts as a writer is his sense of place. Whatever be it—a landscape, a city, a village on the edge of a beach, teak forests, and rubber plantations and so on—he describes them all with a wonderful ease and proficiency and magnificently drawing our attention to their distinct beauties and minor details. For instance let us see the description of Collector's house in Ratnagiri:

> It was a large bungalow with a colonnaded portico and a steep, red-tilled roof. It stood on the crest of a hill, looking southward over the bay and the valley of the Kajali river. It was surrounded by a walled garden that stretched a long way down the slope, stopping just short of the river's gorge.... One morning Uma discovered a narrow entrance hidden behind a thicket of bamboo at the bottom of her garden...Uma was amazed by the view: the meandering river, the estuary, the curve of the

> bay, the windswept cliffs...she could see more of the valley from here than from the Residency. (*The Glass Palace*, 110)

And when during the course of the novel Amitav Ghosh introduces us to the ruined chandis of Gunung Jerai of Malaya we are left with no option but to marvel at his keen and minute observation, deep knowledge and understanding of the things of historical and archaeological importance. And the magnificent use he puts all his knowledge and skill blending it into a perfect whole with his master craftsmanship is simply arresting:

> The stream lay below and its surroundings were exactly as he remembered: there was a shallow ford, bridged by flat stones. A little lower down the slope, the stream widened into a pool, ringed by massive boulders. On the far side, a narrow path led into the jungle.... He was awed by the serene beauty of the place: the colours of the moss-covered chandis were even more vivid than he remembered; the vistas in the background even more sweeping. (*The Glass Palace*, 333-34)

Such are the depictions that even when we are done reading the novel the images of the places described in it, keep lingering in our memory. Perhaps this is what makes Amitav such a great master of the travel narrative, a form whose contours are shaped by places and their histories.

To conclude we can say that *The Glass Palace* by Amitav Ghosh is one of those emphatic, successful, moving and influential novels which touches us deeply not only on account of the tremendous waste of blood and power, and money and life that it pictures but also inspires and moves us by the keen awareness of the stark realities of life of its characters, by the unyielding faith in struggle for existence by both its men and women. It encompasses in it not only the sufferings and fate of the rulers of Burma after their defeat but also depicts the chaos which falls upon the life of its subjects and other common people during the war period. It covers well enough the spirit of endurance and zest for life and tremendous struggle of the people of Asia during the most tough and trying times of the World Wars and their struggles for independence from the imperial rules during the most baffling periods of modern history in its making.

WORKS CITED

Ghosh, Amitav. *The Glass Palace,* Harper Collins Publishers, India, Ninth impression, 2010.

All subsequent references are to this edition.

12

Opium and India in *Sea of Poppies*: A Socio-Environmental Study

A. Sujatha

...those eat now who never ate before;
And those who always ate, now eat the more.

—Thomas De Quincey

The object of this paper is to discuss the role played by opium in India, particularly during the Raj from a socio-environmental perspective, with reference to Amitav Ghosh's *Sea of Poppies*. The paper, at the outset, discusses the general opinion of people towards opium and goes on to present facts regarding opium in India. It then presents the role played by opium during the Raj and reasons for opium's popularity. Next, the paper discusses the various issues addressed in Ghosh's *Sea of Poppies* and focuses on the socio-environmental issues involved in the cultivation of poppy that are discussed in the novel.

Soma, afeem, abhin, Plant of Joy, Milk of Paradise, Destroyer of Grief—like the names of Gods in the Hindu Pantheon the names of this plant are diverse. A peek at English/American Literature shows that opium has always held sway over some of the most prolific and creative minds—Coleridge, Thomas de Quincey, Edgar Allan Poe, Charles Dickens, E.B. Browning, Francis Thompson, Wilkie Collins—to name a few. But, as Jim Hogshire in Opium for the Masses rightly points out, "A love affair with opium cannot be taken lightly. The same poppy that can take its lovers to the gates of

Paradise has the power to send its slaves to a hell on earth, should they ever try to leave her" (3).

Opium made its way into India as a crop for cultivation as early as the eighth century B.C. But scholars affirm that poppy cultivation dates back to the Vedic period. Often it is assumed that soma ras, mentioned in the Vedas, is the drink made from poppy. During the Mughal period, poppy cultivation flourished. According to the Ain-i-Akbari, in 1590, poppy was the staple crop of the spring harvest in the provinces of Agra, Oudh, and Allahabad (http://www.unodc.org/unodc/en/data-and-analysis/bulletin/bulletin_1954-01-01_3_page002.html).

But this crop became one of the key factors that influenced Indian economy during the Raj. The reasons were simple and obvious. The British deciphered the kind of spell opium could exert over the masses and the consequent financial gain. Little did the British realize what a massive threat they were posing to the environment through this monopoly? As Santella rightly points out, "The story of opium is one of both individual and global conflict. It is a story of alleviating pain and inspiring genius, of addiction, escape, and freedom, of contradictions and mystery" (Opium, 8).

The paper aims at analysing the role played by opium in the novel *Sea of Poppies* from a socio-environmental perspective. In doing so, the paper intends to focus on concepts like environmental ethics and environmental justice. The word environment should be taken to mean merely the flora and fauna, for that would mean limiting the sense of the word. Instead, in a broader sense, the word environment refers to society and human beings in relation to their surroundings. These days, the term environmental justice is used almost synonymously with the concept of the environment. According to Robert Figueroa and Claudia Mills, "...environmental justice refers to the conceptual connections and causal relationships between environmental issues and social justice" (426-27).

Ronald Sandler and Phaedra Pezzullo outline the principles of environmental justice some of which are relevant to the scope and outlook of the paper:

> Environmental justice mandates the right to ethical, balanced and responsible uses of land and renewable sources in the interest of a sustainable planet for humans and other living things....
>
> Environmental justice affirms the right of all workers to a safe and healthy work environment, without being forced to choose between an unsafe livelihood and unemployment. It also affirms the right of those who work at home to be free from environmental hazards....
>
> Environmental justice opposes military occupation, repression and exploitation of lands, peoples and culture, and other life forms....
>
> Environmental justices requires, that we, as individuals, make personal and consumer choices to consume as little of Mother Earth's resources and to produce as little waste as possible.... (321-23)
>
> Amitav Ghosh's *Sea of Poppies* deserves noteworthy praise because it has stirred and aroused the Indian readers by urging them to peruse pages of Indian history and perceive the concept of colonisation from ecological/environmental and postmodernist perspectives. The novel was not meant to be centred on opium, but, as Ghosh himself states, "...once I started researching into it, it was kind of inescapable—all the roads led back to opium". (http://news.bbc.co.uk/2/hi/south_asia/7460682.stm)

The novel focuses on the lives of Indians, particularly the farming class, and how opium succeeds in storming into their lives and creating havoc. Ghosh, through snippets of narrative, succeeds in presenting the problems that opium poses to the environment. The first instance is when Deeti glances at her hut that is badly in need of thatching:

> The hut's roof was urgently in need of repairs, but in this age of flowers, thatch was not easy to come by: in the old days, the fields would be heavy with wheat in the winter, and after the spring harvest, the straw would be used to repair the damage of the year before. But now,

> with the sahibs forcing everyone to grow poppy, no one had thatch to spare—it had to be bought at the market, from people who lived in faraway villages, and the expense was such that people put off their repairs as long as they possibly could. (*Sea of Poppies*, 29)

This clearly throws light on the status quo of agriculture in India thereby emphasising the environmental injustice caused to land and to people. In 1773, the British Government declared that the first Governor General of Bengal, Warren Hastings, would maintain monopoly over opium produced in Bengal, Bihar and Orissa. From then on, opium reigned supreme in Indian fields as a principal cash crop, fortified to the greatest extent possible by laws, the most significant among them being the Opium Act (1878). As a result, food crops were cultivated on a comparatively small-scale basis. Whatever little was cultivated was exported to other countries, leaving farmers barely anything to stock for hard times or for the future. This explains the cause for the famines and the poverty-stricken situation in colonial India.

According to B. Chaudhuri, opium cultivation was not forced. The main reason for choosing opium was that it was more remunerative to the cultivators and the advance paid to the cultivators was interest-free. But that was not all. "...The vulnerability of the poppy to fluctuations in the weather, quite a common occurrence in the poppy-growing regions, and the rigidity with which the opium advances were recovered by the government...forced the cultivators into indebtness, and it was partly because of this that a number of them remained tied to opium cultivation" (146). This apparently accounts for the low cultivation of food crops like wheat, dal, and vegetables and for the transition from a monopolistic market to a monopoly.

Ghosh has a definite purpose in introducing Deeti as one of the central characters in the novel. Deeti's life is subject to physical exploitation mainly because of opium although everyone initially attributes it to the influence of Saturn in her horoscope. The very first night of her wedding proves shocking to her when she discovers that her husband Hukam Singh is an afeemkhor, an opium addict. Matters become worse for Deeti when she realizes that she was given opium by her impotent husband on her wedding night so that her brother-in-law Chandan Singh could impregnate her. "It was useless, she knew, to be seized by regret now, on the very night when her fate had been wedded to his: it was as if the shade of Saturn had passed over her face, to remind her of her destiny" (*Sea of Poppies*, 34).

Ghosh's subtle hint on the environmental pollution that opium causes is indeed remarkable. When Deeti and her daughter Kabutri go to the opium factory to get her husband who has had a seizure, they start sneezing,

> ...for they had now drawn abreast of the godowns where farmers came to dispose of their 'poppy trash'—leaves, stalks and roots, all of which were used in the packaging of the drug. Ground up for storage, these remains produced a fine dust that hung in the air like a fog of snuff. Rare was the passer-by who could brave this mist without exploding into a paroxysm of sneezes and sniffles.... (*Sea of Poppies*, 91)

Environmental injustice is portrayed at its best in Ghosh's description of the opium factory, particularly the mixing room. The people inside are subject to the most deplorable working conditions in the mixing room. Besides being made to toil for hours together without rest, they are subject to the most inhuman treatment. They are hardly treated like human beings but a herd of cattle. The opium factory looms like a demon in the lives of the workers and their families and becomes the very symbol of colonial oppression:

> The air inside was hot and fetid, like that of a closed kitchen, except that the smell was not of spices and oil, but of liquid opium, mixed with the dull stench of sweat—a reek so powerful that she had to pinch her noses to keep herself from gagging...she discovered... bare-bodied men, sunk deep in tanks of opium, tramping round and round to soften the sludge.... These seated men had more the look of ghouls than any living thing she had ever seen. (*Sea of Poppies*, 94-95)

Working conditions in those days were so pathetic and more deplorable than these was the treatment meted out to those miserable workers who worked in the most unhygienic and unhealthy conditions. They were caned or whipped even for trivial mistakes. The scene at the factory where a worker is caned mercilessly for dropping a poppy ball is relevant in this regard. When Hukam Singh falls sick and is bed-ridden, Deeti encounters the horrors of opium addiction:

> Hukam Singh's condition, after his seizure at the factory, was so enfeebled that he had not the strength to protest even when she took away his pipe and his brass box. But instead of initiating an improvement, deprivation provoked a dramatic turn for the worse: he could neither eat nor sleep and he soiled himself so often that his bed had to be moved out of doors. Drifting in and out of consciousness, he would scowl and muter in incoherent rage. (*Sea of Poppies*, 153)

This depiction is truly reminiscent of De Quincey's description of the pains of opium addiction. "...He curses the spell which chain him down from motion; he would lay down his life if he might but get up and walk; but he is powerless as an infant, and cannot even attempt to rise" (Confessions of an English Opium Eater, 55).

Deeti is plagued by ill-luck further when she starts working in her poppy field during harvest. Amitav Ghosh provides a vivid picture of the exploited farming class when Deeti goes to sell the poppies that she has harvested. When she finds that her husband had borrowed money and the harvest returns would never suffice even to feed her child, she protests. But the muharir brushes her aside:

> Do what others are doing, he snapped. Go to the moneylender. Sell your sons. Send them off to Mareech. It's not as if you don't have any choices.
>
> I have no sons to sell, said Deeti.
>
> Then sell your land, said the clerk, growing peevish. You people always come her and talk about being hungry,

> but tell me, who's ever seen a peasant starve? (*Sea of Poppies*, 155)

Deeti is not the only person whose life is ravaged by opium. Aafat is yet another victim of opium addiction. When he is first introduced in the novel, he is described as a living nightmare. Neel is warned that there is no escape from the nightmare and that he will have to learn to live with it. The disgusting condition in which Neel finds Aafat is so vividly picturesque that one can almost visualise the scene in one's mind. Neel's initial sense of shock and repulsion on seeing Aafat, pale into insignificance when he encounters the pain of drug addiction:

> His paroxysms of shivering, for instance, would begin with a mild, almost imperceptible trembling.... But these gentle shivers would mount in intensity till they became so violent as to tip him off his charpoy, depositing his convulsing body on the ground. The outlines of his muscles would show through the grime on his skin, alternately contracting into knots and then briefly relaxing, but only to seize up again: it was like looking at a pack of rats squirming in a sack. (*Sea of Poppies*, 321)

Providence however comes to his rescue in the form of Neel to help him and it is with utmost difficulty that Aafat is brought to normalcy.

The novel undoubtedly is an interpreter's paradise, but to delve deep into those perspectives would be beyond the purview of this paper. The incidents cited in this paper only go to strengthen the fact that monetary benefit is the focal point of any colonial rule. The colonised are mere pawns in the game of political chess. There is no turning back. On the other hand, if one is lucky, like Kalua, Neel, Serang Ali, and Aafat, he may escape unscathed. But, not everybody turns out to be so lucky in such wretched conditions. H.H.T. Cleiffe in his book on England's Greatest National Sin: Selections and Reflections on our Asiatic Opium Policy and Traffic aptly remarks:

> The vices were there, the drink was there. To a great extent, the eating and smoking of opium and ganja was

> there, but it was there, not because of, but in spite of, the highest principles inculcated by native religions, and we have just taken it and we have formulated it, and we have financed it, and we have so effected it that the Indian people clearly see that, whatever may be the nominal standard of our integrity, we practically consider finance first and morality second, and in that way we are doing a deep and terrible injury to India. We are lowering their standard of morals. We are placing ourselves in the position of tempters to India. (3-4)

Sea of Poppies is no tragi-comedy like most movies of the present day. Since Amitav Ghosh had intended a trilogy while writing this, the ending of the novel clearly indicates that the sequel will throw more light on the lives of the central characters. Again, if one were to ask if there was a solution to the environmental injustice during the Raj, there is no definite answer except the fact that the swadeshi protests and revolts were the only ways by which Indians could project their frustration and sense of dissatisfaction. Amitav Ghosh too has no intentions of offering solutions. His aim is to portray the lives of Indians caught in the whirlwind of colonial oppression all of which centred on the monopoly of opium.

WORKS CITED

Asthana, N.S. *The Cultivation of the Opium Poppy in India*. http://www.unodc.org/unodc/en/data-and-analysis/bulletin/ bulletin_1954-01-01_3_page002.html. 16 Dec. 2011.

Chaudhuri, B. "Eastern India." Dharma Kumar and Tapan Raychaudhuri. *The Cambridge Economic History of India*. Vol. 2. New York, Melbourne: Cambridge University Press, 1983. 86-176.

Cleiffe, H.H.T. *England's Greatest National Sin: Selections and Reflections on our Asiatic Opium Policy and Traffic*. London: E. Whitby and Son, 1892.

De Quincey, Thomas. Confessions of an English Opium Eater (1822). Digitized and Typeset by Supervert 32 C Inc, 2002.

Figueroa, Robert and Claudia Mills. "Environmental Justice." Dale Jamieson. A Companion to Environmental Philosophy. Blackwell, 2001. 426-38.

Ghosh, Amitav. *Sea of Poppies*. New Delhi, New York: Viking, 2008.

Hogshire, Jim. Opium for the Masses. Washington: Loompanics Unlimited, 1994.

Opium Financed British Rule in India. http://news.bbc.co.uk/2/hi/south_asia/7460682.stm. 02 Dec. 2011.

Sandler, Ronald and Phaedra C. Pezzullo. *Environmental Justice and Environmentalism: The Social Justice Challenge to the Environmental Movement*. Cambridge, Massachusetts: The MIT Press, 2007.

Santella, Thomas M. Opium. Consultant Ed. David J. Triggle. New York: Chelsea House Publishers, 2007.

13

Vainness Demarcation in Amitav Ghosh's *The Shadow Lines*

Dalvir Singh Gahlawat and *Suman Yadav*

India has made a payment considerably to the overall world literature. This sum of India has been so enormous that novelists of Indian English Fiction occupy a unique place and in this respect Amitav Ghosh has made a discrete score on the world literary scene with his literary legacy and gifted language control. He carries on as an outstanding and optimum writer in Indian English Fiction. Many Indian novelists have turned to past to trace the depending mood of nationalism as to cherish the memories of the bygone days. He writes many of his personal experiences in his novels. He himself says in an interview with John C. Hawley in the summer of 2004 which is one of the central themes in his novels:

> He was deeply interested in the methods of knowledge and in our ways of knowing.[1]

Amitav Ghosh was born in Calcutta in 1956. He grew up in Bangladesh (then East Pakistan), Sri Lanka, Iran and India. He completed his graduation from Delhi University; and thereafter he went to Oxford to study Social Anthropology and received a Master of Philosophy and a Ph D in 1982. In 1980, he also went to Egypt to do field work in the fellaheen village of Lataifa. The work he did there resulted in *In an Antique Land* (*IAAL*, 1993). Ghosh has been a journalist and published his first novel, *The Circle of Reason* (1986), and his second, *The Shadow Lines* (1988) won the central Sahitya Akademi

Award, New Delhi. He did his fieldwork in Cambodia. He lived in Delhi and written for a number of publications. He currently lives in New York and teaches at Columbia University. Ghosh has won France's Prix Medici Etranger, India's prestigious Sahitya Akademi Award, the Arthur C. Clarke Award, and the Pushcart Prize. He now divides his time between Harvard University, where he is a visiting professor, and his homes in India and Brooklyn, New York.

Ghosh's second novel *The Shadow Lines* (1988) is a story of such demarcation which is vainness because he is in the view that demarcation separates man from man, nation from nation. In modern world the whole world should live together, work in co-operation and have friendly relation. Then only this world can be saved from the impending catastrophe. The story revolves round the theme of nationalism in an increasingly globalize world. What the question rises in the mind of the readers is the real meaning of the Political liberty and borders which almost seem both institution and division. Here it would be apt to take the allusion of Ramakrishna who travels to the space *Beyond Knowledge and Ignorance* and says:

> God laughs twice; first, when the doctor says that he would save the patient's life and second, when two brothers fight and place a demarcation indicating each other's share in the property.[2]

The novel is a narrative of the family and friends of the nameless narrator which has its roots in broader national and international experience of the past, present and future and they combine and melt together rubbing out any kind of line of demarcations. The title is a good example for showing us the symbolist and the realist elements. The novel is not only rooted in reality but also it looks beyond. There is the use of simple language and the main characters are very real, almost rounded. The text deals with the concerns of our period, the search for identity, the need for independence, the difficult relationship with colonial culture. *The Shadow Lines* interweaves fact, fiction and reminiscence. It is a continuous narrative which replicates the pattern of violence not only of 1964 but also of 21st century.

The novel deals with insecurities in the survival of human race. As the title suggests Amitav Ghosh's *The Shadow Lines* centers on the shadowiness of existing borders that divide people. The interest of the author as an Indian born American lies in making the lines between the personal and public shadowy. The narrator's researches are made by his indigenous effort to transform his private story into public history. The novel accommodates at different places like war-devastated London, civil-trouble in post-partition East-Bengal and the riot-hit Calcutta and plans a major analysis of the emotional composition of the existing man that thrives on aggression. There are two families in the novel—one English, one Bengali—their lives intertwine in tragic and comic ways. The narrator, Indian born and English educated, outlines the events from side to side, i.e. from the outbreak of Second World War to the late twentieth century.

In this novel, the character, Tridib recapitulates his life in the act of saving May from Muslim mobs in the communal riots of 1963-64 in Dhaka as the story is based mainly in Kolkata, Dhaka and London. The novel seems reverberating the feelings of Whole South-East Asia with coherent suggestion of Independence and pangs of division. In this way the symbolic meaning of demarcation is a barrier among the nations.

The Shadow Lines narrates the past of an Indian family living in Calcutta but with roots in Dhaka on the Pakistan side of the border and their relations in Britain. It is all about personal relationship. Fundamentally there's the narrator's family and the family of their close English friends. Three generations are covered in this novel. Grandmother and Mayabai are sisters, who grew up in Dhaka before the separation while Mayabai, more social of two, marries a diplomat and enjoys a life importance overseas. Grandmother loses her husband in Kolkata and has to manage for herself and her only son the narrator's father. She is combatant, declines any charity, and manages to raise her son, the narrator's father, who finally becomes a triumphant administrator.

The story starts about thirteen years before the birth of the narrator and ends on the night preceding his departure from London back to Delhi. He spends less than a year in London, doing research for his doctorate work, but it is London he knew very well even before he puts a step on its pavements with the help of two people—Tridib, the second son of his father's aunt, his real mentor and inspirer, and Ila his beautiful cousin who has traveled all over the world but has seen little compared to what the narrator has seen through his mental eye.

Narrator enjoyed London as a real place because of Tridib's and Ila's friends—Mrs Price, her daughter May and son Nick. Alike comes alive because of all the stories of her childhood told to him by his incomparable grandmother who was born there. It is Dhaka which he never visits that affects him most by the violent drama that take place on its roads taking Tridib away as one of its most unfortunate victims. Some of the most important questions the novel probes are the various faces of violence and the extent to which its fiery arms reach under the guise of fighting and freedom. Ghosh's treatment of violence in Calcutta and in Dhaka is valid even today. The narrator says, talking of the day riots tore Calcutta apart in 1964:

> I opened my mouth to answer and found I had nothing to say. All I could have told them was of the sound of voices running past the walls of my school, and of glimpse of a mob in Park Circus.[3]

The mesh of life in *The Shadow Lines*, which takes in lot of countries, religions, is a collection of recollections, the narrator's own and others', dusty photographs, staining newspaper trimmings but cared for above all by thoughts. While nations, religions, war, violence and division separate people, reminiscence does not. Thoughts generate a world that cannot be divided any more than nations break and drift away when ecological boundaries are randomly recreated.

Tridib is an archaeologist, who has spent a significant time of his early days in England, and who is in love with an English girl. He prefers to see truth in the course of thoughts rather than in the course of his sanity and is aware of the relativity of reality. In according with him, everybody lives in a story, "because stories are all there are to live in" (*TSL*, 184). As Meenakshi Mukherjee has observed: The realignment of the sense of geography happens through "an acknowledgement of the subjective space that all human beings inhabit" as well as by "plotting the different points of the Bartholomew Atlas" with its Euclidian space.

The narrator has combined the lines and statistics on the map he has looked at in Calcutta with the images of the region he had created from Tridib's stories of war-time Lyminton Road. For him history is spoken through actual people living through actual historical understandings. History finishes to be a mere statistics or a anthology of abstract details as each disposition in the novel clear, through their own story, phases of history. In the end the uselessness of sub continental and political affairs intending to rub out the reality of human lives by discovering "shadow lines" of separation materializes deeply all the way through the work. Therein lies its maximum achievement.

Finally, when members of the family are ready to start a journey from Calcutta to their former home in Dhaka, the narrator's grandmother asks whether she will be able to see the border between India and East Pakistan from the plane, a candid reply which however foregrounds the irrationality of the revisionists map-making of the elected officials accountable for separation. The family voyage to Dhaka for liberating an aged relative and, in the climax of this episode, the narrator, when Tridib, who has until the end of time worked out a mostly powerful grip on his thoughts, is killed in the middle of the communal sadism, thinks about the lethal effects of borders. Although he admits that the political map-makers were well-intentioned, he is struck by the fact that the connections that connect Dhaka and Calcutta are closer than ever. Shadow-lines are more than just the borders constructed by politicians. They have other significances in the text as the lines of demarcation that separate colonizer and colonized, present and past, self and image. Ultimately they are the signifying acts that build philosophy of detached self. As always, Ghosh is not only at pains to reveal the porousness of geographical borders, but also the hypocrisy of a range of double classifications of society and region of the soul consciousness.

The demarcation is in fact a demonstration of the touching barrier that separates the neighbours from neighbours and nation from nation. The narrator wants to show how societal groups are unwilling and incapable of living without the constraint of demarcations and yet even some that have lived within those norms are capable of realizing that people should be able to coexist without any demarcations. No doubt, the philosophy of Robert Frost's poems "Mending Wall" and "Good Fences Make Good Neighbours" are also correct. As they say: too much intimacy breeds contempt. People can support the idea of demarcation because they guarantee security and safety. People cannot encroach upon the legitimate rights of others. There will be no misunderstanding once there are demarcations. There will very little litigation in the court over boundary disputes. There are international boundary disputes because boundaries have not been properly demarcated.

But on the other hand Amitav Ghosh's message to society in this novel is that all the barriers between man and man are redundant. All men could live together in peace, harmony and universal brotherhood as the demarcations are more dangerous than harmful. These keep people like unconnected and uncommunicative boxes. There is no cultural and human give and take once demarcation erected. Demarcations make people enemies and people suspect those living other side of the demarcation. These suspicions are by and large baseless but then they are believed to be true. Many international disputes could have been over had there been no borders between states. How have international borders between India and Pakistan made them better neighbours? They continue to exchange fire almost every month. Demarcations are divisive and ruinous and they make people bitter enemies.

NOTES

1. John C. Hawley. *Contemporary Indian Writers in English: Amitav Ghosh*, 2005, Foundation Books Pvt. Ltd., p. 14.
2. Anup Mitra. "Beyond Knowledge and Ignorance", *The Time of India*, 29th January, 2012.
3. www.amitavghosh.com/shadowline_r.html

14

Harmony versus Conflict in Amitav Ghosh's *The Shadow Lines*

Saykar Satish Govind

The Shadow Lines, written by Amitav Ghosh, was published in 1988 and welcomed by the whole world with open arms and warm hug. It attracted the attention of the readers and critics interested in the study of Indian Writing in English. The present paper focuses on the themes of Partition and communal conflict. The novel deals with the memories which remained forever in the minds of those who witnessed all these horror, terror and violence, caused by the Partition of India.

To Anu Chopra *The Shadow Lines* is "a powerful adolescent love story and a story of unrequited love". According to Nutan Damor, it is a novel "about Partition and immigration". Novy Kapadia describes it as "a critique of certain issues such as time, freedom and history", says Nirzari Pandit. It stresses "the need for a syncretic civilization to avoid a communal conflict".

Alpana Neogy compares *The Shadow Lines* with Sunil Gangopadhyay's *Purba Paschim* and finds that both the novels focus on the partition of India and consequent trauma of East Bengali psyche. She is of the opinion that the agonies of displacement, the sense of alienation in the adopted land and constant dream of a return to one's land are the common themes in both the novels. R.K. Dhawan describes the book as novel that resists classification:

> It is basically a memory novel that weaves together past and present, childhood and adulthood, India and Bangladesh and Britain, Hindu and Muslim. It is a social document and a political novel, a Bildungsroman and a postmodernist work of fiction. (R.K. Dhanwan, 23)

The present paper focuses the themes of the Partition and communal conflict in *The Shadow Lines*. It is a novel which covers the history of the three generations of the narrator's family spread over Calcutta (now Kolkata), Dhaka and London and the Prices, his English family friends. The Partition of India and the riots aroused out of it is the main concern of the novel. The murder of Mrs. Gandhi caused the riots in India and it made Amitav Ghosh to express his thoughts which were suppressed in his mind.

The Shadow Lines is divided in two part—"Going Away" and "Coming Home". The novel starts with the incident happened in 1939, thirteen years before the narrator is born, Tridib, who was eight years old, went to England with his parents. The unnamed narrator of the novel identifies himself with his uncle, Tridib. Who was Tridib?

Tridib had given me world to travel in and he had given me eyes to see them with...to me a boy who had never been more than a few hundred miles from Calcutta—I could see that those names, which were to me a set of magical talismans because Tridib had pointed them out to me on his tattered old Bartholomew's Atlas (Amitav Ghosh, 20).

Throughout the novel it is Tridib through whose eyes the narrator looks at the things. Tridib is a son of Mayadebi and Saheb (her husband). He has two brothers—Jatin-kaku an economist with the U.N. and Robi, who later joins the Indian Administrative Service. Jatin-kaku use to live somewhere in South Africa or South East Asia with his wife and a daughter named Ila, who is of the narrator's age.

The narrator's grandmother is Mayadebi's elder sister. His family consists of his grandmother and his parents. The narrator lives with his family in Gole Park. Tridib is the only members of Mayadebi's family lives in Calcutta in his vast old family house in Ballygunge Place with his aging grandmother.

The narrator always thinks of Tridib as a guide, a mentor, etc., but his grandmother calls him a loafer or a wastrel. She is of the opinion that there is nothing in the world Tridib can't do with his connections. She thinks that he can even run the country, but she doesn't approve his living in that old crumbling house. It doesn't mean that he had done nothing. He was actually working on a Ph D in Archaeology of the Sena dynasty in Bengal.

The family friendship between the two families began when Mrs. Price's father Lionel Tresawsen and Tridib's grandmother, Mr. Justice Chandrashekhar Datta Chaudhuri, a High Court Judge, met in Calcutta. Then in 1962 May comes to India for a visit where the narrator met her for the first time. She has come to India, perhaps to meet Tridib where he wanted to. He wishes to meet her in the following way:

> ...as a stranger, in a ruin. He wanted them to meet as the completest of strangers—strangers—across—the—seas.... He wanted them to meet for from their friends and relatives—in a place without a past, without history, free, really free, two people coming together with the utter freedom of strangers. (Amitav Ghosh, 144)

The narrator—Ila relationship runs parallel to Tridib—May relationship in the novel. The narrator is very much attracted to Ila. He thinks that Ila loves him, but really she doesn't. She loves Nick Price and thinks of marrying him. She wants to be free, free of the bloody culture. So she lives in London. The narrator's grandmother criticizes Ila and says that she has no right to live in London because her contribution in building London as a nation is zero. She also criticizes Ila that she wants the freedom to do what she pleases to do. The narrator's grandmother and Ila are in contrast to each other. The grandmother also wanted a freedom in her life when she was in a school. She has thought of killing someone for freedom.

> I would have been frightened.... But I would have prayed for strength, and God willing, yes, I would have killed him. It was for our freedom: I would have anything to be free. (Amitav Ghosh, 39)

She was brought up on stories of Khudiram Bose and Bagha Jatin. She believes in militant nationalism. She believes in war and bloodshed to build a nation. The narrator is different from both—Ila and his grandmother. He says:

> ...I thought of how much they all watched to be free; how they went mad wanting their freedom. I began to wonder whether it was I that was mad because I was happy to be bound: whether I was alone in knowing that I could not live without the clamour of the voices within me. (Amitav Ghosh, 89)

The narrator is learnt to see the world through the eyes of Tridib. Tridib is a 'mentor' to the narrator. The story of the novel ends with the death of Jethamoshai, Khalil and Tridib. It means that Tridib became a victim of the communal riots aroused in 1964. Amitav Ghosh has tried to point out as to why the riots were aroused in Calcutta, Khulna and Srinagar, what were their effects on the private and public life. *The Shadow Lines* is a story of the grandmother who is a middle-class woman. The narrator says about her that she believes in militant nationalism. She says once to the narrator:

> It took those people a long time to build that country; hundreds of years, years and years of war and bloodshed. Everyone who lives there has earned his right to be there with blood: with their brother's blood and their father's blood and their son's blood. They know they're a nation because they have drawn their borders with blood...war is their religion. That's what it takes to make a country. Once that happens people forget they were born this or that, Muslim or Hindu, Bengali or Punjabi, they became a family born of the same pool of blood. That is what you have to achieve for India, don't you see? (Amitav Ghosh, 77-78)

Her views on nationalism are perhaps influenced by Nazism or Fascism in Germany and Italy respectively who regards the individual inferior than the nation. Her views are not the views of common middle-class woman, but of a soldier in the army who is ready to die and ready to kill someone for the nation. She also thinks that those who want to live in the country should earn the right to live with the blood and she says to the narrator that Ila has no right to live in London. She expects the Indians to forget their religion and be the responsible members of united India.

Born in 1902 in Dhaka, she grew up as a member of the joint family, but after the death of her grandfather, the ancestral house had to be partitioned because of the conflict between her father and her uncle. From the larger house in Dhaka she lives in various houses with her husband who died in 1935. Then she accepts a job as a school teacher in Calcutta and she could not go back to Dhaka. In 1947 the Partition of India took place and Dhaka became the capital of East Pakistan (now Bangladesh). She has educated her son declining the help from her rich sister, Mayadebi, who married Datta Chaudhuri who is a diplomat in the Indian Foreign service. When her son is promoted as the General Manager of his firm the family shift to a large new house on Southern Avenue, opposite the lake. Once when the narrator's grandmother comes to know from her poor relation that her uncle is alone in their old family house and has given shelter to a Muslim family. She is now very eager to go to Dhaka to bring her uncle, Jethamoshai, back to India. Fortunately, Saheb, Mayadebi's husband has been transferred to Bangladesh. The grandmother is very confident about her plan to go to the country of her birth. She wants to bring Jethamoshai in India to let him die in his own country. She thinks very sympathetically about him.

> Poor old man...Imagine what it must be like to die in another country, abandoned and alone in your old age. (Amitav Ghosh, 135)

She wants to support her uncle in his old age. He lives in his own country, but the grandmother thinks that he is in another country. The same problem occurred when the time came to leave for East Pakistan. She thinks that she is going for the first time to her home as a window. There was a problem whether someone is going or coming:

> You see, in our family we don't know whether we're coming or going—it's all my grandmother's fault. But of

> course, the fault wasn't here at all: it lay in language. Every language assumes a centrality, a fixed and settled point to go away from and come back to, and what my grandmother was looking for was a word for a journey which as not a coming or a going at all, a journey that was a search for precisely that fixed point which permits the proper use of verbs of movement. (Amitav Ghosh, 153)

She is unable to decide whether she is going or coming home. India is for her an invented country like Lala Kanshi Ram in Azadi. Even in sunlight on a broken column Saleem, Nadira, Zahid, Naseer and Zahra—all think that Pakistan is their country for which they should die. The nationalistic favours is the same, but the difference is that the grandmother and Lala Kanshi Ram think of India as their home and Saleem, Zahid, etc., think of Pakistan as their home. Like a common woman, she thinks that it would be difficult to go to Dhaka as she was going to cross the national border; but when she is told that there is nothing of that kind, she is confused. She says in a state of confusion:

> But if there aren't trenches or anything, how are people to know? I mean, what's the difference then? And if there's no difference both sides will be the same. It'll just like it used to be before, where we used to catch a train in Dhaka and get off in Calcutta the next day without anybody stopping us. What was it all for then—Partition and the killing and everything—if there isn't something in between? (Amitav Ghosh, 151)

She even is unable to understand how her place of birth had come to be so messily at odds with her nationality. It means the Partition of India lost the identity of an individual. Though so, Tridib, the grandmother and May go to Dhaka. She had passed the time of her life in Dhaka and Calcutta as well. For her Dhaka is the past and Calcutta the present. She deviates from her thoughts. She is a woman who tells the narrator to forget the past, could not forget her own past at all. The narrator writes:

> She hates nostalgia, my grandmother, she has spent years telling me that nostalgia is a weakness, a waste of time, that it is everyone's duty to forget the past and look ahead and get on with building the future. (Amitav Ghosh, 208)

She couldn't forget her past and even couldn't ignore the present. And how could she forget her past? Can we say that after Partition she must forget all the things related to Dhaka? No, she can't do it. We can divide the nations but can't memory. In this connection Robi says in the novel:

> Why don't they draw thousands of little lines through the whole subcontinents and give every little place a new name? What would it change? It's a mirage; the whole thing is a mirage. How can anyone divide a memory? (Amitav Ghosh, 247)

When the grandmother, May and Tridib left for Dhaka, within a few days narrator experienced a trouble in Calcutta. When he was going to school by bus, no friends of him were present at the bus stop. He felt that perhaps their parents might have allowed them to stay home to listen to the commentary of the India—England cricket match starting that day in Madras (now Chennai). There was a rumor that the whole of Calcutta's water supply had been poisoned. Montu, a Muslim friend of the narrator, was also absent and was watching them from behind a curtain in his window. When the narrator entered the class, only few students were present. While the class was going on, the students heard the noise near the school but they couldn't see anything as the school had high walls. Then Mrs. Andersen informed them that their classes were being cancelled for the rest of the day and they will be sent home. When the narrator was on his way to home in the bus, he found that the streets had been changed in the couple of hours. The narrator describes:

> ...it seemed somehow unfamiliar. The pavements, usually thronged with vendors and passers—by, were eerily empty now—except for squads of patrolling policeman. All the shapes were shut even the paan—

> stalls at the corners: None of us had ever seen those shut before. (Amitav Ghosh, 202)

The bus driver turns the bus into another narrower street and then towards Park Circus where the narrator sees a scattered mob milling around the circus. Then one group from the mob came towards them. The men began to throw stones against their windows. When the boys looked at them, they were laughing. What kind of pleasure is this? The narrator writes that they were stupefied with fear:

> It would not be enough to say we were afraid: we were stupefied with fear.... It is a fear that comes of the Knowledge that normalcy is utterly contingent, that the space that surround one, the streets that one inhabits, can became, suddenly and without warning, as hostile as a desert in a flash flood. It is this that sets apart the thousand million people who inhabit the subcontinent from the rest of the world not language, not food, not music—it is the special quality of loneliness that grows out of the fear of the war between oneself and one's image in the mirror. (Amitav Ghosh, 204)

When May, Tridib and the grandmother reach Dhaka and meet Mayadebi, the grandmother asks her: "Where's Dhaka? I can't see Dhaka" (Amitav Ghosh, 193). Let us deal with the things those happened in Dhaka. At first, we shall focus on what had happened in Srinagar. One afternoon in 1979, soon after the narrator began work on his PhD, he attended a lecture in the Teen Murti House Library in New Delhi. The speaker was and Australian specialist on Asian affairs who spoke on India's war with China in 1962. He was not a good speaker and did not say anything new, but it jogged their memories. Then his friends and the narrator went to the canteen and found themselves talking about their recollections of that time. Then the narrator remembered the terrible riots in Calcutta in 1964. He said to his friends about the sound of voices running past the walls of his school, and of a glimpse of a mob in Park Circus. After looking in the newspaper file he came to know the reality. He found the headline in the newspaper which said: "Twenty-nine killed in ratios" (Amitav Ghosh, 224).

The news said of the riots happened in Khulna, in East Pakistan, across the border from Calcutta. As the narrator turned the pages to the edition of Saturday, 11 January 1964, and found the headline which said: "Curfew in Calcutta, Police Open Fire, 10 dead, 15 wounded" (Amitav Ghosh, 224).

He also found another headline: "Sacred relic reinstalled" (Amitav Ghosh, 224). It said that the sacred hair of the Prophet Mohammad was reinstalled in the Hazratbal Shrine in Srinagar that amongst a tremendous upsurge of popular joy and festivity throughout Kashmir. Then he understands all the details about the riot.

It is said that the sacred relic known as the Mu-i-Mubarak was believed to be a hair of the prophet Mohammad. It was purchased by a Kashmiri Merchant called Khwaja Nur-ud-din in Bijapur (near Hyderabad) in the year 1699. Then it was transported to the valley of Kashmir. The arrival of the relic was greeted by a great tumult of joy in the valley. In order to get a glimpse of the relic, the people marched in their thousands from every part of Kashmir. Later, the relic was installed at the picturesque Hazratbal Mosque near Srinagar. This mosque became a great centre of pilgrimage and every year multitudes of people—Hindus, Muslims, Sikhs and Buddhist would flock to Hazratbal on those occasions when the relic was displayed to the public. Over the centuries, the shrine became a symbol of the unique and distinctive culture of Kashmir. But unfortunately the Mu-i-Mubarak disappeared from its place. When the people came to know, despite the bitter cold thousands of people, including hundreds of wailing women, took out black-flag demonstration from Srinagar to the Hazratbal mosque. Schools, colleges and shops pulled down their shutters all over the valley and buses and cars vanished from the streets.

There were huge demonstrations in Srinagar in which Muslims, Sikhs and Hindus took active part on Sunday, 29 December 1963. There were a number of public meetings which were attended and addressed by members of all the major religious communities. There were some incidents of rioting and a curfew was quickly declared by the authorities. But the targets of the rioters were not people—neither Hindus, nor Muslims, nor Sikhs—but property identified with the government and the police. The theft of relic had brought together the people of Kashmir as never before. The people from all the religions came together under the leadership of Maulana Masoodi, who persuaded the first demonstrators to march with black flags instead of green and thereby drew the various communities of Kashmir together in a collective display of mourning.

Prime Minister Nehru dispatched the highest officials of the Central Bureau of Intelligence and Home Ministry to find the missing relic. The Premier of Kashmir declared that the theft was a mad act of the anti-nationalist. At the same time, there were meetings and demonstrations in towns and cities in both—East Pakistan and West Pakistan. The religious authorities declared that the theft was an attack upon the identity of Muslims. In Karachi, 31st December was observed as the black day and other cities followed it. The Pakistan newspapers declared it as a part of a deep laid conspiracy for uprooting the spiritual and national hopes of Kashmiris.

The Mu-i-Mubarak was recovered by the officials of the Central Bureau of Intelligence on 4th January 1964. The city, Srinagar erupted with joy. People danced on the streets. There were innumerable thanks giving meetings. Muslims, Hindus and Sikhs marched together in demonstrations demanding that the conspirators be revealed. The celebratory slogan "Central Intelligence Zindabad" (Amitav Ghosh, 226), for the first and perhaps the last time, rang out on the streets of an Indian city.

But in Khulna, a demonstration that was marching against the theft of relic turned violent. Some shops were burnt down and a few people were killed. The Government of East Pakistan lost no time in sending the army there to stop the riots. But within few days the riots spread into the neighbouring towns and districts and towards Dhaka and the Hindu refugees began to pour over the border into India by trains or foot convoys. The Pakistani government provided enough security but sometimes the trains were stopped by mobs. The towns and cities of East Pakistan were now in the grip of frenzy of looting, killing and burning. The riots in East Pakistan (Bangladesh) were the same as they were in West Pakistan in general and Sialkot in particular, which are well described in Azadi by Chaman Nahal. Amitav Ghosh doesn't deal with particulars of riots like Khushwant Singh who described in detail the atrocities perpetrated against women:

> They had heard of gentle women having their veils taken of, being stripped and marched down crowded streets to be raped in the market place. Many had eluded their would be ravishers by killing themselves. They had heard of mosques being described by the slaughter of pigs on the premises and, of copies of copies of the holy Koran being torn up by fiedels. (Khushwant Singh, 105)

A few Calcutta dailies printed the pictures of weeping Hindu refugees along with the accounts of the events took place in East Pakistan (Bangladesh) and there was a rumour in Calcutta that the trains from Pakistan were arriving packed with corpses on 8th and 9th January 1964. So on 10th January, Calcutta erupted. Mobs went through the city killing Muslims, and burning and looting their shops and houses. The police opened the fire on mobs and curfew was imposed in some parts of the city. On 11th January, the army was called out of Fort William and several battalions were deployed throughout the city. Though so, the stray incidents of looting, burning and killing went on for a week. But the reliable estimates of how many people killed in riot of 1964 are not there. The number of the dead could not be less than the people killed in the war of 1962. Amitav Ghosh praises the newspaper and other people, who worked their level best to restore the normalcy. He writes:

> The university communities of both Dhaka and Calcutta took the initiative in doing relief work and organizing peace marches and newspaper on both sides of the border did some fine, human pieces of reporting. As always, there were innumerable cases of Muslims in East Pakistan giving shelter to Hindus, often at the cost of

> their own lives, an equally, in India, of Hindus sheltering Muslims. But they were ordinary people, soon forgotten not for them any Marty's Memorials or Eternal Flames. (Amitav Ghosh, 229-30)

The leaders like Maulana Masoodi are now forgotten. Only those leaders came ahead who had partitioned the country on the basis of religion only for their own benefits. Every novel written on the theme of partition deals with the communal conflict and the communal harmony as well aroused out of it. We know how Sita and Ranjit in *Sunlight on a Broken Column*, hurling their lives in danger came to help Laila and her daughter. Even the relationship between Lala Kanshi Ram and Chaudhri Barkat Ali is the well-known example of communal harmony where they used to call as brothers to each other. Thus it was 1979; fifteen years later he could find that there was a connection between his nightmare bus-ride back from school and the events that killed Tridib and the others in Dhaka. He says:

> Every word I write about these events of 1964 is the product of a struggle with silence. It is a struggle I am destined to lose—have already lost for even after all these years, I do not where within me, in which corner of my world, this silence lies. All I know of it is what it is not. It is not, for example, the silence of an imperfect memory. Nor it is a silence enforced by ruthless state nothing like that no barbed wire, no check points to tell me where its boundaries lie. I know nothing of this silence that it lies outside the reach of my intelligence, beyond words. (Amitav Ghosh, 218)

The narrator is of the opinion that he has no words to describe the riots and the death of Tridib. When he was reading the report of the recovered Mu-i-Mubarak for the fifth time, it struck him that May, Tridib and his grandmother must have left for Dhaka the day before. We know how the grandmother asked where Dhaka is. She was in search of Dhaka that has surrounded their old house. She was searching for Kana—babu's sweet shop. She was not fascinated by the Plaza Picture Palace, the Gulshan Palace Hotel, Rama Race course and so on. She was in search of Dhaka as was in her memory. She felt herself a foreigner in the land of her birth.

Though the Saheb said that there might be a danger to their lives if they go on that time, she felt the need to rescue her uncle who was living alone in a foreign country. But what was there on the other side? Her uncle was looked after by Khalil, a Muslim cycle rickshaw driver and his family. He made Dhaka his home. He did not cross the border, though he was unsafe there. He adjusted himself in the circumstances, ignored his principles and lived happily with the Muslim family. He was an orthodox Hindu. While talking with Robi, the grandmother throws light on her uncle's orthodoxy:

> ...There was a time when the old man was so orthodox that he wouldn't let a Muslim shadows pass within ten feet of his food? And look at him, now, paying the price of his sins. (Amitav Ghosh, 210)

An objective interpretation of the acts of Jethamoshai, the uncle may be positive. It was a positive change in the mentality of an orthodox person. This means that this was the positive effect of the Partition. Once the person who didn't believed his own sons, became one with the strangers. When he was asked to go to India, he rejected the offer of his sons by saying:

> I don't believe in this India-Shindia. It's all very well, you're going away now, but suppose when you get there they decide to draw another line somewhere? What will you do then? Where will you move to? No one will have you anywhere. As for me, I was born here, and I'II die here. (Amitav Ghosh, 215)

He is ready to change himself to live there where he was born. He is ready to continue his life in the same land as was Kemal in Sunlight on Broken Column. Uncle Jethamoshai can best be compared with Gangu Mal in 'Azadi' who accepts Islam for the sake of retaining his property in the city. Both are ready to scarify something. The difference lies in that Gangu Mal was to retain his property and Jethamoshai was to share it with the refugees. He was now known by the name—Ukil Babu.

Even the grandmother requested uncle Jethamoshai to come with her to India. But he was not ready. He was even, at first, unable to identify her. When Khalil introduced her to him, he said that she was a foreigner and came to take you. He didn't approve the plan of the grandmother. We know that the grandmother also was unable to identify the Dhaka which was her past. So she says in distress to May: "Yes, I really am a foreigner here—as foreign as May in India or Tagore in Argentina" (Amitav Ghosh, 195).

But Tridib pointed out to her that she was more foreigner than May, because she didn't require visa to get there. This again shows that the British people were very closer to the Indian than their own people. This can be called the second effect of the Partition that an individual turns into a state of exile in his or her own country. The narrator's grandmother is the best example of that.

When the grandmother and the others were discussing the matter, the driver shouted and said to be quick as there was going to be trouble outside. Then Khalil asked them to go by their car and was ready to follow them bringing uncle Jethamoshai in his rickshaw. Then they quickly got into the car and set off slowly down the empty road with the rickshaw following close behind. But within a few minutes the scene was changed:

> There were dozens of them stretched all the way across the road. They had lit a fire in the middle of the road, with a few broken chairs and bits of wood. Some of them were squatting around the fire, others were leaning against the lampposts and the shop—fronts.... They were waiting for the car. (Amitav Ghosh, 217-18)

This is how the trouble came to them. The car was stopped by the mob and some of them broke the windscreen and injured the driver. Their armed security guard shot at them. Grandmother's uncle was following them. Khalil was driving his rickshaw. The narrator's grandmother asked the driver to drive fast, but May got off the car. So Tridib followed her and ran towards the rickshaw. The mob had surrounded the rickshaw, pulled the old man off it. Then Tridib ran into the mob and vanished. In a moment the men began to scatter. What May had seen there is very horrible: "...I saw three bodies. They were all dead. They'd cut Khalil's stomach open. The old man's head had been hacked off. And they'd cut Tridib's throat from ear to ear" (Amitav Ghosh, 251). This is how the trouble resulted into the death of the three—Tridib, Khalil and Jethamoshai.

Tridib's death had a great impact on almost all the characters. His dead body was brought to Calcutta and was cremated. At that time, Tridib was sent to his mother's brother's house. Then in the Dakshineshwar temple, for the first time, his father told him the news of Tridib's death. Then through Robi and May he got the details of Tridib's death.

When Ila, the narrator and Robi went to Clapham to have a dinner, they met Rehaman-Saheb. While talking with Rehaman-Saheb; Robi told the sad and pathetic story of the death of Tridib. Then he said that he couldn't get rid of that dream ever since it happened. He wanted to get rid of it, but he still did not. He is ready to do anything to get rid of that memory. He says about the effect of memory:

> But it wouldn't go, it stayed. I used to think: If only that dream would go away, I would be like other people: I would be free. I would have given anything to be free of that memory. (Amitav Ghosh, 246)

Robi himself confesses that he is abnormal; he is different than other people. He is not freed of that and so still have the hands shaking like a leaf, though he is thousands of miles away from that place and fifteen years already passed since it happened. He stresses the point that though they draw thousands of lines, it's an illusion, it doesn't change anything. One cannot say that when one is in another continent he or she has nothing to do with his or her past because one cannot divide one's memory. The narrator says how these two cities Calcutta and Dhaka became too close to each other which did not happen in the past:

> There had never been a moment in the four thousand years old history of that map, when the places we know as Dhaka and Calcutta were more closely bound to each

> other than after they had drawn their lines—so closely that I, in Calcutta, had only to look into the mirror to be in Dhaka, a moment when each city was the irreversible symmetry by the lines that was to set us free—our looking glass border. (Amitav Ghosh, 233).

The narrator also, though after fifteen years have passed, couldn't get rid of that riot which had hurt his heart. He went on thinking. Then he thought of the distance between Khulna and Srinagar which was about 2,000 kilometres. He drew a circle on a map placing Khulna as its centre and Srinagar on the circumference and discovered that half of the mankind had fallen within it. But the incident which happened in Srinagar in case of Mu-i-Mubarak had given a kind of turn to the history and the world saw that the distance is not important, closeness is important.

The grandmother was touched by the death of Tridib. She had a feeling of hatred against Muslims. She was very fond of jewelry. In the year 1965, she gave her gold chain, the first thing her husband had given, to the fund for the war. She explains as to why she has given it: "I had to, don't you see? For your sake; for your freedom. We have to kill them before they kill us; we have to wipe them out (Amitav Ghosh, 237).

When she was wounded, she said that she should not waste her blood. She wanted to donate it to the war fund. She would hardly left her room. But she had strong feelings against the Muslims. She wanted the Muslims be killed. She is similar to Debi Dayal in 'A Bend in the Ganges'. They both have faith in militant nationalism. Difference lies in the fact that Debi Dayal is himself involved in terrorist activity, whereas the grandmother did not or could not.

May is also touched by the death of Tridib. She thinks that she was responsible for his death. She used to think that he wouldn't have got out of that car if she hadn't made him to do so. She was an English woman, and so was safe. Though Tridib did know very well that he was going out of the car into that mob to die, he did it to satisfy her. It was a sacrifice in a love. Now May works for philanthropic causes and she has joined a couple of small relief agencies, which provided housing for survivals of an earthquake in Central America. The work satisfies her. The work became a religion to her and so she collects money for it moving from road to road. But now she thinks that she didn't kill him. She tells the narrator:

> But I know now I didn't kill him. I couldn't have, if I'd wanted. He gave himself up; it was a sacrifice. I know I can't understand it, I know I mustn't try, for any real sacrifice is a mystery. (Amitav Ghosh, 251-52)

For years, she thought that she made Tridib to die for the sake of an old man who was unable to get up on his own, or unable to identify the people who were once dear to him. But at last when she spends a night with the narrator where they lay in each other's arms and were glad to be so. It may be the indication of that both May and the narrator is now free of that memory. This is how we may say that the novel ends happily. The narrator says: "...And I was glad too, and grateful, for the glimpse she had given me of a final redemptive mystery" (Amitav Ghosh, 252). Like many other novels *The Shadow Lines* deals with the themes of Partition and the communal conflict. It deals with the causes and effect of the riots spread in North India.

WORKS CITED

Chopra, Anu. *May and Ila—The Two Faces of Woman,* Edited by Indira Bhatt and Indira Nityanandam, Interpretations of Amitav Ghosh's *The Shadow Lines,* Creative Books, New Delhi, 2000, p. 61.

Damor, Nutan. *The Quest for Freedom,* Edited by Indira Bhatt and Indira Nityanandam, Interpretations of Amitav Ghosh's *The Shadow Lines,* Creative Books, New Delhi, 2000, p. 76.

Dhanwan, R.K. *Introduction,* The Novels of Amitav Ghosh Edited by R.K. Dhawan, Prestige Books, New Delhi, 1999, p. 23.

Ghosh, Amitav. *The Shadow Lines,* Educational Edition, Oxford University Press, New Delhi, Thirteen Impressions, 2005, p. 20. (All the references in the parenthesis are from this book.)

Kapadia, Novy. *Communal Frenzy and Partition: Bapsi Sidhwa, Attia Hosain and Amitav Ghosh,* The Novels of Amitav Ghosh Edited By R.K. Dhawan, Prestige Books, New Delhi, 1993.

Neogy, Alpana. *The Partition of Bengal: A Comparative Study of Amitav Ghosh's The Shadow Lines and Sunil Gangopadhyay's Purba Paschim*, The Novels of Amitav Ghosh Edited by R.K. Dhawan, Prestige Books, New Delhi, 1999, pp. 81 to 86.

Pandit, Nirzari. *Freedom, Time and Narrative in Amitav Ghosh's The Shadow Lines*, Creative Books, New Delhi, 2000, p. 82.

Singh, Khushwant. *Train to Pakistan*, India Book House, Pvt. Ltd. Bombay, 1975, p. 105.

15

Amitav Ghosh's *Sea of Poppies*: A Story of Troubled People

Neeta Dhumal

Sea of Poppies is a story set prior to the Opium Wars, on the banks of holy river Ganges and in Calcutta. The characters in the novel are like poppy seeds that outgrow the field as if they form a sea. It is a story about undemanding, common and ill fated people. Deeti, a simple lady is introduced at the very beginning of the novel. She is a dutiful mother and a housewife. Her husband Hukum Singh is a crippled man who works at Ghazipur Opium Factory. Deeti is given opium at the time of her marriage so that her brother-in-law could consummate the marriage in place of her infertile husband. Deeti begets a daughter, Kabutri, from her brother-in-law. After the death of her husband she prepares to go through Sati ritual but a well-wisher of Deeti, Kalua, comes to her help. He rescues her and they elope and stay together. For the conventional villagers this is not acceptable. As both of them cannot return they become indentured servants on the Ibis, the ship.

Zachary Reid, a sailor wants to live on Ibis for his lifetime. He is a son of a slave mother and a white father. He admires Ibis so much as if Ibis were his mother. With the help of Serang Ali, the head of the lascars, he becomes the second in command of the ship which carries labour to the island of Mauritius.

Another character Neel Rattan Haldar is a wealthy rajah whose dynasty has been ruling Rakshali for centuries. Mr. Burnham confronts him. He wants Halder to sell out the property but he refuses to do so as the zamindary is his family's ancestral property and selling it meant his shrinking away from his responsibility. He is tried for forgery but it is a part of plotting of Burnham. Consequently he is sentenced to work as an indentured labourer for seven years in Mauritius. There he meets Ah Fatt, an opium addict and his only companion in prison and both of them would be transported by Ibis.

Paulette, a French woman is brought up in India. She is an orphan and her father was a botanist. Mr. and Mrs. Burnham take Paulette into their home after her father's death. As Mr. Burnham tries to misbehave with her, she determines to runaway from them. Besides Mr. Burnham wants that Paulette should marry his elderly friend, Justice Kendalbushe. Coincidently, Paulette and Zachary Reid meet at a dinner at Burnhams. Both of them get attracted with each other and they decide to travel to Mauritius. Along with her childhood friend Jodu she boards the ship. She disguises herself as an Indian woman. She knows Bengali well and she feels at home with Indian way of life.

The Ibis becomes a refuge to the people who are troubled for one reason on another. All the characters undergo great strife. There is bloodshed on the ship caused by sudden and unpredicted storm. Somehow Neel, Ah Fatt, Jodu, Serang Ali and Kalua manage to escape. They are unaware of their future. At the centre of all there is a vast ship, the Ibis whose prime purpose of journey is to trade and the destiny of Ibis is its tumultuous voyage across the Indian Ocean.

Sea of Poppies is about seeking freedom. Ghosh uses typical polyglot language to narrate the story. It is a first novel of trilogy about the Ibis, a ship that sails between India and Mauritius. A galaxy of characters like poppy seeds arises in the context and most of the characters are transgressors and they experience class or race discrimination. They are exotic and psychologically rich as well as complex and each character helps portray the novel colourfully. These men and women are having limited capacity and they are powerless and cannot establish themselves as individuals. They go through ordeals in their crusade of search for identify and their right to survive according to their own will. Their stories compel us to think about the culture, heritage, history and identity of individuals as well.

These characters go through various experiences of life that expose subtleties of human nature and the age old prevailing customs. There is mention of heartless sati or widow burning custom, raping, kidnapping and floggings where women are treated as commodities without taking into consideration the fact that they are basically human beings. Consequently, these women rebel against the prevailing customs and try to establish their own world. Deeti and Paulette try to choose their own world of their choice. Deeti while bathing in Ganga, an inland at the distance of four hundred miles from Calcutta, hallucinates a tall-masted ocean-going ship, which Deeti realizes is linked-up with her destiny. Orphaned Paulette seeks solace in the company of Zachary Reid on the board of the ship. These characters put their fate on sail with Ibis. Ghosh's gentler tale 'kindles an adventurous optimism in defiance of its protagonists' privations'. These characters appear complex at the outset but as they board the ship they are found easier to comprehend. Ghosh puts his characters in a more sympathetic way though the novel is flooded with characters and different languages but there is no ruthless commotion. Ghosh brings individual experiences under the pressures of history and exploitation of life and the characters are not unnecessarily put into various dimensions.

Amitav Ghosh came across a collection of letters written by medieval Jewish traders where he got reference of Bangalore trader's "slave and business agent". After that Ghosh spent several years and what he found there has been put by him in his books. In *Sea of Poppies*, Ghosh introduces those characters whose social and cultural mobility is dependent on British colonialism and the trading opportunities it brought. Ibis, the ship docked in Bay of Bengal draws together these disparate characters and Ibis allows them to fashion new identities. It is a heterogeneous group of multi-cultured people.

Englishmen presented in the story are quite typical whereas Indian characters bear their own stance. Some of them want to merge themselves in others' culture. These characters embody the ghostly subject with great care and they exhibit their heroic guts. Like poppy fields their lives are colourful but not two lives are identical. In nineteenth century British regime, the crops were replaced with poppy fields that changed the whole scenario. The simplistic agrarian culture had been changing into ghostly mercantile community. Factories were established and exported the opium to the opium den, China. In this process of change common Indian had been crushed and this common man was exploited and humiliated largely. The Englishmen became wealthy and consequently Chinese authorities realized the harm causing to their population and they laid down strict measures to control. The poor Indian was treated merely as 'coolie' to serve the colonists' purpose. In this devastating tumult outcastes like bankrupt Raja, an opium addict, a forlorn woman and many more voyage and the slave boat, Ibis, becomes a shelter for them. These are the misfits in their society but Ibis supports them generously. The novel's grandeur is noteworthy but along with its magnitude its minute detailing of the characters is also significant. These characters become vehicle of the different cultures and the novel becomes a living document of social, economic and political ethos of the era. There is also a record of brutal oppression but all the same it gives optimistic stance.

These characters alienate themselves from their established ways of life and enter into a new realm. The journey of these characters is engrossed with pain and pleasure and they do not merely coincide but relate to each other symbolically. Fate has thrown together these characters and among the crew there are sailors, coolies and convicts and the protagonists of the novel are misfits among the boarders. Their old families' ties are washed away. Like their historical counterparts they view themselves as 'Jahaj-Bhais'. Very strangely enough the unlikely dynasty becomes part of the fate of Ibis. The Diaspora of these characters 'Encapsulates the colonial history of the East'.

WORKS CITED

Review: *Sea of Poppies* by Amitav Ghosh, *Observer Review*, Sunday 8 June, 2008, p. 25.

Ghosh, Amitav. *Encyclopaedia Britannica.*

"Amitav Ghosh Re-emerges with *Sea of Poppies*". *The Hindu* (Chennai-India), May 24, 2008.

16

Micro-narratives of Fever and Discovery in Amitav Ghosh's *The Calcutta Chromosome*

Shyam Chothani

Amitav Ghosh's famous novel, *The Calcutta Chromosome* carries an alternative title *Of Delirium, Fever and Discovery*. These three aspects of the title also become the narrative principles of the novel and hence the novel has in it, at various stages, three different styles of expression, corresponding to them.

Firstly, all the main characters in the novel are affected by malaria at one point or the other. Then they get into a feverish hallucination which is then reflected in the narrative which moves in restless jumbled fits. For instance, when Antar speaks about Murugan, his fits of anger and frustration overcome the cohesion of the narrative. Secondly, every single character is involved in a quest or discovery. Antar searches for Murugan and his theory. Murugan searches for the past of Ronald Ross, and Ross himself is in search of microscopic parasites. Thus, the novel becomes a collection of searches and discoveries. Further, delirium is a state in which past and present get mixed. So is the case of the narrative in *The Calcutta Chromosome*. In places it begins in the present with Antar's consciousness but it shifts constantly back into the past by exploring the memories of various characters. It opens by exploring Antar's memory of Murugan and then, Murugan's memory of Ross, Cunningham and Farley, Phulboni's memories revealed in his stories, and interestingly, the mechanical memory of Antar's supercomputer—Ava.

The novel also uses the technique of telescoping, i.e. use of narrative to merge one consciousness with another. For instance, when Murugan disappears, his memory is reduced to Antar's memory. Similarly, Phulboni's memory is internalized by Murugan. This device is like a Russian doll, keeping one narrative within another. The Russian doll also explains the inter-locking narratives of the novel that move across time and space.

The novel also employs the technique of narrative refrain. Same or similar incidents are experienced by many characters in the novel. For instance, the Renupur incident is recalled by Cunningham, Phulboni and Murugan. However, these characters were not present at Renupur at the same point of time. This refrain creates a reality out of fantasy.

Amitav Ghosh also uses a rhizomic pattern in the narrative. Rhizomic pattern is the use of multi-layered horizontal narratives, with each level intersecting the other. For instance, the narratives of Antar, Murugan, and Phulboni are horizontally placed and they create three focal characters. At the same time, these three narratives overlap as Antar's quest includes Phulboni's life. Three narratives are further connected together by two quests—those of Antar and Murugan.

Spread narrative is another term that can be used in the context of *The Calcutta Chromosome*. This term was used by Andrew Gibson to describe a non-linear narrative that moves like fluid, horizontally. It indicates constant exchange between levels, forces, and voices similar to the concept of rhizome. For instance, in the novel, one finds a constant exchange between the forces of science and the forces of counter science, represented by Ronald Ross and Mangala respectively. Similarly, voices get exchanged among the characters even when they do not meet each other. For instance, Murugan's voice becomes Antar's voice even when Murugan is reported missing. Similarly, Phulboni's oriental silence becomes Murugan's pregnant silence later in the novel when he disappears.

Ghosh has also used a geo-narrative in *The Calcutta Chromosome*. Geo-narrative is a kind of narrative that carries cartographic features by converting words and expressions into geographical features. In *The Calcutta Chromosome*, the narrative keeps shifting the geographical settings that include the United States, Egypt and places in India like Chennai, Calcutta and Renupur. Such shifts indicate the diasporic experiences of the characters. For instance, Ronald Ross's journey from England to India and then to different places create a context for narrating colonial diaspora. Antar and Murugan too are diasporic subjects, and their experiences are narrated with similar shifts in the settings.

One significant aspect of any narrative is focalization, i.e. creating a focal character either from a first person point of view or an omniscient point of view. In this novel, one can find multiple focal characters. For instance, Murugan is focal character in Antar's point of view. Ronald Ross is a focal character, initially, in Murugan's perspective. However, Murugan focalizes Phulboni later; then Lutchman; and still later, Mangala. The narrative in *The Calcutta Chromosome* traces secrets of places by cracking the codes and mysteries of these places. It is expressed very clearly in the novel.

Every city has its secrets, the voice began, but Calcutta, whose vocation is excess, has so many that it is more secret than any other. Elsewhere, by the workings of paradox, secrets live in the telling: they whisper life into humdrum streetcorners and dreary alleyways; into the rubbish strewn rears of windowless tenements and the blackened floors of oil-bathed workshops. But here in our city where all law, natural and human, is held in capricious suspension, that which is hidden has no need of words to give it life; like any creature that lives in a perverse element, it mutates to discover sustenance precisely where it appears to be most starkly withheld—in this case, in silence (Ghosh, 2008, 22).

Ghosh explores this paradox of telling and keeping the secret alive. Even at the end of the novel the secrets about Phulboni, Mangala and Ross remain secret, despite narrating them. Phulboni tries to tell these secrets in the form of encrypted secret, in his stories.

The title is justified with the narrative of *The Calcutta Chromosome* which moves like chromosome with its jumps (skipping one generation), changes and mutations. Further, like the chromosome the narrative has disruptions, interruptions, distortions, secrecy and silences. For instance, Antar's story is interrupted by Murugan's story, and Murugan's story, in turn, is interrupted by Phulboni's story. Distortions are also common in the narrative as for instance, the history of identifying malaria parasite. Ghosh gives at least three versions of the identification of the parasite—one, Ronald Ross's laboratorial finding; two, the tribals' finding that mosquitoes spread malaria; and three, Mangala's use of malaria parasite as a cure for syphilis-induced paralysis.

Amitav Ghosh uses frame narratives to subvert the mega narrative or the master narrative in the novel. Each character's life is framed partially in the consciousness of another character. Antar, for instance, frames Murugan; Murugan frames Ross, Mangala and Lutchman. The readers are drawn into all these micro narratives that imply the plurality and incompleteness of truth.

The Calcutta Chromosome is also a postcolonial/ postmodern historiography. It considers the possibility of merging various discourses like fiction, history, and science. It is also built upon historiographic details like letters, diaries, personal memory and the history imagined. Ghosh mixes scientific history with stories to expose the fictionality of history and the historicity of fiction. For instance, Ghosh creates a blur in the boundary between the real and the unreal. To illustrate this point, one can talk about Murugan's identity. He exists in the unreal space or in cyber space in hyper reality. The whole identity of Murugan is a reconstruction of his partly burnt I-card with the help of Ava. Later, the computer also recovers Murugan's once deleted message in the form of an oral narrative. Similar is the state of Farley's letter which is not only uncatalogued in the library but also disappears after Murugan reads it. These developments indicate an anxiety for truth in the narrative. At one stage, Murugan expresses this anxiety to Urmila:

> You've got me there Calcutta, Murugan said. That's where I keep coming short. All I have is bits and pieces—no beginning, no middle and definitely no end. (Ghosh, 2008, 215)

Amitav Ghosh too seems to articulate the same anxiety as the whole narrative offers only bits and pieces of history and truth, which are based on visions and speculations.

The narrative in *The Calcutta Chromosome* changes the readers as the chromosomes undergo mutation. Further, every single receiver of some information in the novel also undergoes changes. This possibility of changing something by knowing is articulated by Murugan to Antar:

> You took the words out of my mouth, Murugan said. 'Not making sense is what it's about—conventional sense that is. Maybe this other team started with the idea that knowledge is self-contradictory; maybe they believed that to know something is to change it, therefore in knowing something, you've already changed what you think you know so you don't really know it at all: you only know its history. Maybe they thought that knowledge couldn't begin with without acknowledging the impossibility of knowledge. See what I'm saying?' (Ghosh, 2008, 91)

Thus, the main purpose of the narrative in *The Calcutta Chromosome* is to tell the readers that they only know the received history of malaria research and not the truth of the same.

WORK CITED

Ghosh, Amitav. *The Calcutta Chromosome.* New Delhi: Viking, 2008.

17

Homespun Wisdom and Axiomatic Aspects in Amitav Ghosh's *River of Smoke*

Vivekanand Jha

Amitav Ghosh is not a novice and amateur name in the arena of English Fiction that I should begin a critical article on him with his biographical detail and the number of honours and awards bestowed to him. Whosoever have interest in Amitav Ghosh, I think, must be aware of such accounts and details pertaining to Amitav Ghosh. Therefore, I would straightway like to take you to the tour of the sum and substance on which the present article is based. Those readers who are ambitious of reading the novel, *River of Smoke* must have read the first and inaugural of Ghosh's ibis trilogy, *Sea of Poppies* and if they have they must be aware of one of the central characters of the Novel, Deeti. And Amitav Ghosh opens the accounts of his second novel of proposed trilogy, *River of Smoke* with the characterization of Deeti and the very beginning of the novel has been done with following paragraph:

> Deeti's shrine was hidden in a cliff, in a far corner of Mauritius, where the island's eastern and southern shorelines collide to form the wind-whipped dome of the Morne Brabant. This site was a geological anomaly—a cave within a spur of limestone, hollowed out by wind and water—and there was nothing like it anywhere else on the mountain. Later Deeti would insist that it wasn't chance but destiny that led her to it—for the very

> existence of the place was unimaginable until you had actually stepped inside it. (3)

Amitav Ghosh has almost touched upon all the frequencies and wavelengths of humanitarian spectrum in the novel, *River of Smoke* but I would be dealing with only one aspect of such comprehensive contour. The novel is replete with domestic and widespread wisdom, maxim and established facts which mesmerize the readers with their unbound wit, sense of humour and the knowledge they garner by virtues of reading them. The very commencement of the proverbial statement comes out from the fresh breath of Deeti:

> Repetition is the method through which the miraculous becomes a part of every life. (14)

The nuptial tie between Bahram and Shireenbai was mere a marriage of convenience and this marriage brought about no positive changes in the life of Bahram other than scaling disproportionate materialistic marriage. The living standard of Bahram was rustic and inappropriate in comparison with that of the Seth's family and it was a cause of gaucheness and embarrassment for him. Even his in-laws were deeming him with an eye of contempt and derision. Bahram's mother though a widow is woman of high self-respect and blue blood family. Many ups and downs in life have made her to achieve unfathomable insights into the practical and realistic mode of life and she made a stiff opposition of the circumstances under which Bahram had to remain as a house-husband in the family of Seth because of pitiable and wretched economic condition of his family. Her mother did know ill and side effects of being house husband and promulgated a pertinent proverbial pronouncement in Gujarati:

> *Kutra pos, bilara pos per jemeina jeniyane varma khos* —Rear a dog, rear a cat, but shove the son-in-law and his offspring into the gutter. (48)

All that Bahram needed was an opportunity to show his mettle and once he grabbed it he glittered like gold. The very first visit of Bahram to Canton brought incredible accomplishment and success not only for his family but even for Bahram himself. Now, he was totally changed from old to new

Bahram and in a short notice he became one of the most highly acclaimed businessmen of Bombay and a man of high esteem in Canton of China. Rather than continuing as a house husband he became capable to paddle his own canoe and prosperous enough to lead a separate life but due to homesickness and obstinacy of his wife he deferred the decision to change his residence. The in-laws of Bahram were now envious of his success and watching him with eyes of suspicion, distrust and derision. Despite considerable achievements he was unable to get due respect from them and a kind of restlessness was conspicuous in the psyche of Bahram which reminded him the homespun wisdom of her mother that she generally spoke to:

> *Palelo kutro peg kedde*—It's the pet dog that bites you in the leg. (53)

The father-in-law of Bahram passed away and his brothers-in-law irritated by his leaping progress brought a proposal to dispose of the export division founded by their father. Though it was owned by their brothers-in-law but Bahram had great role in making this export division one of the leading companies of Bombay at the cost of his own intelligence and diligence. Thus, the export division was for Bahram as for the mother a child and he once decided to buy it at the cost of selling off all his lifelong earnings and even the jewellry of Shireenbai. But after long debate, discussion and contemplation they defer their decision to sell off the export division by a year that will allow Bahram to purchase the division himself. Seeing the situation working in his favour, Bahram turns superstitious and placing his hands on his heart he spells out:

> *Hak naam te Saahebnu*—Truth is the name of the Almighty. (57)

Unlike other boys of Canton, Bahram never wanted his illegal son, Ah Fatt to be a boat-children swimming into broth and water but he wanted him to become a well read man. The rules and regulations of Canton give no more right to boat boys other than scholarship to fish and sail and handle boats. But his mother, Chi-mei was well aware of these facts and therefore she had exhibited no interest in educating her son as:

> What use was calligraphy to him when boat people were banned by law from sitting for the Civil Service examinations? (89)

Fitcher Penrose earns prestige, laurels and money by virtue of his repeated visit in Canton in the quest of rare and precious plants and his success in garnering those plants and transporting it to Britain established him as a one of the most renowned botanists and horticulturalists of Britain. Attributing his success to his visit to Canton Mr. Penrose acknowledges:

> 'Canton's placed many a foot on the ladder of fortune,' said Fitcher, 'and I was fortunate that mine was among them'. (103)

After departure of his father-in-law Bahram found it a difficult task to carry on relationship and rapport with his brothers-in-law as they were just jealous of his surprising success fort they themselves were unable to step into the shoes of their father. They got even excuse to put spoke into the wheel of Bahram as they came to know that China is likely to put ban on imports and trading of opium even at the cost of fighting and war. Bahram discharges his anguishes on his brothers-in-law and regrets the exit of his father-in-law through following dictum:

> when the wise one goes, things fall apart.... (112)

Shireenbai is a superstitious woman and she has a great belief in miracle-mongering, palmistry and chiromancy and even she is hell bent to restrict Bahram from going to China this time due to rumour of war and other ill and evil omens that she comes across due to her superstitious conviction. Under the escalating pressure of his wife Bahram defers his decision to depart for China by few days and as he observes no unusual things taking place in Canton he appointed an ultimate date for his departure and declared that he would no more wait after that as he would miss to start the trading season in Canton. When a point of his departure arrived everything went wrong through the superstitious eyes of Shireenbai so much so that the crying of owl supposed to be heard at night but:

> An owl was heard at daybreak. (112)

The love of Chi-mei was drawing Bahram towards Canton and this was the reason he was adamant to set out for Canton even though all the circumstance, were adverse and he no more yielded to the credulous cries of Shireenbai. But he found sudden love and cares for him into the eyes of Shireenbai and he assured her that he would return safe from china as:

> A wife's prayers will never be wasted. (113)

Since Canton is not allowed for European and foreign women and therefore the foreigners discharge their ignited passion on the local girls of easy virtue popularly known as sing-song-girls. Such is the havoc of sing-song-girl in Canton Ah Fatt, a friend of Neel is observed warning him before Neel was likely to set out for Canton:

> In China people say "everything new comes from Canton". Better for young men not to go there—too many ways for them to be spoiled. (145)

Bahram has been in China for long and he is now well acquainted with how and where abouts of China. Napoleon Bonaparte, a French military and political leader during the later stages of the French Revolution, is a prisoner on the island of China and he wanted to meet Bahram personally to know what is politically and economically going on in China at present. But he was afraid of facing Napoleon Bonaparte singlehandedly and he decides to accompany his friend Zadig Bey who is well versed in French and world politics. The thought of facing the authoritarian General reminds Bahram of the pertinent dictum that her mother used to utter:

> If you put your head on a grindstone, then you must expect the pestle. (159)

Bahram and his friend and interpreter Zadig Bey meet Napoleon Bonaparte and while both Zadig and Napoleon were busy conversing with each other; Bahram gave a close look on the gesture, posture and profile of the General Napoleon Bonaparte. When the eyes of Bahram fall on the neck of the General he was quickly reminded of the often repeated saying of his mother:

> *tukki garden valo haramjada ni nisani*—a short neck is a sure sign of a haramzada. (169)

Chinese authorities are disappointed with expanding opium business by William Jardine from one region of China to another and they are planning to send William Jardine out of China and Mr. Jardine is wise enough to go through the impending situation and before he could have insulted and ousted he himself announces to leave China and he produces a lame excuse that he will have to return to England to engage himself in wedlock. John Slade, the founder and editor of the newspaper, *Canton Register,* is a daring fellow and for making vociferous and raucous remarks he was well-known as Thunderer. In a get-together party of General Chamber of Commerce he ultimately goes on to ask Mr. Jardine of his sudden departure from China with following idiomatic expression:

> Since no one else will dare ask, it falls to me to bell the cat. (235)

The ship, *Lord Amherst* is talked about in the novel as a flash back of six years ago when "the *Lord Amherst* was one of many British ships to be sent to forage along the northern coast of China, in the hope of finding new ports through which to funnel opium and other foreign goods into the country"(290). The peculiarity of the ship lies in the fact that it was successfully able to meet out her purpose through false pretension and even eye washing the hawk eyes of Governor Lin Zexu. Bahram reminisces this incident with a hearty laugh followed by utterance of following established belief:

> England-fellow speakee plenty lie. (291)

Mr. Inns is famous in the novel for his notorious acts and he is transporting opium despite severe and strict ban on smuggling of opium has been declared by new representative of Chinese government in Canton, Commissioner Lin. In a raid made by Chinese administration and soldiers he is caught red handed indulging in opium trafficking and they order him to leave Canton in no time and without any terms and conditions. But Mr. Inns is adamant not to leave canton despite all attempts of pleading and requesting of Chamber of Commerce fails to convince him and ultimately the president of Chamber of Commerce conveys the message to Chinese authority that Mr. Inns is not the member of the organization run by them and therefore they have no jurisdiction over Mr. Inns. But the fact is that all foreign traders clandestinely do their trading of opium through Mr. Inns despite the restriction on the trading and trafficking of opium is on its zenith. Bahram smiled such way of befooling the Chinese authority and he introspects:

> Really, there was no language like English for turning lies into legalisms. (349)

All these upheaval, hassle and tug of war on trading and trafficking of opium in Canton have warmed up the political atmosphere of Canton and it has adverse effect on the day to day life of both Chinese and foreigners in Canton. While Robert Chinnery tries to convey to Miss Paulette through letter what has been happening in Canton on the issue of opium treading, he emphasizes sum and substance of his letter through following epigrammatic sentence:

> Since news needs no boats to travel in. (369)

Mr. Charles King, an American trader, is in good terms with mandarins, Chinese merchants in Canton and he was also made one of the members of Canton's General Chamber of Commerce to represent the views of foreign traders to them. But instead of supporting the issues of foreign traders, he worked in disobedience of them and hand in glove with mandarins. He has been dead against the trading and smuggling of opium by the foreign entrepreneurs right from the beginning to the end of the novel. He supports open heartedly the strict and stern official measures taken by Chinese against the trafficking of drug and opium by foreign traders in China and he is of the view that

> The smuggling of opium has lost us the affections of the good, has made us panders to the appetites of the bad, and we may well fear lest we one day suffer by the outbreakings of passions to whose excitement we ourselves have ministered. (371)

Canton is the place that opened the floodgates of opportunities for Mr. Robert Chinnery who had to struggle for his survival in India and he proudly pronounce over his stay in Canton: "How could I abandon the one place that had offered me the treasure I had always sought and never found- Friendship?" (375). This place has filled his life with all the feasible happiness and he keeps on grabbing chance after chance in making his name and fame in the field of painting. Though it is another thing that once he thinks of leaving Canton which is presently undergoing opium crisis as

> It was Wrong and Unconceivable to remain in a place where one was unwelcome. (375)

China is the most flourishing and economically affluent Country in the East by virtue of their diligence and power and perseverance to struggle. Amitav makes use of this fact in the novel, *River of Smoke* through the mouthpiece of Mr. Robert Chinnery who in a letter to Miss Paulette deems China distinct in diplomatic approach and technique:

> One thing you have to say about the Chinese is that unlike others in the East they are a practical people. When faced with a problem they try to find a solution. (380)

Bahram was not fanatic and superstitious follower of God, theology and mysticism like his wife Shireenbai and at the same time he was not blasphemous by nature. Even being in Canton he was observing routine worship with lighting of incense, wick, and offering of fresh flower and fruit. He was well contemplated by some standing chanting that was inculcated to him in his childhood:

> *Humata, Hukhta, Hvarshta*—good thoughts, good words and good deeds. (382)

The new governor of Canton, Commissioner Lin issues warning after warning against trading of opium through a series of letter written in Chinese which is interpreted by professional translator, Mr. Fearon to the members of General Chamber of Commerce in Canton run by foreign traders. Once he saw his words are falling flat to the ears of them, he issues an ultimatum to them with beginning of following line:

> Our words have filled your ears as the empty wind. (390)

The warning of Commissioner Lin against trafficking of opium remains replete with flowery, ornate and deconstructive diction and example of such sentences can be observed when Mr. Fearon reads out his message "Mark my words: the squeeze, when it comes, will be all the tighter because it is more subtly applied" (419). In the course of reading the messages of Commissioner Lin by Mr. Fearon, the members of General Chamber of Commerce in Canton don't refrain from making mockery of Commissioner Lin and Chinese in general. While cutting a joke, Mr. Burnham reminds the members of the address of Lord Napier on Chinese:

> Chinese are a race remarkable for their imbecility. (420)

Mr. Slade is one of the strongest and vociferous members who plead trading and trafficking of opium in legitimate and rightful manner. But at the same time he turns diplomatic too and advises all members to observe restrain and lets Chinese to take first the aggressive and offensive steps and he further persuaded them with a quaint aphorism:

> We must be the willow, not the oak, in the lowering storm. (428)

Commissioner Lin issues ultimatum to all opium traders to surrender all opium on board of their ship and in the case of failing to do so they must remain ready to face the consequences. The members of foreign traders cudgel their brain to dispose of the impending crisis imposed by Commissioner Lin. Mr. Dent comes out with a great idea of dealing with such threatening and he plans to tell Chinese authority that this is such a grave and important decision that it cannot be taken in hot haste and it requires plenty of time and serious deliberation. Mr. Dent thinks that if he could carry this matter for long, Commissioner Lin would automatically turn lenient on the issue of Opium as

> An ultimatum is easy to issue but difficult to act upon. (437)

Such idea of Mr. Dent was applauded and welcomed by every member of Chamber of Commerce and Mr. Burnham especially is disproportionately excited and he calls this idea a genius of stroke and in the intoxication of enthusiasm he goes on to promulgate:

> Let us see if this Commissioner's bite is as bad as his bark. (437)

All members of General Chamber of Commerce convene meeting after meeting to come out with viable solution before the deadline of Commissioner Lin's ultimatum expires. But in such a meeting, the absence of Charles King was conspicuous which gave Mr. Slade an opportunity to let loose harsh irony and satire on Mr. Charles King. Mr. Slade makes a cryptic promulgation: "Well, if our Achilles is to sulk in his tent, I suppose he cannot be without his Patroclus" (448). He further goes on to decipher and decode this enigmatic pronouncement:

> Ab ore maiori discit arare minor/ From the older ox the younger learns to plough. (448)

Bahram and Zadig finishes a feast and suddenly eyes of Bahram fall on the portrait of his mother hanging through the wall that reminds him of his childhood days. He reveals to Zadig Bey how he had to remain contented with the meal made for poverty stricken child. He said that if his mother were surviving he would have been very happy to see sumptuous and materialistic lifestyle of his son now. On this Zadig Bey cuts a joke: And what would she have said, Bahram-bhai, if she'd known that it had all come from opium? To this question Bahram gives ready witted reply: She would have said that

> A lotus cannot bloom unless its roots are planted in the mud. (452)

Commissioner Lin is hell bent to make surrender all the opium that were secretly and securely stored on board of their warehousing vessels while the foreign traders hand in glove with local merchants claim that they have no opium stored in the vessel. Commissioner Lin is well aware of the fact that this is nothing but a lame excuse projected by foreign traders of opium and he calls this pretext nothing but to

> Shut the ear while the jingling bell is stolen. (462)

While rest of the members are resolute and immovable in their decision to not yield to authoritarian call of Commissioner Lin to surrender all opium in possession of them but Charles King makes his all attempts to let decision go in the favour of Commissioner Lin. Because of such attitude he has been at logger heads with hot headed people like Mr. Slade and Mr. Burnham. During exchange of such hot words between two factions, Mr. Charles King resorts to offensive attack of words through following sentence:

> Any murderer could claim that he is but exercising his natural rights. (464)

In these war of words on the issue of opium dealing and trafficking Mr. Charles King further goes on to unleash potentially and rationally charged irony:

> A few rich men, in order to grow richer, are willing to sacrifice millions of lives. (466)

Despite tug of war on dispute of opium, Mr. Charles King doesn't give up his hope to convince and persuade the perpetrators of opium to accede to the proposal postulated by Commissioner Lin. He warns them that the situation is still under their control and

> Once a chain of events is set in motion, it is not in our power to make reparation or atonement. (468)

In a counter reply to Mr. Charles King, Mr. Burnham raises a question on the masculinity of Asian itself and he further claims that opium is required by them to bolster their potency and they are indispensably susceptible to the opium. Thus, Mr. Burnham is of the view that the Western traders of opium are doing an obligatory and congratulatory work rather than earning disproportionate assets by trading opium and thereby spoiling the life of millions of innocent:

> Effeminacy is the curse of the Asiatic. (468)

Even though Bahram indulges in trading of opium but he is a truly benevolent man. Neel had deep reverence and esteem for him for his humanitarian disposition. He is the man marred by the impending circumstances and any person in his position and place couldn't be better than him in decency and demeanour. He is like others in only one respect and that is in opium trading and in all other aspects he is philanthropic, pioneer and genius. According to Neel only tragic and serious drawback of Bahram is that he is a pure Hindustani and he works by his empathies, emotions and feelings, not by crafty and diplomatic wit and wisdom:

> It is his misfortune that he comes from a land where it is impossible even for the very best men to be true to themselves. (485)

The opium fiasco has resulted into war like situation in Canton. Mr. Slade and Mr. Dent who were dead against approach and intervention of Captain Elliott into the affairs of General Chamber of Commerce in Canton, are now bound to seek his help and involvement in this regard. But Mr. Charles King is quick enough to remind them once they were wanted Captain Elliott miles away from Canton and when now it comes to their safety and security he is most needed. Mr. Charles King ridicules them with a smile on their sudden change of stance:

> The government is to you what God is to agnostics—only to be invoked when your own well-being is at stake! (493)

The situation in Canton is ominous and the news of impending war like situation hovers in every nook and cranny of Canton. Though Mr. Robert Chinnery has no connection, directly or indirectly, dealing with opium but he is also one of its sufferers for he does stay in Canton. He conveys to Miss Paulette regarding the recent development in Canton on the fiasco of opium that has dispossessed the sleep of both the innocent and perpetrators of opium. The hangover of this impulsive and impetuous situation looms large on the psyche of Mr. Robert Chinnery when he begins the fresh letter after a long period of time something in this way:

> Bad news is always hard to convey, but never more so than one is hard-pressed for time. (498)

Mr. Robert Chinnery is a professional painter and he has been bestowed upon special responsibility of finding rare plant for Fitcher Penrose. Even amid the hours of opium crisis he doesn't refrain from performing the task assigned to him though it is another thing that by the end of novel he is unable to trace out the rare plant which Fitcher Penrose is in dire need of. The task of finding this rare plant, I think, has been earmarked by Amitav Ghosh for the possible theme of his third and last of his ambitious trilogy. But despite his failure to achieve his objective and tragic precipitation of opium conflict Mr. Robert Chinnery is still full of hope and optimism for the future of Canton and he renders this city a life of immortality:

> The flowers of Canton are immortal and will bloom for ever. (537)

Going through the whole book between the lines one can effortlessly come to the conclusion that the novel, *River of Smoke,* by Amitav Ghosh has been meticulously written after a great deal of dissertation, deliberation, debate, discussion, sophistication and erudition. Though living in plenty Ghosh has thought of shanty and he has included themes in his novel from all strata of life where village-town, rural-urban, male-female, rustic-refined, etc. equally play their role in furthering the plot of novel being extended into the pages of 553. These homespun wisdom and axiomatic aspects make the readers to chuckle and arouse into them supplementary interests and curiosity and this repository of universal and household adages and axioms reminds the readers of their interactions with their own mother and other people they come across in their formal, informal and day-to-day life.

WORK CITED

Ghosh, Amitav. *River of Smoke.* New Delhi: Penguin Books India, 2011. All the textual references with page number(s) that are cited in the article are from this edition of the book only.

18

The Voice of the Subaltern in Amitav Ghosh's Fiction

Ambarish Sen

Amitav Ghosh is one of the pioneering figures in the field of recent Indo-Anglican fiction in general, and the fictions of Indian Diaspora in particular. Like Salman Rushdie, Amitav Ghosh seeks to create a nuanced novelistic perspective in his fictional world with the help of vibrant characters innovation in themes and intricately structured narrative. Ghosh weaves in his novels a complex pattern where history, personal memoire and social anthropology have a constant interplay and overlap.

The new Indian English fiction of the eighties is free from the self-consciousness, shallow idealism, and sentimentalism that characterized the works of Raja Rao, R.K. Narayan, or Mulk Raj Anand. In Stead, the contemporary Indian ethos with all its pressing and realistic concerns is reflected with well thought out analysis of various problems in his fictions. The problem of rootlessness and identity, migrancy and the quest for root along with the diasporic nostalgia for a lost world become the dominant concern in Ghosh's fictions. One of the distinctive features of Indian Postcolonial studies is the socio-political inequalities and marginalization which finds adequate literary attention in his works. In this article, I would like to focus Ghosh's treatment and projections of the voice of the subaltern that adds to his works and additional vibrancy and intense human flavour. With the help of his major works, I would like to substantiate how Ghosh attempts to justify that the plight and oppression of the disempowered or the Subalterns becomes a pressing issue in the globalized world/society and to the development of a modern welfare state. Ghosh has a cosmopolitan world view and he accomplishes his task of illuminating the hitherto unlit pages of history with his cross-cultural, transnational and transcontinental networking.

Let me tell at first a few general statements as to what does the word subaltern signifies. It is a much discussed umbrella term in the recent Postcolonial/Third-world historical literary and socio-political studies. It is a complex multi-dimensional and comprehensive peonage open to a wide range of socio-cultural and economic issues. It refers to persons who are socially, politically and geographically oppressed, cornered and remains outside hegemonic power structure. In the seventies this term started to be used as a reference to colonized people in the South Asian subcontinent. It provided a new perspective on the history of a colonized place from the perspective of the colonized rather than from the perspective of the hegemonic power. In general it refers to marginalized people and marginalized groups and the lower classes to person without any social status.

Ghosh's venture into the world of fiction starts with the publication of his first novel *The Circle of Reason* (1987) in which the author interweaves a well patterned narrative incorporating a wide range of thematic strains. In it Ghosh weaves a complex pattern of stories juxtaposing lives in rural Bengal and remote Al Ghazira with a linguistic verve and technique. In this book the problem of the marginal is explored in context with forced or circumstantial migration. In the course of the story we confront with the misery of the dispossessed people who starts their voyage to Al Ghazira in quest of a utopian community. In this group we see the protagonist of the story Alu (Nachiketa Bose) and the migrant body of women sex workers who constitutes a community in the boat Mariamma, based on elemental human concern among themselves. Some of them expect to achieve their due social importance in the imaginary land of Al Ghazira which they were denied to them in their homeland.

These marginal women characters led by Jindi are the victims of both the patriarchal oppression and social malpractices in their homeland. The word Mariamma, by its etymological meaning means mother. In reality the boat offers them at least a temporary respite from their traumatic past and uneven future. It is Ghosh's design of the narrative that the principal marginal figures meet in this temporary shelter that is the boat Mariamma. There are other characters like Rakesh and professor Samual who are also in this group of dispossessed subalterns, though with different motives and different social background. Yomuna Siddiki in her essay "Police and Postcolonial Rationality" in *The Circle of Reason* attempts to categorize the different factors, responsible for the problems of the marginal in the perspective of postcolonial rationality.

In an Antique Land (1992) is Ghosh's attempt at exploring the submerged voice of medieval history and investigating into certain unlit yet interesting events of medieval trade exchange between India and Egypt through the route of the Middle-East. The book renders Ghosh's arduous research experience in Egypt. As a social anthropologist Ghosh has a fascinating interest in exploring the continuous process of human evolution through rereading and rewriting history beyond the Western or colonial historiography. In the course of his anthropological research Ghosh chanced to come across an eight hundred years old Ganiza document, originally written in Jewish-Hebrew where he found the details of medieval trade network and cross-cultural communication between India and Middle East. He was fascinated to see the details of a Jewish merchant Abraham Benuzu and his Indian slave Bomma who was named as The Slave of MS.H.6. The search for the details of that slave of MS.H.6 and the relation between the master and the slave Ghosh discovered many illuminating facts about this marginal slave and how significant his role was in the commercial career of Benuzu. Going beyond the master-slave relation, there was an intimate personal proximity between Bomma and his master. This exploration of the unheeded pages of history constitutes the central aspect in Ghosh's quest for an investigation into the Subaltern historiography beyond the borders of western hegemonic discourse.

In an Antique Land is a fascinating fictionalized historical record in which travelogue, social anthropology and personal memoir are intermingled. The story shifts forth and back between Lataifa and Nashway (two Egyptian provinces) in space and between twelfth century Egypt and the present day in time. Robert Irwin in his illuminating review on *In an Antique Land* complements Ghosh's technique of comparing and contrasting present-day and twelfth-century Egypt. (Irwin, Robart. "Intimately Egyptian", in *Times Literary Supplement,* No. 4685, January 15, 1993, p. 7, from Gale contemporary literary criticism, Vol. 153). Ghosh's descriptions of his experiences in Egypt are equally vibrant and constitute another thematic line of the story. Ghosh was in a remote village of Lataifa during his anthropological field work. He gives beautiful pictures of the elemental pre-occupations of the simple village folk or working class people and his day to day encounter with them. Boys wander through mazes of mud-colored houses, date-palms under washed-out skies as in every other nineteenth century English print, women carry baskets of vegetables on their heads. The sense of agelessness and placelessness is the driving force behind *In an Antique Land.*

A book that appealingly excavates a little-known corner of Middle Eastern history (the Jewish traders commuting between the Arab world and India in the twelfth century), and beautifully lights up the laws and losses of typical Egyptian village today. (Irwin, Robert. *Out of the Dustbin of History,* in Washington Post Book World, Vol. XXII, No. 13, March 28, 1993, p. 6).

The Western hegemonic historical discourse is usually negligent to various fascinating and illuminating episode of Third World or colonized history. *In an Antique Land* like his other fiction and nonfictional works is Ghosh's attempt of reconstruction and rewriting of these dust covered episodes of history from the perspective of Subaltern historiography. From an almost irrecoverable Cairo Geniza document, he starts his search for Bomma or The Slave of MS.H.6. This research opens before him vistas of interesting and illuminating world of medieval Indo-Arab trade—the Arab traders maintaining their trade route from the Malabar cost of Southern-India (Mangalore) to Gulf areas of Iraq, Iran and Egypt. In this reinterpretation of history Ghosh as an able anthropologist offers an ironic rejoinder to conventional Eurocentric construction of Third World history that is biased, one-sided, blinded by orthodoxy and age-old colonial misconceptions.

In spite of his anti-Western and anti-colonial interpretation of subaltern history and the quest for the silent voices of the antic land and time, Ghosh is deeply sensitive to the ironies of history that have survived both medieval and modern crises. On leaving Egypt for the last time, Ghosh found his way to the tomb of the medieval saint Sidi Abu-Hasira, where there was a famous annual festival. It was carefully controlled by the authorities. To his surprise, he discovered that the saint was a Jew who had been venerated by Jews and Muslims alike. Ghosh's difficulty in explaining his interest in the tomb to a suspicious policeman also signaled the end of the legacy of Ben Yiju: "The remains of those small, indistinguishable, intertwined histories, Indian and Egyptian, Muslim and Jewish, Hindu and Muslim, had been partitioned long ago" (*In an Antique Land*, p. 339). Still, he felt the tomb was a victory of sorts:

> It seemed uncanny that I had never known all those years that in defiance of the enforcers of History, a small remnant of Bomma's world had survived, not far from where I had been living. (*In an Antique Land*, p. 342)

Ghosh's next novel *The Calcutta Chromosome* (1996) is written in the frame of a science fiction. In this book Ghosh's central concern is the discovery of the parasite of malaria by Sir Ronald Ross. In dealing with this story, Ghosh explores the contribution of certain native subalterns behind Ross's achievement. In this way Ghosh attempts to recast the history of the discovery of malarial parasite as an alternative to Western interpretation of it. It is his quest for the hitherto unlit pages of history of human knowledge which may render a glorious version of the arduous efforts of the subalterns which play a vital role behind the achievements and inventions of the Europeans. The traditional discourse of Western knowledge system based on the binary of colonizer and the colonized, is abandoned here by Ghosh in the process of glorifying the alternative versions of history.

The Calcutta Chromosome is an ingenious and bewitching novel that gives a unique treatment to that sinister episode that lies hidden under the veil of glorious research on the parasite of malaria. The story moves forward and backward in time. There are certain missing links of history which connects the actual time of Ronald Ross's research on mosquitoes and the present retrospection of it. Discovery of this missing links helps the author a lot in throwing light on the dark secret pages of history.

It opens in a near-future New York, where a computer clerk named Antar is having his daily battle of wills with his computer, Ava. Ava has no qualms about reporting him to his employer, the International Water Council, if she senses she doesn't have his full attention, and they have already threatened to reduce his pension. Today, Ava has trawled up a mystery item in one of her filing inventories, which Antar recognizes as the burned remains of an ID card; more than that, he recognizes the man it belonged to, Murugan, an eccentric colleague who went missing in Calcutta back in 1995. Western discourse of the history of science records glorifies Sir Ronald Ross, the great white man of science, as the successful researcher of malaria, but Ghosh's quest and logical investigation into the details of the research reveals the fact that there is a group of poor native marginal who assisted Sir Ross to a great extent. Without their active involvements Ross's research involvement and Ghosh's research could not have been successful. This group is led by Mangala an illiterate woman who becomes the priestess of a malaria cult still active in the 1990s. There is also a poor deformed boy named Lakhan or Lakshman on whom the experiments was done. This poor boy remains a fascinating subaltern figure, shrouded in mystery. He was found destitute from Shialdaha station and disappears mysteriously like the other missing links after the research is over. There is also a native poet Phulboni who also is an interesting character in the story as he fascinates the author to a great extent.

The Western or colonial historiography projects the Orient as the domain of ignorance, a land of perpetual superstation, mystery, fairytale romance and narrow religious dogma and doctrines. So it is the responsibility of the white European to civilize the Third World. As a result the colonial annals of history represent the colonized countries as the symbol of irrationality and wander. The Western discourse strategically and deliberately excludes the indigenous knowledge system from the pages of the statistical records of human achievement. Ghosh's rendering of the alternative version of the history of malarial research thus constitutes the counter of colonial or postcolonial analysis of knowledge system. The analytical reading of the text of *The Calcutta Chromosome* from the subaltern perspective represents the orient as worthy research and study. This quest for an alternative rendering of the Eurocentric historical or scientific discourse represents the Indian indigenous culture as glorious and praiseworthy as the West. This complex counter cultural representation of the secret dark pages of research on the anopheles mosquito—the carrier of malarial virus makes the novel stunningly vibrant and intensely human. *The Calcutta Chromosome* thus suggests that we re-read the historical record, uncover its subtexts and rewrite its narratives so as to come up with a 'whole new story' about the meaning and value of science from a properly post-colonial perspective.

Let me now turn to the projection of the subaltern characters and concern in Amitav Ghosh's *Sea of Poppies* (2008), the first volume of "Ibis trilogy", it revisits in new, breathtakingly detailed and compelling ways some of the concerns of his earlier novels. Among these are the incessant movements of the peoples, commerce, and empires which have traversed the Indian Ocean since antiquity. The novel dramatizes the stories of insignificant men and women with little power to alter the malignant design of destiny, the hostile social force and the course that history takes. Their stories are framed against the grand narratives of history; invite other ways of thinking about the past, culture and identity.

In order to discuss Ghosh's treatment of the subaltern in the *Sea of Poppies* I will attempt to analyze the miserable condition of the poor indentured labourers during their transport to Mauritius as Girmitias. I will try to substantiate my argument by analyzing the pathetic fate of some of the borders of Ibis who in spite of their different social backgrounds, have been marginalized and made powerless by the arbitrary action of East India Company regarding the cultivation and export of opium. The central character of the novel is Deeti Singh—a woman, from a poor peasant community from Bihar whose husband is a worker at the Gazipur opium factory and a victim to opium. It is Ghosh's exploratory skill of writing that brings the tragic story of Deeti into the foreground of the narrative. The poor peasants were compelled to stop cultivation of sugarcane and other edible crops under the pressure of East India Company for the cultivation of opium which added capitals and increased the company's trade outside India to China, Mauritius and Malay, while the poor land owners were denied their legitimate rights to their lands and appropriate wages. All these poor characters are the victims of fate and were hitherto denied their position in the elitist discourse of history.

In this fiction, like previous ones, Ghosh deals with the Subaltern figures with profound human sympathy and make them eloquent in the story. Like Lakhan or lakshman in *The Calcutta Chromosome* and The Slave of MS.H.6 (Bomma) *In an Antique Land,* the story of Deeti and Kalua, a gigantic figure from the lowest run of society becomes interesting and subject to exploration and socio-psychic analyses. Deeti's and Kalua's fate are indispensably tied by circumstances and their feelings for each other strikes a sympathetic chord in our hearts and their rebellious attitude against orthodox Hindu conventions like 'Sati' shows the sign of construction of a counter historiography.

Kalua rescues Deeti from her husband's pyre from being burnt and they two unite in a wedlock and start a voyage into a territory that is unknown and undiscovered. The future is opaque and uncertain and in the Ibis along with other migrant labourers they form a community with a profound feeling of love, sympathy and homeliness and in the schooner a new world is forged together. It is a world constituted by peoples from different cross-sections of nineteenth century Indian society. It brings together north Indian women, Bengali Zemindars, Black men, rural labourers and Chinese seamen.

Ghosh in this novel deals with one of the central problem of nineteenth century colonial history of India that is the incessant flow of rural labourers of Bihar and Bengal to the sugarcane plantations of the European colonies outside in Mauritius, China and Africa. This is one of the recurrent concerns of Post Colonial Diasporic literature, discussed and debated frequently in Ghosh's earlier novels like *The Glass Palace*, *In an Antique Land* and *The Circle of Reason,* etc., and in *Sea of Poppies* this favourite theme of Amitav Ghosh is given a more humane treatment and discussed at length with a more critical insight. The hitherto silent "voice of the subaltern" becomes eloquent and centrally significant in the texture of the novel.

One of the recurring themes in Ghosh's work is that globalization in terms of trade, migration and cultural contact. Ghosh believes that although European colonialism constitutes a great rupture in the histories of Asia and Africa, out of these great upheavals the third-world communities were destroyed and regenerated again. The heterogeneous group of migrants that were shaped in the Ibis demonstrates this in a microcosm. Ghosh's novel projects the fact that how helpless an individual is against a cataclysmic historical phenomenon that marks an indelible impression in the history of a nation. His novels ranging from *The Shadow Lines* to the latest *Sea of Poppies* share this concern to a great extent. His novels in general, and *The Shadow Lines* in particular conveys that no arbitrary border that separates two countries can wipe out the memories and the emotional bond that exist between the two neighboring countries. Therefore certain nostalgic individuals have no specific home; they live "in no home but in memory".

The travelers on the Ibis represent their individual cultural legacy, yet they have different priorities. Some are the victims of orthodox social conventions-casteism or the puppets in the hands of inscrutable blow of destiny, while others are driven by their profession or in specific colonial context to seek fortune in new lands. There are others, who have odd individual history or peculiar and shady past to be concealed. In the words of Bibhash Choudhury:

> There is, in a way, an inclination on the part of the characters to carry-forward aspects of cultural history, which they recognize as significant to their personalities and even in moments of extreme crises, these aspects leave their mark in the narrative. ("Amitav Ghosh: *Critical Essays*", Bibhash Choudhury, p. 165)

Sea of Poppies is imbued by a profound human significance and a commitment to human values. Ghosh's endeavour is to demonstrate the gradual evolution of human community and to reclaim all that in the diversity of our cultural legacy is valuable and ultimately indispensable.

This is how the plight, crises and the heart rending story of the subalterns or the marginal is projected into the centre of narrative attention by Ghosh in most of his novels. As a social anthropologist, Ghosh made a good research on the evolution of human society in the face of adversities and natural calamities. He was well read in history and tried to throw light into the unheeded pages, illuminating the oppressed lives of working classes. The story of Deeti, Kalua, Neel, Lakhan (Lakshman) and Bomma (The Slave of MS.H.6) are set against a grand narrative of history and "they are people with little power, caught in their private world of memory and desire" (Shirley chew, professor emeritus of English at Leeds University). I would like to conclude this discussion on the representation of subalternity in Ghosh's fiction by mentioning the lines from Hardy's two touching short stories which in my opinion is an echo in Ghosh's sympathy for the powerless Subalterns: "War's annuls will fade in to night/ Ere their story die". (*In Time of the Breaking of Nations*) Or "Come hither, Son", I heard Death say;/ "I did not will a grave/ should end thy pilgrimage to-day,/ But I, too, am a slave!" (*The Subalterns* by Thomas Hardy).

WORKS CITED

Bose, Brinda. *Amitav Ghosh: Critical Perspectives*, Published by Anurag Jain for Pencraft International, 2005.

Chakrabarty, Dipesh. "*Habitations of Modernity:* Essays in the Wake of Subaltern Studies", Published by Permanent Black, 2002.

Choudhury, Bibhash. *Amitav Ghosh: Critical Essays*, Published by Asoke K. Ghosh, PHI Learning Private Limited, 2009.

Dhawan, R.K. *The Novels of Amitav Ghosh*, Published by New Delhi: Prestige Books, 1999.

Khair, Tabish. *Amitav Ghosh: A Critical Companion*, Published by Permanent Black, 2003.

Mondal, Anshuman A. *Amitav Ghosh: Contemporary World Writers*, Published by Vinod Vasishtha for Viva Books, 2010.

19

The Map was in my Head: The Cartography of an Experiential City in Amitav Ghosh's *The Shadow Lines* and *The Calcutta Chromosome*[1]

Somdatta Bhattacharya

> He did not have to tell me where it was. I knew already, for the map was in my head. (*The Shadow Lines,* 56)

Amitav Ghosh's celebrated novel *The Shadow Lines* (1988) begins with a short paragraph that describes a journey: "In 1939, thirteen years before I was born, my father's aunt, Mayadebi, went to England with her husband and her son, Tridib" (3). This is a much underplayed description of a journey that has enormous implications for the narrative of *The Shadow Lines*—a narrative about/of journeys. The novel, in very simple terms, is about the journey of a boy/narrator—growing up in Calcutta, and then moving to Delhi and London and his unique vision of looking at the world, a trait which was gifted to him by his eccentric uncle, Tridib. A closer look at the narrative will reveal the spatial quality of the vector field, to borrow the concept from Physics, of these journeys—*The Shadow Lines* is about journeys "away" and "to" Calcutta. A look at the chapter titles—"Going Away" and "Coming Away"—provides further evidence for this argument. In other words, at the centre of a complex grid of border crossings and cultural/spatial travels that make up this novel, lies one city—Calcutta.[2] This essay looks at the representation of this city space and its cultural practices in Ghosh's *The Shadow Lines* and, very briefly, in *The Calcutta Chromosome* (1995).

Let us begin our discussion of *The Shadow Lines* with a look at the narrator himself. As we have specified above, *The Shadow Lines* traces the narrator's journeys across vast and varied urban and cultural landscapes. His recollections regarding three generations of his relatives also consist of vast expanses of landscapes traversed in acts of migrations. The narrator himself, as Robert Dixon points out, finds a "dwelling in travel" (18). But it is in his trajectories within the city that I am interested in. And I would argue that his journeys "away" from the city Calcutta also trace his essential location in the caste/class hierarchies within the city, and consequently, become representations of the city that is written onto his character.

Writing about *The Shadow Lines*, Meenakshi Mukherjee seeks to "emphasize the concreteness of the existential and emotional milieu in which Tridib and his reflected image—the unnamed narrator—are situated" (259). This spatial/cultural milieu (Calcutta) and its cultural practices define the fate of the unnamed narrator. His family belongs to the class of the Bengali *bhadralok*—a class distinguished for its high culture, education and its essentially urban (read Calcutta) moorings. Ghosh carefully defines their values, beliefs and aspirations. For instance, note the narrator's career graph. He does his schooling from a good school in central Calcutta—most probably a convent school. This is revealed by simple comments made casually. From the description of the route taken by his school bus when returning home on the day of the riot reveals that his school is somewhere between Park Circus and Park Street, an area where most of the "good" English medium Calcutta schools are located. Again, his mathematics teacher is Mrs. Anderson, an Anglo-Indian lady—a prominent figure in convent schools in Calcutta. From Calcutta he moves to Delhi for further education. Ghosh carefully locates the college that the narrator goes to (92). The landscape of affluent Delhi University campus comes through unmistakeably in the spatial coordinates of Delhi. After Delhi, the narrator leaves for London for further education. London is a dream destination for most Calcuttans—a sign of the "relentless educational compulsions" (Mukherjee, 259) of his/her class and the residual effect of colonialism. These journeys, I argue, are mapped onto the narrator and they, in turn, map out the narrator's Calcutta moorings.

The class aspirations of the Bengali *bhadralok* that have defined the trajectories of the narrator's journeys "away" from home also find spatial representations within Calcutta. One way in which it comes through is in the representations of the dreaded "other"—in the representation of a landscape that stands for the failure to fulfil the class aspirations, the *bhadralok*'s fall from grace. This fear of failure and its association with spaces is poignantly revealed when the narrator and his family go to visit his grandmother's relatives living in the humble dwellings in Garia (in the deep south of the city):

> It was true of course that I could not see the landscape or anything like it from my own window, but its presence was palpable everywhere in our house; I had grown up with it. It was the landscape that lent the note of hysteria to my mother's voice when she drilled me for my examinations; it was to those slopes she pointed when she told me that if I didn't study hard I would end up over there, that the only weapon people like us had was our brains and if we didn't use them like claws to cling to what we'd got, that was where we'd end up, marooned in that landscape: I knew perfectly well that all it would take was a couple of failed examinations to put me where our relative was. (134)

The same fear is evoked in the grandmother's distaste and fear for people occupying certain city spaces:

> Part of the reason why my grandmother was so wary of him [Tridib] was that she had seen him a couple of times at the street corners around Gole Park [in south

> Calcutta] where we lived. She had a deep horror of the young men who spent their time at the street-corner addas and tea-stalls around there. All fail cases, she would sniff; think of their poor mothers, flung out on the dung-heaps, starving. (7)

This passage brings out a fascinating cityspace, perhaps, peculiar in India to the city of Calcutta—the space for *adda*. *Adda* is a curious word, it both means the action of chatting and also the space where the chat is held. *Adda* is almost synonymous with Bengali *bhadralok* culture, where the participants meanderingly touch upon the eclectic topics of politics, cinema, economy, theatre, food and so on over food and drinks. But *adda* is also the space of refuge for unemployed youth, who in want of more productive activities, gather at street corners or neighbourhood clubs and chat over tea and smoke. And it is this latter *adda* that the narrator's grandmother has a distaste for. The narrator maps out a landscape of *adda* through the streets and by-lanes of Calcutta, in search of Tridib—that "conversation-loving stretch of road between Gariahat and Gole Park":

> But if I happened to hear that Tridib was around I would double back through the park and the back lanes. Someone would always be able to tell me where he was: he was a familiar figure within the floating, talkative population of students and would-be footballers and bank clerks and small-time politicos and all the rest would gravitate towards that conversation-loving stretch of road between Gariahat and Gole Park. (8)

As for Tridib, these *adda* sessions become occasions for mapping new territories through stories and anecdotes of far-flung places. Through his stories these locales get superimposed on that stretch of Calcutta:

> But occasionally, when he was in the mood and somebody happened to say something that made a breach in his vast reservoirs of abstruse information, he would begin to hold forth on all kinds of subjects—Mesopotamian stellae, East European jazz, the habits of

> arboreal apes, the plays of Garcia Lorca, there seemed to be no end to the things he could talk about. (8-9)

The Shadow Lines is a narrative that weaves an interesting grid of migrations in and out of Calcutta. Going further, I would argue that the narrative also brings out a view of Calcutta as a landscape fractured by forced migrations. Let us look at an extract that occurs at the beginning of the novel where the narrator describes how the streets where he grew up have changed over the years:

> When I go past Gole Park now I often wonder whether that would happen today. I don't know, I can't tell: that world is closed to me, shut off by too many years spent away: Montu [his childhood friend and neighbour] went away to America years ago and Nathu Chaubey, I heard, went back to Banaras and started a hotel. When I walk past his paan-shop now...somehow, though the paan-shop hasn't changed, I find myself doubting it. At that time, in the early sixties there were so few cars around that we thought nothing of playing football on the streets around the roundabout—making way occasionally for the number 9.... There were only a few scattered shacks on Gariahat Road then, put up by the earliest refugees from the east. Gole Park was considered to be more or less outside Calcutta: in school when I said I lived there the boys from central Calcutta would often ask me if I caught a train every morning as though I lived in some far-flung refugee camp on the border. (7-8)

In this one paragraph that occurs very early in the narrative, Ghosh tells us a lot about the narrator—apart from the obvious fact that he has stayed away from Calcutta for quite some time, it hints that he and his family have migrated from erstwhile East Bengal, now Bangladesh. In its very few words, it encapsulates the history of displacements across the border and the inevitable demographic and cultural changes and the conflicts it wrought on the city. After 1947, Calcutta had increasingly grown into a city of migrants—mainly coming into the city, but also leaving it. The Chinese and the Jewish populations of the city were majorly depleted after the independence (Dutta, 169-70). Although there is no authentic statistics on the number of refugees who entered West Bengal from East Pakistan, "by the time of the 1951 census a mere one-third (33.2 per cent) of the inhabitants of Calcutta were recorded as having been born in the city, with everyone else being an immigrant" (Dutta, 171). Though the major wave of migration was an immediate aftermath of the partition, in 1950, another one million refugees crossed over to West Bengal, in the sixtees migration was associated with events of communal unrest like the 1964 riots and the 1965 India-Pakistan war, and another major influx came during the 1971 Bangladesh Liberation War (Dutta, 169-72). Relief camps were set up, which were known as "colonies". "In 1949, there were more than 40 colonies in southeast Calcutta and some 65 in the north. Their 'housing' consisted of temporarily built thatched huts, water drawn from a standpipe, and sanitation arrangements that were insufficient" (Dutta, 171).

The paragraph quoted above maps out the sections of the city inhabited by the immigrants—the stretches that constitute the "South Calcutta" (The narrator is curiously silent about North Calcutta). The West Bengalis (or *Ghotis*, as the slang would have it) living in "Central and North Calcutta" would come to look at this landscape as a suburb, or as "some far-flung refugee camp on the border". This landscape, the "other" of the bustling, "central city", came to be associated with the squalor that represented the fate of the immigrants struggling to survive the scars of displacement. Krishna Dutta draws a vivid picture of this scene:

> The refugees were camping in the streets, scratching a living by setting up tea shops and tiny kiosks selling cigarettes and *pan*. Listless and bored, they spat the blood-red juice from chewing *pan* all over the city's walls and pavements, not bothering with a spittoon. Lacking any kind of sanitation, they defecated in the open gutters. Babies were born on the railway platform and open streets without much ado, let alone medical treatment. The streets were alive with rats, cockroaches and flies, and scavenging dogs and vultures. (172)

Many of those who had migrated to Calcutta before Partition had family connections and financial backing that helped them establish themselves as the *bhadralok* before the wave of impoverished immigrants began to lash on the shores of the city post Partition. And it was inevitable that they wanted to distinguish themselves from the poorer lot. Thus, this landscape becomes further fractured, as is reflected in the narrator's grandmother:

> My grandmother, looking out of her window in amazement, exclaimed: When I last came here (Garia) ten years ago, there were rice-fields running alongside the road; it was the kind of place where rich Calcutta people built garden houses. And look at it now—as filthy as a babui's nest. It's all because of the refugees, flooding in like that.

Just like we did, said my father, to provoke her.

We're not refugees, snapped my grandmother, on cue. We came long before Partition (131).

Cities are manufactured in imagination, by popular discourse and writing. This point is elaborated by Tuomas Huttunen in his essay "Representation of London in *The Shadow Lines* by Amitav Ghosh". He cites Fredrick Jameson's discussion of the change from market to monopoly capital, where Jameson detects "a growing contradiction between lived experience and structure, or between a phenomenological description of the life of an individual and a more properly structural model of the conditions of existence of that experience". Carrying this argument forward into literature, Huttunen says that the immediate experience of an individual subject, which according to Jameson was previously the primary raw material of fiction, is now reduced to only one of the sectors in the social world. What is more, the way this sector of immediate sense-perception is realised does not necessarily coincide with its actual socio-cultural present. He elaborates his point by showing how in *The Shadow Lines*, the representation of the narrator's imaginary London is different from the lived experience of the other characters. Moving along the same argument, while discussing the representation of Calcutta in the novel, I will argue that this representation of Calcutta differs from and excludes certain lived experiences.

While speaking of London in *The Shadow Lines,* the narrator says, "I wanted to know England not as I saw her, but in her finest hour—every place chooses its own and to me it did not seem an accident that England had chosen hers in war" (57). If the London that Ghosh describes is the city in its finest hour, then the Calcutta that he speaks of is also the city in its finest hour—the sixtees Calcutta. It was time when Calcutta was the most fashionable—with the cultural scene in the city bustling with activity—but it was also the decade that witnessed the tragic Naxalite movement. It is the Calcutta that many would want to know and several refer to with a deep sense of nostalgia. However, interestingly, though Ghosh describes much of the sixtees Calcutta, he is silent about the Naxalite movement that rocked the city towards the end of the decade. It is a little strange that an observant and sensitive character like the narrator of the novel was not at all affected by this movement. One wonders whether this is an attempt to cleanse the cityscape of a kind of violence that left the city scarred for life. However, this is not to say that Ghosh's novel is censored of all violence. Rather it is a novel that exposes the face of brutality with ease. One instance of this is the narrator's—then just a school boy returning from school with his friends—experience of the 1964 riots in the city. Interestingly, the narrative here has little action. However, it conjures up a cityspace that is hauntingly still and menacing in its silence, a contrast to the lively, bustling cityspace:

> Tublu shook my elbow and pointed at a rickshaw that had been pulled across the mouth of a narrow lane. The others saw it to and turned to stare. We couldn't take our eyes off it, even after we left it far behind. There was no reason for us to stare: we saw rickshaws standing at untidy angles in the streets every time we went out. And yet we could not help staring at it: there was something about the angle at which it had been placed that was eloquent of an intent we could not fathom: had it been put there to keep Muslims in or Hindus out? At that

> moment we could read the disarrangement of our universe in the perfectly ordinary angle of an abandoned rickshaw. (203)

The rickshaw, an innocuous everyday sight in the city space, turns into a menacing object fracturing the cityscape, into a boundary dividing the city along the lines of religion.

In *The Calcutta Chromosome* (1995), Ghosh continues to engage with the landscape of Calcutta. The Calcutta that Ghosh presents here is mainly the Calcutta of the 1990s—a period when the city was in a process of re-invention. It was a time when the city was realising its inadequacies and was desperately trying to re-create itself. And as in *The Shadow Lines*, here too the city is carefully mapped by Ghosh. When the character of Murugan is introduced, he is carefully worked into the landscape of the city. The passage is so accurate in its spatial specificities that anyone who is slightly aware of Calcutta roads will immediately locate Murugan:

> Walking past St Paul's Cathedral, on his first day in Calcutta, August 20, 1995, Murugan was caught unawares by a monsoon downpour. He was on his way to Presidency General Hospital, on Lower Circular Road, to look for the memorial to the British scientist Ronald Ross. (20)

Such descriptions of the city abound in the novel. As in the case of *The Shadow Lines*, the narrative here continues to evoke landscapes that are specifically constructed to convey various images of the city. Some of these landscapes, one may argue, perpetuate stereotypes associated with the landscape of Calcutta. Thus, for instance, we have Ghosh carefully constructing the landscapes of sinful desires erected on the debris of colonial ruins:

> On Free School Street, I was walking past New Market, on my way home, when a guy came up to me and whispered in my ear. I guessed he was a pimp.... It was irresistible. All I had was five rupees but that was enough. He led me down one of those thin alleys around Free School Street, just around the corner from the Armenian school, where William Thackeray was born. (237)

Interestingly, the spatial imagery of the city here, once again, ignores north Calcutta. The whole action of the novel unfolds between Chowringhee, Alipore, Gariahat, Rabindra Sadan, Kalighat, Robinson Street and PG Hospital. The narrative seems curiously inhibited about north Calcutta, while spreading itself over south and central Calcutta, the areas of the city that have risen to economic prominence and hubs that were once the refuge of the migrant populations. Also, the Calcutta that finds representation in Ghosh is undoubtedly a very 'Bengali' Calcutta. It is a landscape that is curiously cleansed of the non-Bengali populations. As figures suggest, more than 50 per cent of this bustling cosmopolitan city's population comprise non-Bengalis. But they hardly find a place in Ghosh's novels. *The Shadow Lines* has only two non-Bengali Calcuttans—Mrs Anderson (the narrator's school teacher) and Nathu Chaubey, the *paanwala*—and they are quite forgettable in the entire scheme of the novel. *The Calcutta Chromosome* has only one non-Bengali Calcuttan—Mrs Aratounian. Murugan is from Calcutta but has lived away in New York for a long time and his is a character that cannot be localised, much like those of Sonali and Urmila. The only reference to any migrant community is restricted to the Nepali workers at Romen Haldar's construction site. This makes the representation of Calcutta hardly cosmopolitan. This silence about, and the erasure of, the "others" of the city, one is compelled to argue, runs parallel to Ghosh's attempt to recover a pristine urban landscape untouched by violence or invasions by the "other", as seen in *The Shadow Lines*.

This romanticisation of the city, I argue, helps in the re-invention of Calcutta, but while doing so, Ghosh fuels the Western imagination of the exotic, oriental "other". *The Calcutta Chromosome* has been dubbed as science fiction. The central thematic of the novel is built around the idea of the transmigration of souls. Ghosh vaguely refers to the fact that Mangala might have chanced upon a chromosome that enabled her to transmigrate. But this explanation is hardly scientific. The ceremony in which transmigration takes place is replete with elements that evoke the sense of the oriental "other"—

cymbals, incense sticks, chants, trance, etc. The powerful character of Mangala is reminiscent of "Shakti"—the female principle—but the way the West would see it. And the city—dark, mysterious and often menacing—inevitably has these elements written over it. As the writer Phulboni mentions, he has "wandered the darkness of these streets, searching for the unseen presence that reigns over this presence". Phulboni's dark, mysterious city, in a sense, could easily have been the city the nameless narrator's grandmother was afraid of in *The Shadow Lines*—the city that might consume the unemployed, aimless youth who fail to measure up to the *bhadralok* ideals of success.

In these two Ghosh's novels, I have read themes of displacement, migration, etc., and a landscape of the city that carries within itself these burdens. The nameless narrator in *The Shadow Lines* decodes in this landscape the various tropes of the refugee experience and he also maps the city in its various "peculiar" elements—the locations of *adda*, the landscapes of failure defined in *bhadralok* terms and the intersection of the mythical and the real. The inscrutable, dark landscape of the chromosome of Calcutta, and the bewildered characters who try to decode it and fail also talk about one experiential aspect of the city. The romanticisation of the city where the city space is cleansed of historical and political violence, and the mythicisation where the city is shrouded in the unexplained phenomena of primeval forces, also point to the possibilities that narratives of the city space present. Here the effort is not to point to the fissures between the 'actual' and the 'narrative'. In fact, the 'narrative' is also a 'real'. "At the same time that the city is experienced as a physically factual built environment, it is also, in the perception of its inhabitants, a city in a novel, a film, a photograph, a television programme, a comic strip, and so on" (Burgin, 175). My study points to this same narrative facet of the "urban"—we narrate the cities that we live in and we live in the cities that we narrate.

NOTES

1. This essay largely draws upon my PhD research on the representations of post-Independence Calcutta in literature,

films and popular arts. And I would like to acknowledge my indebtedness to my research supervisor Professor Supriya Chaudhuri who has helped me hone the ideas that go into this essay.

2. While the city's name was always pronounced as "Kolkata" or "Kolikata" in the Bengali language, in 2001, the English name of the city was changed from "Calcutta" to "Kolkata", reflecting the Bengali pronunciation. The argument behind the move was to erase the burdensome legacy of a colonial past. The move also had its detractors. I would argue that this act of renaming remains an insufficient and feeble attempt at re-imagining the city, especially since 'post-independent' is never coterminous with 'post-imperial' and since Independence is never a complete break from colonialism. For this ideological reason/reality and also for reasons of convenience, my analysis will, from here on, continue to call this cityscape 'Calcutta'. This preference also reflects the fact that the texts that I analyse here represent a city in a historical, political and ideological continuum.

WORKS CITED

Burgin, Victor. *Some Cities*. Berkeley: University of California Press, 1996.

Dixon, Robert. "Travelling in the West: The Writing of Amitav Ghosh." *Journal of Commonwealth Literature,* 31.1 (1996): 3-24.

Dutta, Krishna. *Calcutta: A Cultural and Literary History*. New Delhi: Roli, 2003.

Huttunen, Tuomas. "Representation of London in *The Shadow Lines* by Amitav Ghosh". *Literary London: Interdisciplinary Studies in the Representation of London,* 2.1, 2004.

Kumar, Priya. "Testimonies of Loss and Memory: Partition and the Haunting of a Nation". *Interventions: International Journal of Postcolonial Studies,* 9.1, 2007, 99-105.

Mukherjee, Meenakshi. "Maps and Mirrors: Co-ordinates of Meaning in *The Shadow Lines*". *The Shadow Lines*. New Delhi: Oxford University Press, 1988.

———. Elusive Terrain: Cultural and Literary Memory. New Delhi: OUP, 2000.

20

Amitav Ghosh: A Raconteur of Existence

Rashi Saxena

Modern Indian authors have great interest in humanity and civilization. In the same order, Amitav Ghosh entered in the ocean of words to go more deep with human tendency. Basically he is an anthropologist educated in India, Alexandria and Oxford. At the outset his primary theme is the Diaspora and later on he continues with related themes like emigration, exile, cultural displacement and transnational cultural flow and so on. Conversely, "nation" is not the only subject to Ghosh's imaginary it deserves numerous interpretations. By choosing nation he weighs against Salman Rushdie, yet he deals many other habitat of human life. He puts important value to familiar life either to joint or nuclear. For him it works as the central imaginative unit. To highlight it he employs variety of narrative techniques, genres and storytelling styles to invent a "neverland" which again sticks together to reality. In this way he abruptly merges the borders of narrative aesthetics and effects radical transformation of reality. Amitav's fiction repeatedly works to patch up the edge between literary facet and political dogma of contemporary world.

Ghosh is the author of *The Circle of Reason* (his 1986 debut novel), *The Shadow Lines* (1988), *The Calcutta Chromosome* (1995), *The Glass Palace* (2000), *The Hungry Tide* (2004), and *Sea of Poppies* (2008), the first volume of The *Ibis trilogy*, set in the 1830s, just before the Opium War, which encapsulates the colonial history of the East. Ghosh's latest work of fiction is *River of Smoke* (2011), the second volume of the *Ibis trilogy*.

Amitav Ghosh's fictional world is a twitchy description of social activities and his protagonists are explorer and deals with diasporic exiles. They can be marked for the good replica of "the migrant sensibility". Salman Rushdie termed it as one of the central themes of this century of displaced persons. Unlike Rushdie's metaphor "the past is a country from which we have all emigrated", Ghosh's motto is to give parallel consideration to time and space (covering of distinct times and distant places). For him national margins and abstract boundaries are permeable fictions to be constantly lapse. Through the various crises-crossings enabled by a free-ranging narrative, discrete binaries of order and category give way to a realm of mirror images and hybrid realities. Reason becomes passion, going away is also coming home, and the differences between us and them, now and then, here and there are interrupting by the itinerant maps of a roaming imagination.

Ghosh is remarkable in his use of narrative structure to exemplify thematic interests. *The Circle of Reason*'s itinerant and wayward picaresque echoes the intellectual caprices of its characters. The first novel, *The Circle of Reason* basically is a comic tale of dodgy juxtaposition and its protagonist Balaram follows an obsessive combination of Hindu ideas of purity and Western notions of cleanliness with Louis Pasteur's microbiology. However, the eccentric version of reason is almost wiped out in the novel by forces of unreason: ambition, paranoia, territoriality, and violence. The scientific approach and Balaram's hallucination of social progress reflects Gandhi's nationalistic self-sufficiency and a global multinational economy in which technology recognizes no continents and no countries.

The description provided by Balaram's last disciple, the mysterious Alu, reflects the diasporic theme of the novel respectively followed by a picaresque story span across the nation. In al-Ghazira, Alu's charismatic, socialistic and quixotically approach zooms at fundamentals of the elimination of money. The final scenes in El Oued are more earnest and down-to-earth, favouring the migrant's adaptive "making do" and "being human" over the purist strictures of science and religious tradition. Nevertheless, reason and the past both circle back in the form of Balaram's favourite book, *The Life of Pasteur*, which has also traveled from Bengal to Algeria, and which Alu can now "reverently" cremate.

Amitav Ghosh seems more intellectual in his second novel *The Shadow Lines* which makes impossible coexistences and disrupted metaphysical boundaries into real struggles both for its narrator and its readers. Thematically, it is comparative study of three generations of two different families. Those families are the followers of different cultures and reflect different tones of life. As *The Shadow Lines* traces nearly a half-century of interlocking relations meanwhile it also acknowledges the fact that nations are "imagined communities". The presence of unnamed narrator gives novel its way to accomplish its theme of existence. The questions come in natural way that whether the cities and borders of country can make limited human effort to live his life without any attachment. Amitav realizes that the gist of human life is that after looking so much here and there man only wants to relax, to come home to take rest. In fact, no boundaries of physical map mean to a common man. This thinking ultimately takes its place in the novel. This novel is more somber, less fanciful in its politics, and quite stunning in the power with which its formal experiments in sequence and location resonate thematically. The narrator is an imagined shadow of cosmopolitan cities. He often swings from story within story to place within place and finally to memory within actuality. In this way a clear looping can be traced here. The basic point which is considerable here is the meaning of *The Shadow Lines*. The blurred boundaries are mere a pseudo-treatment of politics but at last all boundaries seem to be same when it is the question of their existence.

The anonymous narrator, with his internationalized consciousness, keeps amused in an authorized sense of simultaneity and connection. Growing up with Tridib in Calcutta, he can "know" war-time London neighbourhoods and see the English boy Nick Price as a spectral mirror image. His grandmother's confusion between her childhood Dhaka and the present-day foreign city becomes symptomatic of the violence done to people by artificial borders and partitions (poignantly allegorized in her family's divided house). If the novel valorizes the search for unbounded space and co-existing time, however, it refuses to endorse self-serving appropriations of "other" realities. Ila's globe-shrinking project enables not only integration but also juxtaposition. The controlling metaphor of the airport lounge makes this point brilliantly: as replicated space (they all look alike) and individual place (each one is distinctive); as both attached to and detached from its national home; as a place where departures rub shoulders with arrivals, where everyone is always on the move. Full of complex cross-cultural encounters, *The Shadow Lines* makes a unique contribution to the debates over "difference" and "otherness" that have galvanized the contemporary post-colonial world.

Ghosh's interesting and wonderful third novel, *The Calcutta Chromosome*, deals with the experiences of Ronald Rass and, swings the readers into the colourful medical history of European research into malaria a century ago. It begins with the unlikely discoveries of Ronald Ross, an imperial army doctor in India who, despite ignorance of microbiology and erroneous ideas about how malaria is transmitted, nonetheless managed to win a Nobel Prize for helping understand the disease. In an ingeniously plotted narrative, Ghosh unravels some mind-boggling alternative possibilities for where Ross's knowledge really came from and what it might—very radically—entail. Full of outrageous fantasy and "decentering" impulses that speculatively reroute European knowledge through Indian ones, the book imaginatively ventures into what Brian McHale, in *Postmodernist Fiction*, calls "secret" or "apocryphal" history. It does so through a genre—the mystery—that makes unlikely mental journeys, startling discoveries, and the revelation of secrets into its narrative life-blood.

The theme of *The Calcutta Chromosome* can be entertained through a careful glance over the novel. The use of the controlled surprises and circuitous discoveries of the mystery-thriller reflects human enterprise and exhibits the progressive strides towards the surprising discoveries. Through Ghosh's craftsmanship story becomes a feverish literary journey into a promising world. The new zone of thinking takes Ghosh to that point from where he achieves new mastery over the future agendas of oneself and others.

The modernisation of literature is a quality of Amitav Ghosh. The use of modern gadgets and devices exemplify modern approach of Ghosh. His protagonist, the Egyptian researcher Antar, works in a near-future New York on a highly advanced computer. The machine, Ava, outlandishly blends the visionary empowerment of recent Internet hype—it really can do anything, speak any dialect, find any document—with the oppressive scrutiny of Orwell's Big Brother—it won't let Antar stop work early, and its invasive hologram technology respects no bounds of privacy. Antar and Ava investigate the disappearance of the long-lost Murugan, a self-styled authority on Ronald Ross, who went to Calcutta in 1995 on the trail of some suspicious anomalies he'd found in Ross's work; he was last seen the day after his arrival. The narrative follows Murugan through two days of unsettling encounters and strange coincidences that augment and clarify his incipient theories; he also discovers an inextricable link between himself and one of Ross's research subjects.

The discovery process shared by Murugan, the reader, and Antar is define with a zig-zag narration which attracts readers meanwhile its careful designing with a carefully timed sequence of grotesque surprises popping out at every turn. In stylized prose emphasizing dialogue and description, Ghosh employs conventional devices of the mystery, the high-tech thriller, the "hard-boiled" detective novel, the science fiction adventure, and the Victorian ghost story—all with such boldness and panache that it can be hard to tell if he is parodying the genres or "doing" them in earnest.

But after the novel's controlling plot lays down the last bit of secret knowledge, it turns out to be very much *about* control, and about knowledge. Although Ghosh typically does not use implicit devices, explain his point of view yet he shapes his theme and plots in a way that there is always something new remain. Understanding of the issues and problem like malaria is reclaimed and redefined on distinctly Indian terms; in Ghosh's version it has significance not just for science and bodily health, but also for spiritual health and worship, fate and predestination, reincarnation, time cycles and other notions more dear (by and large) to Indians than Westerners.

Another experiment by Amitav Ghose is his Ibis trilogy. This is might be of his expanded criteria of understanding the human attitudes and their reflection against such artificial boundaries. The first urging book titled *Sea of Poppies*. This book breezes the memories of historical adventure through the lush poppy fields of the Ganges, the rolling high seas, the exotic backstreets of Canton. Moreover this is the landscape decorated with vivid characters, whose diaspora encapsulates the vexed colonial history of the East itself, that makes *Sea of Poppies* so breathtakingly alive—a masterpiece from one of the world's finest novelists.

Postmodern themes are the base of Amitav Ghosh's fiction. He constantly weaves his magical realistic plot with postmodern themes. Self-reflexes and confessional elements characterize fictional works of Amitav Ghosh. Displacement has been a central process in his fictional writings; departure and arrivals have a permanent symbolic relevance in his narrative structure. Post modernism gives voice to insecurities, disorientation and fragmentation. Most of his novels deal with insecurities in the existence of humanity, which is one of the postmodern traits. In *The Glass Palace*, the havoc caused by Japanese invasion in Burma and its effect on the Army officers and people—a sense of dejection that deals with so much human tragedy, wars, deaths, devastation and dislocation (Meenakshi Mukherjee, 153)—has been penned. In *The Shadow Lines*, Tridib sacrificed his life in the act of rescuing May from Muslim mobs in the communal riots of 1963-64 in

Dhaka. Pankaj Mishra describes Amitav Ghosh in the *New York Times*, as one of few postcolonial writers, "to have expressed in his work a developing awareness of the aspirations, defeats and disappointments of colonized people as they figure out their place in the world".

Amitav Ghosh discards Western values and beliefs as only a small part of the human experience and rejects such ideas, beliefs, culture and norms of the Western. In *The Hungry Tide,* Ghosh routes the debate on eco-environment and cultural issues through the intrusion of the West into East. *The Circle of Reason* is an allegory about the destruction of traditional village life by the modernizing influx of Western culture and the subsequent displacement of non-European peoples by imperialism. *In an Antique Land*, contemporary political tensions and communal rifts were portrayed.

Amitav Ghosh being a postmodernist acknowledges national boundaries as a hindrance to human communication. For him the Nationalism causes wars and consequently, he is in favour of globalization. Amitav Ghosh's novels centre on multiracial and multiethnic issues; as a wandering cosmopolitan he roves around and weaves them with his narrative beauty. In *The Shadow Lines*, Amitav Ghosh makes the East and West meet on a pedestal of friendship, especially through the characters like Tridib, May, Nice Prince, etc. In *The Glass Palace*, the story of half-bred Rajkumar revolves around Burma, Myanmar and India. He travels round many places freely and gains profit. Unexpectedly, his happiness ends when his son is killed by Japanese bomb blast. The reason for this calamity is fighting for national boundaries.

Amitav Ghosh has been credited for successfully mastering the genre known as 'magical realism' which was largely developed in India by Salman Rushdie and in South America by Gabriel Garcia Marquez. Ghosh is seen as "belonging to this international school of writing which successfully deals with the post-colonial ethos of the modern world without sacrificing the ancient histories of separate lands" (Anita Desai, 1986, 149). Like Salman Rushdie, Amitav Ghosh perfectly blends fact and fiction with magical realism. He reconceptualizes society and history. He is so scientific in the collection of material, semiotic in the organization of material, so creative in the formation of fictionalized history.

Amitav Ghosh is one among the postmodernists. He is immensely influenced by the political and cultural milieu of post-independent India. Being a social anthropologist and having the opportunity of visiting alien lands, he comments on the present scenario the world is passing through in his novels. Cultural fragmentation, colonial and neo-colonial power structures, cultural degeneration, the materialistic offshoots of modern civilization, dying of human relationships, blending of facts and fantasy, search for love and security, diasporas, etc.... are the major preoccupations in the writings of Amitav Ghosh. Postcolonial migration is also valued in Amitav Ghosh's vision. In *The Hungry Tide,* the theme of immigration, sometimes voluntary and sometimes forced, along with its bitter/sweet experiences, runs through most incidents in the core of the novel—the ruthless suppression and massacre of East Pakistani refugees who had run away from the Dandakaranya refugee camps to Marichjhampi as they felt that the latter region would provide them with familiar environs and therefore a better life. In *Sea of Poppies*, the indentured labourers and convicts are transported to the island of Mauritius on the ship Ibis where they suffer a lot. In *The Glass Palace*, Burmese Royal family, after the exile, lives an uncomfortable life in India. Rajkumar who piles heap of amount in Burma is forced to leave his home and business due to Japanese invasion.

The first chunk of this large book has a number of strands, but Ghosh manages to hold the reader's interest easily with the exotic locales and swift changes forced on them and the characters. Meanwhile his language works as an adhesive to hold readers, however, it sometimes becomes weak to tie up their interest yet finally it manages proper readability. In *The Shadow Lines*, the narrative is simple and it flows smoothly, back and forth between times, places and characters. Throughout *The Glass Palace*, Ghosh uses one end to signal the beginning of another so that at one level, nothing changes but yet everything does. There is a strong suggestion of

Buddhist metaphysics in his technique. Life, death, success and failure come in cycles and Ghosh uses the concept of a pair of binoculars early in *The Glass Palace* to sensitize the reading in this perspective. Being a postmodernist, he makes use of very simple language to give clarity to the readers. Many Indians writing in English experiment with the language to suit their story. Ghosh also does it in *The Hungry Tide* using Bangla words like *mohona, bhata* and others, interweaving them with local myths like that of Bon Bibi and her brother Shaj Jangali, the presiding deities of the region. Though *The Glass Palace* and *The Hungry Tide* have their share of non-English lexical items, *Sea of Poppies* in numerous places piles up the Indian (Bengali or Bhojpuri) or lascar-pidgin terms to the point where some readers might to some extent begin to get confused.

For Amitav Ghosh, language in the process of the production of art attains the status of diasporic representation —voicing him and thousands of other uprooted individuals. Language embodies the attempt to create family that has broken and dispersed in the mire of confused identity. Ghosh acknowledges it in *The Shadow Lines*:

> You see, in our family we don't know whether we're coming or going—it's all my grandmother's fault. But of course, the fault wasn't hers at all: it lay in the language. Every language assumes a centrality, a fixed and settled point to go away from and come back to, and what my grandmother was looking for was a word for a journey which was not a coming or a going at all; a journey that was a search for precisely that fixed point which permits the proper use of verbs of movement. (*The Shadow Lines*, 153)

This is a language that Ghosh believes in thus this kind of language he tries to create in his work.

Postmodernists reject elaborate formal aesthetics in favour of minimalist designs. Amitav Ghosh does not give any significance for picturesque description and ornamental use of language. Tabish khair comments on this as, "Ghosh is very careful in his use of English and vernacular transcriptions. He develops a conscious and rich tradition in Indian English fiction, a tradition that includes R.K. Narayan and Shashi Deshpande. The attempt is not to stage Indian Englishes. Ghosh avoids the aestheticisation of language" (108).

Beside it, he does, however, get bogged down at times. As for him, history is part of the problem: Ghosh feels compelled to explain the events not just from the characters' point of view but also to provide a gloss for readers who are unlikely to know the details. He tries a variety of approaches in providing this information, but they rarely fit smoothly in the rest of the story. This continues to be a problem throughout the novel, growing worse towards the end. Ghosh also feels compelled to explain details about logging and elephant-handling and the motor-cars of the day and much else. The information is interesting, but rarely does he integrate it smoothly in his narrative. Certain details—a page on anthrax, for example—read as though they had been cut out of an encyclopedia and pasted in the text: "The word anthrax comes from the same root as anthracite, a variety of coal", etc. Girish Karnad rightly said about him, "Ghosh uses to great effect a matrix of multiple points of view in which memory, mythology and history freely interpenetrate.... A delight to read" (*Indian Express*). *The Glass Palace* is not only a novel but also romance, narrative fiction, adventure fiction, and historical fiction. He combines all the elements of a novel to create fragmentation. Ghosh uses the romantic genre to chart the characters who reflect on the history of colonialism in Burma and the formation of the present Myanmar nation. It is also a narrative fiction that employs a complex spiral narrative structure to texture many characters' identities and experiences in the world where we live in. It can be read in historical point of view, since it is portraiture of history and document of nation. Ghosh invents the third person narrator who relates a story in a spiral fashion that fictionalizes and makes real historical subject and event. *The Calcutta Chromosome* (1995) is "not only a medical thriller but also a Victorian ghost story, a scientific quest, a unique mixture of a 'whodunit thriller', and a poltergeist tale" (Sudeep Sen, 222). To sum up, postmodernism, is a blooming and ongoing area for Ghosh he tries to use its approaches in his work.

At times *River of Smoke* reads like a cross between a Capt. Hornblower tale and a Victorian epistolary novel, yet Ghosh's sharply anti-imperial vision subverts both types. Above all, the novel reclaims a story appropriated for too long by its winners: those who, centuries ago, conquered (or imposed their will on) foreign lands, subjugated and displaced their peoples, replaced their agriculture with deadly cash-crops, thrust addictive poisons on them for profit and enforced all this with the power of the gun masked by a rhetoric of civilization and divine purpose. This book is the story of Amitav Ghosh's decade of intimacy with the village community. Mixing conversation and research, imagination and scholarship, it is also a charged, eccentric history of the special relationship between two countries, Egypt and India, through nearly ten centuries of parochialism and sympathy, bigotry and affection.

The vast sweep of this historical adventure spans the lush poppy fields of the Ganges, the rolling high seas, the exotic backstreets of Canton. But it is the panorama of characters, whose diaspora encapsulates the vexed colonial history of the East itself, that makes *Sea of Poppies* so breathtakingly alive—a masterpiece from one of the world's finest novelists.

Ghosh is as engaging a storyteller in life as on the page, where gun battles, perilous ship passages and the beauty of a newly discovered country are animated vividly. The dialects of the time—British, Indian and Chinese; and the "Laskari" language of the ships' crew from Malaysia and India coalesce into a dizzying polyglot. All the political events in the novels happened, he says: his research has taken him from the National Maritime Museum in London to the Harbour Master's offices in Sydney, where he studied passenger and crew lists from ships travelling between England and Australia more than 200 years ago.

In conclusion it is right to say that Amitav Ghosh is one of the most distinctive and influential writers to come out of India since Rushdie. Throughout his diverse and generically composite *oeuvre* one constant has been his attempt to find connections between seemingly unrelated subjects. Ghosh's fiction challenges the artificial "Shadow Lines" that have been erected to separate, for example, nations from their neighbours, fact from fiction, and academic disciplines from each other. His interrogation of boundaries accords with the preoccupation with hybridity, "in-between" spaces, and diasporas in postcolonial debate. Although Ghosh dislikes being categorized as "postcolonial", in his writing he frequently focuses on the ways the partitioned South Asian subject has been affected by, and yet can to some extent resist, colonialism's legacy. At the heart of Ghosh's corpus is the contention that knowledge is produced by structures of dominance, particularly the military, economic and epistemic strategies of colonialism. His main focus is the impact that Western paradigms of knowledge have had and continue to have on India. Ghosh is also crucially concerned with highlighting filiations and connections which go beyond the (neo) colonial relationship, such as the persistence of pre-colonial trade connections between the Indian subcontinent and the Arabian Peninsula, or the existence of an Indian community in Burma which was almost entirely erased by nationalism. Finally, in his writing Ghosh constantly experiments with form and genre in order to adumbrate a dialogic, non-coercive method of knowledge transmission.

WORKS CITED

Ball, John Clement. *Imagining London: Postcolonial Fiction and Transnational Metropolis*. University of Toronto Press, 2004.

Berry, Peter. *Beginning Theory*. New York: Manchester University Press, 2002, p. 126.

Ghosh, Amitav. *The Circle of Reason*. London: Hamish Hamilton Ltd., 1986.

———, *The Shadow Lines*, Delhi: Ravi Dayal Publisher, 1988; 153.

———, *In an Antique Land*. Delhi: Ravi Dayal Publisher, 1992.

———, *The Calcutta Chromosome*. Delhi: Ravi Dayal Publisher, 1996.

———, *The Glass Palace*. Delhi: Ravi Dayal Publisher, 2000.

Ghosh, Amitav. *The Hungry Tide*. New Delhi: Harper Collins, 2005.

———, *Sea of Poppies*. New Delhi: Penguin Books India, 2008.

Khair, Tabish. *Amitav Ghosh: A Critical Companion.* Delhi: Permanent Black, 2003, 108.

Mukherjee, Meenakshi. "Of Love, War and Empire." *Rev.* of *The Glass Palace.* Indian Review of Books, 10.1 (Oct. 16-Nov. 15, 2000), 151-53.

www.the-criterion.com *The Criterion: An International Journal in English.* Vol. II. Issue. II, 4 June, 2011.

http://www.complete-review.com/reviews/ghosha

http://www.enotes.com/amitav-ghosh-criticism/ghosh-amitav/ sudeep-sen-review-date-winter-1997, 222.

http://www.the-criterion/V2/n2/Suresh.pdf.

www.nytimes.com/books/01/02/11/reviews/010211.11mishrat. html.

21

Amitav Ghosh's *The Circle of Reason*: A Bildungsroman, Picaresque and Detective Novel

Priyanka Vaidya

> *The Circle of Reason* (COR) is an intriguing debut which introduces and explores themes that have been developed in his later works. The novel is ostensibly a bildungsroman describing the journey of Alu, a Bengali orphan, from the obscure village of Lalpukur to Calcutta, Kerala, the Middle-East and Algeria. It incorporates the elements of the picaresque novel, the novel of ideas, the thriller or detective novel and the Hindu epic. (Chambers, 36)

Amitav Ghosh has occupied himself ceaselessly in the task of putting the marginalized and suppressed human beings back in the heart of the narrative, and saving them from getting vanished in the hegemonic narrative of the nation. Particularly concerned with the South Asian Diaspora in the different regions of the world, his novels are attempted recitation of anti-Hegelian olden times of the globe, incorporating the hitherto left-out narratives of the ordinary human beings—the dilemma of individual against the historical milieu, his endeavour to defy the hegemony of the nation through his own narrative and exploration for his own identity. As Rushdie states in *Midnight's Children*, "There are many stories to tell...an excess of intervened lives, events, miracles, places, rumours so dense a commingling of the improbable and the mundane" (15).

Deriving three gunas, Satva, Rajas and Tamas from *Bhagwadgita*, Ghosh names the three sections of the novels. According to the Sankhya philosophy, nature is composed of three forces called, in Sanskrit, Sattva, Rajas and Tamas. These as manifested in the physical world are what we may call equilibrium, activity and inertness. Tamas is typified as darkness or inactivity; Rajas is activity, expressed as attraction or repulsion; and Sattva is the equilibrium of the two. Ulka Joshi asserts: "*The Circle of Reason* has a circular pattern on the lives of Indian philosophy. She describes the metaphors...to emphasize the circles and concludes that throughout the novel the novelist seems to manipulate the circles" (25-33).

Alu is apprenticed as weaver, while his uncle Balaram, the village school master, he is obsessed with Western ideas, epitomized by his passion for phrenology and the writings of Pasteur School of Reason, alternatively born and terrorize people with carbolic acid. Anthony Burgess read the episode as a satire on Western imperialism. While Alu stands for tradition, Balaram 'stands, in a demented way, for progress' (Qtd. in Dixon, *Travelling in the West,* 13). Balaram's enthusiasm for reason can certainly be read as satire on those diasporic Indian intellectuals who enthusiastically embrace the theories of the west. Balaram has made his mind 'a dumping ground for the west' (Qtd. in Dixon *Travelling in the West,* 13).

If Balaram's interest in reason is part of the influx of foreign ideas into the village of Lalpukur, the village is not the symbol of an Indian tradition that can be placed in simple opposition to West. The village symbolizes Orient, the traditional India:

> The people of Lalpukur were 'vomited out of their naïve soil years ago' and dumped hundreds of miles away... borders dissolved under the weight of millions of people in panic—stricken flight from an army of animals'. (*COR*, 59-60)

Ghosh's novel deconstructs any simple opposition between tradition and modernity, or discrete oriental and occidental cultures. When Balaram decides to make the young Alu a weaver, he tells him a history of the technology of weaving that evokes cultural instability and borrowings across borders develop the idea that culture is a process of circulation that has nothing to do with national borders:

> Indian cloth was found in the graves of the Pharaohs. Indian soil is strewn with cloth from China. The whole of the ancient world hummed with the cloth trade. The Silk Route from China, running through Central Asia and Persia to the ports of the Mediterranean and from there to the markets of Africa and Europe, bound continents together for more centuries than we can count.... All through the centuries, in its richness, and variety, bound the Mediterranean to Asia, India to Africa, the Arab world to Europe in equal, bountiful trade. (*COR*, 55-56)

There is no single national root of weaving. There are complex international roots of the craft. Lalpukur is not a traditional village. It is the mixture of technologies, the village is

> Churning like cement is grinder and Balaram was busy chasing its shooting boundaries with buckets of carbolic acid, his hair wafting behind him in the germ-free air. (*COR*, 76)

Many historical events take place in the novel as the Indian nationalist struggle of the 1930s, the Bangladesh war of 1971, and the international tide of migration to the Middle East of the 1970s onwards. The novel is mostly concerned with the period of British colonization of India:

> There are no barriers of time and space in the fiction of Amitav Ghosh. The reader is able to move with the characters "to envision the way in which the past is ever present without his consciousness". (Qtd. in Bhatt, 12)

Ghosh provides several instances of internal Diasporas in this part of the novel. The people of Lalpukur, for example, had been "vomited out of their native soil" in the carnage connected with the partition of India; within the narrative time of the novel they witness once again the spectacle of people being "dumped hundreds of miles away" because of the civil war that led to the emergence of Bangladesh (Jaishree, *Language in India*).

> To which we hav'een left adrift how are those worlds
> How the branch of flower is, how the mansion of fragrance is.
> O, wind! You do pass from there
> How are my foot-prints in that lane
> Those stony people, those tedious houses
> How are those residents and how are those glass houses.
>
> *Sheeshe Ke Maka Vale*, 173

The Circle of Reason about an eight year old orphan, who lives in Lalpukur in West Bengal from where he is on run. Using the motif of journey Ghosh has drama suspense and mystery too. Alu's journey across the Indian Ocean on a mechanized boat allows Ghosh to depict the risks endured by thousands of Indians who leave their native land in search of a prosperous future. Illegal emigrants hazard their lives voyaging on frail vessels. Alu's particular boat also bears witness to the wide range of social types who make the dangerous crossing in pursuit of economic security: among the passengers are a professor, a travelling salesman, and a madam and her girls, one of whom is even pregnant. Asnani describes the novel: "It is also an interesting tale of myriad colourful people of man's relation with the machine, his curse and salvation" (141). Indu Bhatt describes: "The circles, which are inter-connected, and the circle of Alu, which always remains outside.... In tracing the journeys of the main character, she concludes that Ghosh reveals too much of passion and too little of perception" (18-23).

> That it is from those who have suffered the sentence of history-subjugation, domination, Diaspora, displacement —that we learn our most enduring lessons for living and thinking. (Bhabha, 172)

Balaram tries to apply Western theories of Indian life and Alu walks on the path of diasporic Indians. Part II of the novel is set in al-Ghazira on the Persian Gulf. There Alu resumes his craft of weaving, but is accidently buried alive when a new concrete building in which he is working as a labourer collapses. Darshana Trivedi asserts:

> *The Circle of Reason* is not a novel of plot and character but of thought...it deals with modern man's problem of alienation, migration and the existential crisis of life. (34)

The Circle of Reason is a saga of flight and pursuit, this novel deals with the adventures of a weaver, picaro, a wanderer Alu, who faces every tyranny in life as a person who is without any roof and stability in life. His feet are always on his head, he keeps on moving always as a restless person who is in search of identity as a diasporic Indian. He is young master weaver who is wrongly suspected as a terrorist. He is chased from Bengal to Bombay and on through the Persian Gulf to North Africa by a police officer who is having an eagle-eye.

The Circle of Reason is a tale told in beautiful manner. Devy says: "the story-tellers Rushdie, Amitav Ghosh...seems to enjoy the excitement as the poets...enjoy their poetic rhetoric" (115). Language plays an important role in English fiction. To quote Devy, "It is as if these writers are trying to create an Indian English through their fiction, rather than creating fiction out of living Indian English. It is therefore the playfulness and fiction making becomes obsessive concerns" (16). Bhatt says:

> Ghosh's style can be compared with flowering river with all its moods.... A keen interest in Anthropology, in places of today and yesterday makes his novels interesting...he wanders through the ancient land of Egypt as well as war ravaged London during Second World War, through Dhaka before and after partition coming and going, arriving and departing...the novelist has a rowing eye and perceives in depth the events of the world. (11-12)

The novel is Ghosh's analysis of the concept of Reason. Since the Enlightenment, Reason emerged as the sacred beliefs in Western consciousness, relegating irrationality as the undesired 'Other'. This often leads to such simplistic associations where Western philosophy is equated with the desired rationality, while Oriental philosophy becomes inevitably fanciful, irrational and false. In *The Circle of Reason*, Amitav Ghosh makes a critique of these hastily drawn binaries; instead, he investigates the contradiction natural in the concept of reason. The insufficiency of reason is presented through the characters of Balaram, whose obsession for Reason borders on insanity. Ghosh suggests that Balaram's partially unaware absorption of Western dialogue of reason is the source of his breakdown. Reason is never the ultimate truth, it needs to be balanced and countered by emotions that were earlier discarded as Oriental irrationalities. *The Circle of Reason* is an allegory about the annihilation of conventional village life by the invasion of Western civilization and the successive displacement of non-European peoples by imperialism.

WORKS CITED

Asnani, Shyam. *New Dimensions of Indian English Novel*. Delhi: Doaba House, 1987.

Bhatt, Indira and Indira Nityanandam, eds. *The Fiction of Amitav Ghosh*. New Delhi: Creative Books, 2001.

Bhatt, Indira. "Outside the Circle." *The Novels of Amitav Ghosh*. Ed. Bhatt, Indira and Indira Nityanandam. New Delhi: Prestige, 1999.

Chambers, Claire. "Historicizing Scientific Reason in Amitav Ghosh's *The Circle of Reason*." *Amitav Gosh: A Critical Companion*. Ed. Tabish Khair. Delhi: Permanent Black, 2008.

Devy, G.N. *In Another Tongue*. India: Macmillan, 1995.

Dutta, Pradip. "A Voice among Bullet Holes: *The Circle of Reason*." *The Novels of Amitav Ghosh*. Ed. Bhatt, Indira and Indira Nityanandam. New Delhi: Prestige, 1999.

Ghosh, Amitav. *The Circle of Reason*. London: Hamilton, 1986.

Jaishree, N. "Amitav Ghosh's *The Circle of Reason*: A Study of Diaspora."*Language in India*. Ed. J. Sundar Singh. 10. January 2010. www.languageinindia.com.

Joshi, Ulka. *The Circle of Reason. The Novels of Amitav Ghosh*. Ed. Bhatt, Indira and Indira Nityanandam. New Delhi: Prestige, 1999.

Khair, Tabish, ed. *Amitav Gosh: A Critical Companion*. Delhi: Permanent Black, 2008.

Rao, Damodar K. "Magic and Irony as Principles of Structure: A Reading of *The Circle of Reason*." *The Novels of Amitav Ghosh*. Ed. Bhatt, Indira and Indira Nityanandam. New Delhi: Prestige, 1999.

Raza, Rahi Masoom. *Sheeshe Ke Maka Vale*. Ed. Kunvar Pal Singh. Delhi: Vani Publisher, 2001.

Trivedi, Darshana. "Here is God's Plenty." *The Novels of Amitav Ghosh*. Ed. Indira Bhatt and Indira Nityanandam. New Delhi: Prestige, 1999.

22

The Hungry Tide: Amitav Ghosh

Rituparna Datta Roy

The British had precious little idea, when they left India in 1947, that in due time, a virile, tropical beanstalk would sprout from their erstwhile colony, in the form of literature, out of the legacy of the English language they were leaving behind. Today, after 60 years of independence, that stalk has stalked the length and breadth of this country of numerous tongues; though Indian Writing in English has been around only for a century and a half.

Indo-Anglian literature dates back roughly to the 1830s, when Sri Kashiprasad Ghosh, who is considered by many the first Indian poet writing in English, published his first collection of poems. A bevy of contemporary talented poets: Miss Aru Dutt, Miss Taru Dutt, Michael Madhusudan Dutt, *et al.* made the English language the custodian of their emotions and expressions. Prose writing did not lag behind, either. Soshee Chunder Dutt is generally considered to be the father of English prose in India. Sri Bankim Chandra Chattopadhay's very first novel: *Rajmohan's Wife*: was in English. Sri Rabindranath Tagore wrote English with enviable comfort and élan. Smt. Sarojini Naidu wrote poetry in English. Wheeled by a whole gamut of eminent literatures, the language graduated to a vital form of art, shaking itself off the shackles of its once —subaltern status in the subcontinent as a mere tool for communication between the ruler and the ruled: the British and the Indians.

Meenakshi Mukherjee points out in *The Twice Born Fiction,* that the novel came from England, was new in every Indian literature and that the Indian English novel was the last among Indian language novels to get established.[1] Therefore, though the novel in Indian literature had been in existence for more than a hundred years, the development in the Indian English novel could be telescoped into a span of less than 40 years (1920s-1960s) with the various phases of the different regional language novels overlapping.[2] These phases, as broadly identified by Mukherjee are:

Phase I: (1920s): the historical novel

Phase II: (1930s and 1940s): the novel of social reform and political change

Phase III: (1950s and 1960s): the novel of self-identity including the psychological novel.

Indian English novel is rooted in Indian society. It is Indian novels in English that we are getting to read and which are doing us proud with their unique art and rich interpretations of Indian society. The Indian English writer uses the English language to mediate his own uniquely Indian experience. Historically, the objectives of Indian literatures have been to entertain as well as to reform society. The Indian English has, since the beginning, tried to use the form to create new ideals for his or her society without compromising on art. Therefore, for the Indian novelist, the novel has been more than an aesthetic construct.

The three pioneering writers who began their careers almost simultaneously in the 1930s are Raja Rao, Mulk Raj Anand, and R.K. Narayan. The themes handled by the older generation of the novelists in English had for a long-time remained predictably pan-Indian: the national movement, partition of the country, the clash between tradition and modernity, faith and rationality, east-west confrontation, disintegration of the joint family, exploitation of women, etc. In this way they were in a way defining "Indian" concerns as against local or regional issues.

The Indian English novel, speaking in terms of cultural specificity, embraced largely the Hindu world view—brahminical, vedantic to be more precise. An early novelist like Raja Rao did accommodate the marginalized sections of Indian society like the untouchables and the lower castes, though peripherally, in his novel *Kanthapura.* However, it was Mulk Raj Anand, who, in the words of C.D. Narasimhaiah, "brought into fiction the coolie, the cobbler and the untouchable, who form the bulk of the Indian people".[3] The year was 1935, the novel was *Untouchable.* For the first time in literature in English, an underdog, a low caste was made the hero of a novel. Making a harijan the protagonist was a supreme act of courage in a deeply caste-ridden society such as Indian.

Slowly and steadily this began to be almost routine affair. In the last decade or so, that sections of Indian society who were either marginally or hardly represented in Indian English fiction began to find a predominant place, viz. Amitav Ghosh's *In an Antique Land,* Rohington Mistry's *Such a Long Journey* and *A Fine Balance*, Kiran Nagarkar's *Ravan and Eddie*, Allan Sealy's *Trotternama*, and some others. These second generation of writers—Amitav Ghosh, Upamanyu Chatterjee, Rohington Mistry, Shashi Tharoor, Anita Desai, *et al.*, started exploring the hitherto untouched layers of life and experience, which would not have occurred to the novelists of the 1930s, as being capable of lending themselves to creative transmutations. They turned to life and experience as they knew them first hand. The new English fiction thus began to exhibit confidence in tackling new themes and experiments with new techniques and approaches to handle those themes.

Amitav Ghosh is probably the most scholarly practitioner of the by-now-distinct genre of Indian Writing in English. He has authored several highly acclaimed, internationally popular novels: *In an Antique Land, The Shadow Lines, The Calcutta Chromosome, The Glass Palace*, etc. Born in Kolkata, Amitav Ghosh grew up in East Pakistan (now Bangladesh), India, Sri Lanka and Iran. Graduating from Delhi University, he went on to do a Ph.D in social anthropology at Oxford, and came back to Delhi where he taught for some time. His experience as a social anthropologist at the universities of Delhi and Oxford shows in his handling of the characters and the context in which they exist. He reveals a strong sense of history and a firm grasp of socio-cultural and historical material that underlines his narrative. Ghosh's wide travels have contributed to his ability to move his characters in and out of their native settings with confidence and ease. Indeed, journeys are a very real and important part of his fictional landscape. In *The Circle of Reason*, Nachiketa Bose moves from East Bengal to Kerala to the African Sahara. In *The Shadow Lines* the narrator journeys from Kolkata to Bangladesh to England, while Abraham Ben Yiju *In an Antique Land* moves from his small Israeli community in the Middle East to Mangalore on India's west coast to become a prosperous trader. In *The Hungry Tide*, Piyali Roy comes from Seattle, USA, to Lusibari through Kolkata. Ghosh's themes allow this movement to be totally natural.

Describing Amitav Ghosh's story-telling technique, P.K. Datta describes its overall impact as "one of passage rather than of montage".[4] The idea of passage allows Ghosh to constitute his novelistic experience as "oppositions founded on co-existing paradoxes rather than on antagonism", continues Datta.[5] In this way, Ghosh is able to provide the method of describing society, says Datta, for the purposes of narrative meditation.[6]

The Hungry Tide is an intense, intensely memorable novel, expected only from a writer of his stature. Ghosh is a fascinating and seductive writer, who tempts the reader on as if with an unsolved mystery, blending tale into tale in a vast-seeming narrative close to the Bengali tradition of the river-novel. He drags the reader with remarkable ease to the distinct frontier that lies beyond picture postcard realism: the Sunderbans, the backdrop of the hungry hearts of *The Hungry Tide*.

The Sunderbans are an immense archipelago of islands, located at the southernmost tip of West Bengal. Some of these islands are large, some mere specks on the Bay of Bengal; some have just emerged, others have survived through time immemorial. Here, only the truly dispossessed settle down, brave the man-eating tigers and crocodiles, to curve out a precarious existence from the mud. It is in one of these islands, Lucibari (a fictitious name), that Piyali Roy, or Piya, as everyone calls her, arrives to track rare river dolphins.

Piya is by profession a cytologist, one who studies marine mammals. Though she was born in Kolkata, she was brought up in Seattle, U.S.A., from a very early age. As a result, English is her only language. Her profession has brought her back to India. She knows that two species of river dolphins—*Orcaella and brevirostris*—commonly known as the Gangetic dolphin and the Irrawaddy dolphin—"inhabit the Bay of Bengal near the Sunderbans".[7] She is on her "cetacean pilgrimage" as she calls it—to see these dolphins herself, and to occupy herself with a research project about them. Armed with a range finder, binoculars, clip charts, pens and a monitor that is connected with the satellites through the GPS (Global Positioning System), and the sketches of the dolphins, "drawings that were copied from a monograph that date back to 1878",[8] she sets out on her lone journey, in the creeks and rows in the Sunderbans, in a small boat owned and oared by Fokir, and his 5-year old son, Tutul.

Piya shows the sketches of the dolphins to Fokir, and asks him through gesticulations if he has seen any of these creatures, and in case he has, to direct her to the area where she can see them herself. Fokir thus brings her to Garjontola, a place where she sees a whole shoal of dolphins. Excited, she decides to continue her expedition in a big motor boat, in which she can work and rest for about a week—taking Fokir as her local guide. But first, she wants to go to Lucibari, where she has been invited to come and stay by Kanai Dutt, an acquaintance.

Kanai is a sophisticated Delhi businessman, an interpreter by profession, who has come to Lucibari on his aunt Nilima's request. Piya comes to Lucibari and stays in the guest house that Nilima, a local widowed social worker, offers her. Piya talks of her plan, and Nilima arranges for a motor boat driven by Horen, for her. Piya wants Fokir as her guide, and wants him to take his boat, as it is easier for the smaller boat to navigate through the shallow narrow stretches of waters. Piya can communicate with Kanai and Nilima well enough, but not with Fokir, who is an illiterate fisherman. So Kanai offers his services as an interpreter—he would be the interlocutor between Fokir and Piya. Piya does not exactly welcome the idea, but she is too modest and sober to say so.

It is from this moment that the tide begins to turn. Kanai notices that the two 'speechless' creatures—Fokir and Piya—carry on their respective missions—his to show her the dolphins and hers to see them and take notes about them—well enough. Their wordless but evident bonhomie rouses jealousy in Kanai. Moyna, Fokir's wife, becomes suspicious of Piya and Fokir's mutual (though unuttered) attraction. Moyna makes the monetary transactions with Piya. Piya tells Moyna through Kanai that she will pay "all the expenses...the rent for the boat, the provisions and all that...the expedition would last a few days—may be four or five", and at the end of it, Fokir will make about "three hundred US dollars".[9] Moyna is overjoyed at the large sum of money, still she feels the unvoiced call between man and woman—Fokir and Piya. She asks pointblank, "why a highly educated woman like [Piya] needs the help of her husband—someone who doesn't even know how to read and write".[10] When Kanai translates the question to Piya, she "frowned, puzzling over this. Could Moyna really be as dismissive of her husband as her question seemed to imply? Or was she trying to suggest that Piya should hire some one else?"[11] But Piya finally decides that "there was no one else she wanted to work with"[12] and tries to pacify Moyna by saying, through Kanai, that Fokir "knows the river well. His knowledge can be of help to a scientist like myself".[13]

During the expedition on the big motor boat, Megha, silent but hostile cross-currents of tension fly like sparks between Kanai and Piya. Kanai, to whom so far (he is around forty-two) women have been merely substances for amorous dalliances, realizes his true feelings for Piya. He gives her marriage proposal. Piya, though greatly surprised, gently says, "I'm sure one day you'll meet the woman who's right for you.

But I don't think I'm the one"[14]. Kanai nodded "resignedly to indicate that this was more or less what he had expected to hear".[15] But he cannot totally conceal his wound. He snaps that Moyna believes Piya is "in love with Fokir", that Moyna is actually "terrified that Fokir is going to leave" her for Piya.[16] Piya calls Moyna's suspicions "absurd", but she "chafe[s]" when Kanai asks, with a "rasp" in his voice, whether she is indeed in love with Fokir. She answers in a "constricted" voice, "I don't know Kanai. I don't know what to tell you—any more than I know what to tell her".[17] But Piya does realize, "in the depths of her heart, [that] she would always be torn between the one and the other"[18]—between the educated and arrogant Kanai, and the illiterate and sensitive Fokir. The melody of Fokir's Bangla song of "Bon-bibi—Dukhey—Dokkhin Rai"[19] enthralls her, but she gets to understand the language only with Kanai's translation.

Kanai, rebuffed in love, decides to go back to Delhi immediately, and starts for Lucibari, in the middle of the expedition. Piya goes to Garjontola in Fokir's little boat, and it is agreed that Megha will come the next day to fetch them from Garjontola. But, as luck would have it, a big cyclone breaks out early next morning, and Piya and Fokir together cannot row fast enough to reach Megha through the flooded country side. Perforce, they have to take shelter on a tree top. All of a sudden Fokir is hit severely on his back by a big stump of a tree and dies instantly, though he manages to shield Piya with his own body. Piya becomes numb with shock,—not only because of the suddenness of the incident, but also because she now realizes the sudden void that is created in her own world by Fokir's death.

Piya comes back from Garjontola, all alone, through immense struggle. One look at her solitary figure and devastated mien, makes Moyna, who has been awaiting her husband anxiously, lose consciousness. Later, she is told by Piya, that in his last breath, Fokir uttered the names of Moyna and Tutul only. Moyna realizes, too late, that her suspicions have been baseless;—her beloved husband remained faithful to her till his end, he never let Piya dominate his emotions. His undying loyalty provides the much-needed succour to Moyna, already reeling under the trauma of widowhood. She can even sympathise with Piya, whose grief is no less than hers.

Moyna, now, being a widow, cuts off her long hair to short length, and oddly resembles Piya, whose hair has always been short. On the other hand, Piya, who has lost most of her possessions in the seething storm, perforce, has to wear the discarded, colourful sarees of Moyna (Moyna herself wears only white sarees now). Once she dons sarees, Piya's physical identity as an Indian woman becomes securely established. Kanai, who has so far seen Piya in Western clothes only, is astonished to find how much alike these two *Niobe*s look and behave—both wearing sarees and sporting short hairs, both becoming mute—Moyna being shell-shocked, Piya being ignorant of the local lingo, Bangla.

Kanai goes back to Delhi, having lost hope of having Piya, but also with "calm of mind, all passions spent"[20] knowing that Piya could never attract Fokir towards herself. He realizes that along with him, his 'tormentor' Piya also sails on the same boat—of unrequited love.

Piya leaves Lucibari a few days after Fokir's death and goes to Kolkata to finalize the paraphernalia regarding an American citizen staying and working in India. She returns within a month, flogged on by her decision to carry on her research on *Orcaella* in Lucibari itself. She talks to Nilima at length about her intended research project, and announces that she would like to "name it [the project] after Fokir, since his data is going to be crucial to this project".[21] Nilima realizes that though research on dolphins constitutes the crux of Piya's life, she is not in love with dolphins only. Her heart beats equally fast for the man who has made his ultimate sacrifice in making her realize her dream.

The three main characters are immensely memorable, with their edgy exchanges, attraction, involvement, even hunger—for each other. The narrative is taut and packed. But what actually awes the reader is Ghosh's formidable scholarship. It seems that there is no aspect of the Sunderbans that he does not know—the nature of its ebbs and tides, the manner of the foundation of the localities, the legends of Bon-bibi and her brother Shah-Jungli—the patron Goddess and God of the 'tide country', the mode of life of the inhabitants there, an anthropologist by training, Ghosh dredges up lost stories in the way an archeologist would, and analyses them in a way an anthropologist might. The political upheaval of Morichjhãpi in 1979 is well documented, though there is no attempt on his part to squeeze history into a preconceived shape. Ghosh is equally at home with the dolphins and the working patterns of a cytologist. He has been to the Sunderbans himself, he has been on a survey expedition to track dolphins on the Mekong river himself. He mixes so much knowledge with so consummate ease in the main structure of the narrative that it never seems interpolated. The reader never feels that he is reading a textbook, but realizes, nevertheless, that he is being continuously enlightened on one issue or another. After going through the book one can claim to have come to know the 'tide country' reasonably well.

NOTES

Meenakshi Mukherjee. *The Twice Born Fiction: Themes and Techniques of Indian Novels in English*. New Delhi: Arnold Heinemann Publishers, 1971, p. 18.

Ibid., p. 21.

C.D. Narsimhaiah. *Makers of Indian English Literature*. Delhi: Pencraft International, 2003, p. 76.

N.E. Bharucha and V. Nabar. (Eds). *Mapping Cultural Spaces: Post-colonial Indian Literature in English*. Delhi: Vision Books, 1998, p. 65.

Ibid.

Ibid.

Amitav Ghosh. *The Hungry Tide*. New Delhi: Harper Collins India Limited, 2005, p. 32.

Ibid.

Ibid., p. 210.

Ibid., p. 211.

Ibid.

Ibid.

Ibid., p. 212.

Ibid., p. 335.

Ibid.

Ibid., p. 336.

Ibid.

Ibid., p. 360.

Ibid.

John Milton. "Samson Agonists". *The Complete Works of John Milton*. London: McMillan, 1964, p. 288.

Amitav Ghosh. *The Hungry Tide*. New Delhi: Harper Collins India Limited, 2005, p. 398.

23

Colonialism and Postcolonialism in Amitav Ghosh's *The Glass Palace*

L.V. Padmarani Rao and *Githa Bhojane*

Introduction

Colonialism and imperialism are often used for one another. According to the OED, the word colonialism comes from the Roman 'colonia'. It means 'farm' or 'settlement'. Imperialism comes from Latin 'imperium' which has so many meanings as power, authority, command, dominion, realm and empire. Imperialism is understood as a strategy where a state aims to extend its control forcibly beyond its own borders over other State and peoples. Such a control is not only military but also economic and cultural. A ruling state imposes not only its own terms of trade but also its political ideals, cultural values and language upon the subject state. In modern times, there are three major phases of imperialism. The first phase is between 1492 and the mid eighteenth century. The second is between the mid nineteenth century and First World War and the last phase is the period during and after Second World War.

After the end of Second World War in 1945, there was a process of decolonization of the colonized people who were under the control of colonizers. Postcolonial criticism has numerous aims as to re-examine the history of colonialism from the perspective of the colonize, to determine the economic, political and cultural impact of colonialism on both the colonized people and the colonizing power, to analyze the process of decolonization and so on. These postcolonial thoughts came forward by the Marxist critique of colonialism and imperialism from Frantz Fanon to Gayatri Spivak. Among the major figures of postcolonial writers are Edward Said, Homi Bhabha, Frantz Fanon, Gayatri Spivak, Chinua Achebe, Wole Soyinka, Salman Rushdie, Jamaica Kincaid and Buchi Emecheta to name a few.

Amitav Ghosh

Born in Calcutta, grew up in Bangladesh, Sri Lanka, Iran and India, studied at Delhi and Oxford, stayed in Egypt and Cambodia to do the field work, settled in India, Amitav Ghosh in his writings seems to believe that an effective fiction emanates from a particular historical moment which intersects the narrator and the nation at the crucial point of their evolution and growth. As Devy says, 'Alienation between speech and life seems to have disappeared now' and so storytellers like Rushdie, Amitav Ghosh almost are poets enjoying their 'poetic rhetoric'. Ghosh uses English language skillfully and artistically to present the narrator and what is peculiar of Ghosh's novels is that he varies his choice of narrator in each of his novels. Being an anthropologist himself, Ghosh takes the readers through many parts of the work. He wanders through the ancient land of Egypt as well as the war-ravaged London during the Second World War, through Dhaka before and after partition. Coming and going, arriving and departing find a frequent place in his fiction. This is not merely a geographical or physical movement but also a movement from ignorance to knowledge, awareness and understanding. The novelist has a roving eye and perceives in depth the events of the world.

There are no barriers of time and space in his fiction. Ghosh uses 'time' to maximum effect because yesterdays, today and tomorrows fuse into one. To him past, present, and future coalesce into one. He does not arrange events in a historical or chronological order. Instead, the reader is able to move with the characters 'to envision the way in which his past colors his present, in which the past is ever present within his consciousness'. His novels are never limited by clock-time, as they do not deal merely with externals.

***The Glass Palace* (2000)**

The Glass Palace (2000) unfolds over a hundred years of pre-colonial, colonial and postcolonial Burmese history as families are formed and individual characters experience loss and joy. Social organization such as feudalism is destroyed and new ones formed in the guise of the colonial and postcolonial nation-state. The story follows three generations from three families in Burma, Malaya and India. As Firederick Luis Albama quote:

> Amitav Ghosh continues to explore different story telling forms and took complicate the picture of pre and post colonial South Asian identity in his fourth novel *The Glass Palace*.

The text is divided into seven parts with the events beginning and ending in Burma. *The Glass Palace* of the Royal family with King Thebaw, Queen Supayalat of Burma, the British invasion and by 14th November 1885, the complete occupation of the British on Burma, to the Royal family to be transported from Mandalay to Madras and then to Ratnagiri forms the first part of the novel. Dolly is an assistant to the princess of the Royal family and during their movement out of Mandalay, from across sea, Rajkumar, 'the Kalaa, an Indian' is fascinated by her. The later part of the novel deals with Rajkumar-Dolly relationship. Historiographically, the novel also aims at depicting Burma, India and the Japanese invasion.

It is about geographical entities, space, distance and time. There are many characters and many stories merged together. It is a saga of many families, their lives and their connection with each other. *The Glass Palace* is a story of an Indian orphan Rajkumar who is transported to Burma by accident. Rajkumar, the boy who is eleven years old, is remarkable for his exploring sprit, keen perception and his ability to take calculated risks. He works in tea stall of matronly lady Ma Cho. He loves exaggerating his age just to feel like an adult. He is established as bold and remarkable. Once he lands in

Mandalay, his lifelong search for places and people begins. He is taken in by the city of Mandalay.

He is a complete destitute in an alien city with no acquaintances. Finally he goes to Ma Cho for job and he receives rebuke and scolding at the beginning. But then he knew that it wasn't aimed directly at him. He develops his sense of belonging at the new places. As he views the fort of Mandalay, the crystal shining glass palace, he knows that orphans like him can't go there and yet—

> No matter what Ma Cho said, he decided, He would cross the fort before he left Mandalay; he would find a way in. (Ghosh, 2000, 7)

It is a *dhaba* where Rajkumar meets the man in Ma Cho's life, Saya John. In due course of time, Saya John comes very close to what Rajkumar could have called as his father. But this doesn't come in a day. Rajkumar matures fast. Life teaches him its own lessons. At his heart, he is always certain about his success in life. When the British throw down the king of Burma, Rajkumar is told that the British wish to control Burmese territory for wood. And from this point, he starts shaping his future plans. He senses wealth in teak.

When the city is gone berserk by the British, it is the Indian soldiers who come on the orders of their colonial masters. Suddenly Indians become the target of the frenzy mob. Rajkumar is also attacked. He is saved by Saya John. He gets a job at Saya's Company because of his integrity and personality. When the palace of King Thebaw is evacuated, every one rushes into it to loot as much as they can. Rajkumar also goes in. He gets there his future wife Dolly. She is an orphan like Rajkumar. She is a maid who looks after the princesses. Rajkumar uses his free will in building his business. He decides to take a loan from Saya and establish his separate timber yard. Saya is full of doubts, and then Rajkumar gives a few tips to Saya—"If I'm ever going to make this business grow I'll have to take a few risks" (Ghosh, 130).

Having taken much risk, he grows economically very well and becomes a successful and respected businessman. Then he goes in search of Dolly who is living with the king Thebaw and his Queen, who are in exile in India. Usually no one form Burma is allowed to meet the deposed king or staff lest such a meeting may create problems of revolt at Burma. Uma, the collector's wife, who is a good friend of Dolly arranges the meeting between Dolly and Rajkumar. They marry at Ratnagiri and have two sons Neel and Dinu. When Dinu becomes the victim of slight polio in one leg, Dolly spends her day and night in Dinu's care. She cuts herself off from the world including her elder son, Neel and husband. During this period Raj goes into physical relationship with one of the workers forcibly and Ilongo his illegitimate son is the result of this extramarital mating. Rajkumar's life is a story of the struggle for survival in the colonial turmoil. As a colonized subject from Bengal, he becomes a colonizer in Burma transporting indentured labours from South India to other parts of the colonial world. He has even sexually exploited a women worker on his plantations.

Saya John is a fine example of the breed of hybridity. His clothes are western. He speaks English, Hindustani and Burmese. His face looked like that of Chinese. Saya himself makes fun of his mixed identity:

> The soldiers there were mainly Indians and they asked me this very question: how is it that you, who look Chinese and carry a Christian name, can speak our language? When I told and say, you are dhobi ka kutta...a washerman's dog...na ghar ka na Ghat ka.... You don't belong anywhere, either by the water or on land, and I'd say, yes, that is exactly what I am. He laughed with an infectious hilarity, and Rajkumar joined in. (Ghosh, 10)

Saya John throws light on the Indian soldiers constituting the British army. When he was working as an orderly in a hospital in Singapore, Saya John comes across several wounded Indian soldiers who were in their twenties. It was the money that drew them to this profession. They earned a few annas a day, not much more than a dockyard coolie. It always amazed him—"Chinese peasants would never do this allow themselves to be used to fight other people's war with so little profit for themselves" (Ghosh, 29-30).

Amitav Ghosh refers to the phrase "banality of evil" in the context of soldiers fighting for their British masters from neither enmity nor anger, but in submission to orders from superiors, without protest and without conscious. The process of colonization and the state of the colonized are very relevant thought components of this novel. The very word used for Rajkumar—Kaala—is objectionable to the modern generation, which is decolonized at least in the political sense of the word. In this novel, there is the actual process of aggression, capture and colonization. How the Burmese people are robbed off all grace with guns and artillery by the commanding British is the central focus in the novel. The soldiers who are invading Burma are Indians. Instead of fighting their common enemy-the British—the Burmese and the Indians are fighting among themselves. Another interesting point is that those who wait on Queen Supayalat are supposed to do so on all their fours, i.e. both hands and legs on floor. When an English midwife comes, she refuses to crawl. Supayalat fails to make her crawl; "she was an English women" and hence was forgiven. The glass palace is a symbol of power as well as fragility of imperialism. The people in the glass palace do not have the liberty to throw stones at others. The colonized people are always imprisoned in 'the glass palace' and they have lost the capacity to throw stones at the colonial master.

To Arjun 'modern' and 'western' are synonymous. He is boasting of his connection with the west. In his mind he has accepted that the Western style is better and therefore desirable. Dinu is also fascinated for the British. And hence, Arjun in a conversation with Dinu replies:

> To you the modern world is just something you read about. What you know of it you get from books and newspapers. We're the ones who actually alive with westerns.... (Ghosh, 279)

Dinu understands that it was through their association with European that Arjun and his fellow-officers saw themselves as pioneers. Mental colonization is even worse. Arjun says:

> We understand the west better than any of you civilians. We know how the minds of westerns work only when every Indian is like us will the country become truly modern. (Ghosh, 279-80)

Saya John doesn't see the English as usurpers; for him, they are superior. From them, he has learnt the art of using everything for his own benefit. Rajkumar is fully convinced that without the British the Burmese economy would collapse. Many stances can be given where the author has shown the cruelty of colonization and its impact on the lives and mind of the colonized. Decolonization is not easy, perhaps it is not even possible. As Arjun says:

> We rebelled against an Empire that has shaped everything in our lives; colored everything in the world as we know it. It is a huge, indelible stain, which has tainted all of us. We can't destroy it without destroying ourselves. (Ghosh, 518)

The initial description of the palace gives the novel its title. A little before the end of the novel one finds a young researcher of Rangoon University writing a dissertation on the fames of the nineteenth century history of Burma called *The Glass Palace Chronicles*:

> The young girl who'd helped to shelter Dinu when he had passed through Rangoon in 1942. She was now doing in her mid twenties, a student at Rangoon University. She was doing research in Burmese literature, writing a dissertation on *The Glass Palace Chronicles* a famous nineteenth century history, written in the reign of king Bodawpaya, and an ancestor of king Thebaw's. (532)

The Glass Palace of the title indicates both the magnificent hall of mirrors which is the centre piece of the Mandalay residence of Burmese kings and the name of a 'Small photo studio' where the book's action appropriately ends.

One can easily find the theme of an orphanhood in the novel. Rajkumar, Dolly, Saya John, all the maids of Queen Supayalat are orphans. The novel begins in a web of journey, chance, uncertainty and orphanhood. These are all well related. The roadside food stall (dhaba) is a recognized symbol of journey. The roadside food stall is also a place of current news, cheap food and temporary connections. It is a novel about many places, war and displacement, exile and rootlessness. It also depicts human helplessness in such a scenario. All human beings try to adjust, compromise, live and above everything else to form relationship. This forming of new bonds mixing of races and castes is something that doesn't stop. The collector at one point of the novel is intrigued when he comes to know of the pregnancy of Supayalat's first daughter. He is disgusted. He is at a loss. His sense of class and decency is deeply violated—"Was this love for them: this coupling in the darkness a princess of Burma and a Marathi coachman; this heedless mingling of sweat?" (Ghosh 152)

Apart from Characters, there are various ideas in this novel. There are relevant ideas on the process of civilization, wars and their futility, the concept of boundaries, colonization, and journey. In hybridity, rootlessness, childhood and process of growing, etc. one can find loneliness in this novel. Rajkumar is lonely at the beginning of the novel and at the end of the novel. Uma, who is a widow, leads her life lonely and with depression. Her husband, collector Dey, doesn't have a peaceful married life. When Uma leaves him, he feels lonely and commits suicide. In *The Glass Palace*, 'Glass Palace' functions as a metaphor, Glass is brittle and implies transparency; Palace is the symbol of power. Glass Palace is an illusion that is created around power.

Conclusion

The novel is divided into seven parts and each section has its aspects. The first part is called Mandalay. It is the place where the novel opens and it depicts how the British occupied Burma. The second part is named Ratnagiri where the calamitous effects of imperialism are shown. The third section is 'The Money Tree' shows how Rajkumar prospers through timber business. The fourth section is 'The Wedding' deals with the second generation. Rajkumar's son Neel marries Manju and people like Arjun and Dinu show fascination for the British. The fifth section 'Morningside' depicts the consequences of Second World War in Malaya. The sixth part shows how characters suffer due to the outbreak of the Second World War. The last section of the novel entitled *The Glass Palace* deals with the peak of Indian National Movement and its final achievement of independence. Thus, Amitav Ghosh's novel *The Glass Palace* is a fine example of colonial and post colonial over tones.

WORKS CITED

Auradkar, S.P. *Amitav Ghosh—A Critical Study*. Creative Books. New Delhi, 2007.

Barry, Peter. *Begninning Theory—An Introduction to Literary and Cultural Theory*. Vinod Vasishtha. New Delhi Permanent Black. Delhi, 2003.

Bose, Brinda. *Amitav Ghosh—Critical Perspectives*. Pencraft International. Delhi, 2005

Ghosh, Amitav. *The Glass Palace*. Harper Collins Publisher. New Delhi, 2000.

Habib, M.A.R. *A History of Literary Criticism*. Atlantic Publisher. New Delhi, 2005.

Khair, Tabish. *Amitav Ghosh—A Critical Companion*.

Loomba, Ania. *Colonialism/Postcolonialism*. Routledge. London, 2005.

Tiwari, Shubha. *Amitav Ghosh—A Critical Study*. Atlantic Publisher. New Delhi, 2003.

24

Borders, Violence and Amitav Ghosh's *The Shadow Lines*

Rajnish Mishra

> Everyone lives in a story...because stories are all there are to live in, it was just a question of which one you choose. (*The Shadow Lines,* 109)

Amitav Ghosh's *The Shadow Lines* (TSL) is a story that arises out of the narrator's reminiscences, recollected in tranquility and looked at with all the wisdom of the hind sight. It is about essentialization as a process, and its questioning in various ways. Essentialization is a very dangerously deceptive thing, especially when its purpose is a neat compartmentalization of human beings on the basis of subjective traits. Even then, sustaining the definition of water tight compartments of humanity becomes very difficult when homogeneity tends to erase the well-defined boundaries, making them blurred and shadowy. One of the many appealing facets of *The Shadow Lines* is the way it looks at the accident that descended on the pages of history: the creation of two nations on the basis of the incompatibility of two religious groups and their mutual hatred. East and West Pakistan were carved out of the British India on the basis of the two nation theory that totally opposed any possibility of co-existence. Boundaries were created and people were forced to alter their lives and selves to accommodate them to the conceptual nations that the powerful persons had created.

The Shadow Lines shows the plight of the narrator's grandmother and her loss of the sense of secure moorings; a point of reference to which one returns for assurance. Her loss was caused due to the borders imposed on her. In his *Modern Political Geography* Richard Muir defines boundaries that "occur where the vertical interfaces between state sovereignties intersect the surface of the earth.... As vertical interfaces, boundaries have no horizontal extent" (qtd. in Anderson, 172). Tha'mma would have been perplexed with Muir's elegantly defined boundaries that only existed in the conceptual space. In her own simple way she "wanted to know whether she would be able to see the border between India and East Pakistan from the plane" (*TSL*, 90). She wasn't looking for a line as such, but for some indicator of demarcation.

Hindus and Muslims, unlike the White and Black peoples, have no phenotypical inherent traits to tell them from each other. They shared land, culture and more than a thousand years of history. They had lived together, happily or unhappily, peacefully or struggling for survival based on the same resource. They would have kept doing the same had their fates not been manipulated by those who had assumed God-head, with its power, will, means and knowledge. The gods had developed a line of reasoning that showed the two categories of Hindus and Muslims as completely irreconcilable and essentially antagonistic. Their ideas found fruition in the first nation of the world that was constructed purely on the basis of religion: Pakistan, or the land of the holy. One of the prominent websites operating from Pakistan asserts it confidently:

> As early as in the beginning of the 11th century, Al-Biruni observed that Hindus differed from the Muslims in all matters and habits.... The speech made by Quaid-i-Azam at Minto Park, Lahore on March 22, 1940 was very similar to Al-Biruni;s thesis in theme and tone. In this speech, he stated that Hindus and Muslims belong to two different religious philosophies, with different social customs and literature.... He emphasized that in spite of the passage of about 1,000 years the relations

> between the Hindus and Muslims could not attain the level of cordiality. (www.storyofpakistan.com)

The Muslim fundamentalists were inadvertently but ably supported by the Hindu right wing. Leaders ranging from Quaid-e-Azam to Guruji had supported and established in the popular imagination the mutually exclusive and entirely essentialist categories of Hindus and Muslims. Their efforts bore fruit by contributing towards the establishment of these categories as parallels to the imagined communities of nations. Anderson defines nation as "an imagined political community...inherently limited and sovereign" (6). Despite all differences and conflicts, the members of this imagined community have a strong sense of belonging: "It is generally recognized that the intelligentsia were central to the rise of nationalism in the colonial territories...[their] vanguard role derived from their...literacy and bilingualism" (Anderson, 116). It was the intelligentsia who had started the process. Sir Syed Ahmed Khan was one of the first to broach the issue of fundamental incompatibility. Allama Iqbal had called the idea of territorially divided loyalties to nations as one of the modern inventions and an enemy of the solidarity of the Muslim "umma". He was right about the imaginary and inventedness of nations, as Anderson too would assert five decades later. Finally, Quaid-e-Azam Jinnah made Pakistan possible as a geopolitical entity.

History does not prove Iqbal's claim of the solidarity of the inherently heterogeneous Muslim umma that cuts across innumerable linguistic and geographical boundaries right, as is clear from the present unrest in Pakistan itself. One look at the past reveals that the Hindu-Muslim rift was deepened, widened and clearly defined in the decades enveloping 1900. It is from the same time period that one may trace the unbroken lineage of the monster of institutionalized and systemic communal hatred—communal riots—in the Indian subcontinent. The demographics specific to the subcontinent facilitated its origin and growth. Hindus or Muslims, whether they formed an absolute majority in a geographical region and felt secure in their numerical strength, or they were a minority, and the potential victims of persecution on the basis of the religion of their birth: in each case there was a way to communalize masses. The mass paranoia of the inevitable discrimination based on religion was fed and raised to a heightened pitch by those who had the most to benefit from such circumstances. Public fear was roused in order to gain political mileage and what came out of it was natural and logical.

Ironically, the partition of the two nations joined them even more closely and strongly. So strongly, that an event in India's northern most state of Jammu and Kashmir caused riots in both Indian and Pakistani parts of the subcontinent on both sides of the border. The same happened after 8 December 1992, while India was spilling its blood, so was Bangladesh where "Muslims attacked and burnt down Hindu temples and shops.... At least 10 people have died, many Hindu women have been raped, and hundreds of Hindu homes and temples have been destroyed" (Chronology for Hindus in Bangladesh). One strong similarity between the two riots is the presence of the desecration of the religious symbols at their core: "the sacred relic known as the Mu-i-Mubarak—believed to be a hair of the Prophet Mohammad himself" and the mosques at Ayodhya, Mathura and Kasi or Varanasi (*TSL*, 135). Politicians were behind inciting the masses into violent action, and in keeping the government machinery inert while they went on a rampage, on both sides of the borders of time and space. *The Shadow Lines* has a number of lines of action and the one that's red with blood is etched very clearly in its second half.

India's test series against England was to begin on 10th January 1964 in Madras. It was on that fateful date that the narrator of *The Shadow Lines* was to taste what the fear of an unknown "they" meant. In his comparatively empty school bus he was introduced to the faith inducing powers of rumors. Most of the students had not brought water that day because of the rumor of "their" poisoning all the water of Calcutta had already spread. The very psychology of the unchallengeable and pre-validated logic of rumors brings back to my mind the post riot curfew days of 1991, when morning rumors were congealed and solidified by the evening. In those days the two dailies: Aj in the morning and Gandeev in the evening, were the only source of local information for people thirsty for any snippets that could confirm or prove wrong whatever they had heard throughout the day. More than that, they needed objective justification of their own prejudices. Just like the little boys in *The Shadow Lines*, they "did not need to ask any question...[they] knew the answers...it was a reality that existed only in the saying" (*TSL*, 120).

The Shadow Lines shows violence through its presence in the background and its pervading the atmosphere, also through its turning into silence, through its conversion into a recurring nightmare, and finally, through the narration of the one graphical act of violence that left a permanent scar on the lives of its witnesses (Robi, May and Tha'mma). The January 1964 riots, that *BBC* rightly called "the first incident of religious violence since 1950" in India spread on both sides of the border. They are portrayed not so much as direct acts of violence as through the tension and fear created in the minds of the children (the narrator and his schoolmates in one case and Robi in the other). This tension and the unmentioned yet ever discernible fear create an atmosphere that becomes a character in itself—an important determiner of actions and lives. It is this tension and fear in the atmosphere that brings back to my mind a series of reminiscences from the Varanasi riots of 1991-92, the chaos, the heat, and how it was felt by those on the extreme periphery of any active involvement or loss. Fear is central in both the cases: of fictional and real lives. In *The Shadow Lines* there is an elemental fear of violence that the children in the bus feel when they hear the noise of the rioting mob, and later when they were followed by one. They could not compare it to anything else in their experience and the narrator later opines insightfully:

> It is a fear that comes of the knowledge that normalcy is utterly contingent, that the spaces that surround one, the streets that one inhabits, can become, suddenly and without warning, as hostile as a desert in a flash flood. It is this that sets apart the thousand million people who

> inhabit the subcontinent from the rest of the world—not language, not food, not music—it is the special quality of loneliness that grows out of the fear of the war between oneself and one's image in the mirror. (122)

Fear of that kind is ever present. Always ready to rise in the hearts of the trapped people, making them feel cornered enough to plan retaliation and contribute to the vicious cycle of violence that begets violence. A similar fear was in the air back in 1991-92 also. Instead of treating the parallel at an emotional and personal level, the present paper is an attempt to incorporate the analogical streams of 1964 and 1991-92 riots in showing their pattern. It does not try to hide differences, if there, e.g. one major difference between them was that the 1964 riots were relegated to the narrow columns of the last pages of the newspapers, but the 1991-92 riots (coming right after the infamous 1989 Varanasi riot) was very widely covered and reported about. The narrator painfully realized it when he mentioned the riots of 1964 to his friends and they accepted being completely ignorant of it.

"Real" life enters fiction and a history treads cautiously into the orbit of narration when a historical novel touches a real life event. The narrative of *The Shadow Lines* is woven around the historically real incidents with complete details of their occurrence. Everything is treated in such a manner that the reader is forced to suspend all disbelief willingly, effortlessly, even colluding with the narrator/writer; more so, when dates and numbers are woven into the story. 10th January 1964, when the first match of the test series was to begin, and its co-incidence with the riot's entering the life of the narrator is a clever device. A detailed account of the events that led to the riots is given in the novel, *The Shadow Lines*. On 27th December 1963 Mu-i-Mubarak disappeared. There were some incidents of people's damaging public property, but their anger was directed against the government and not against any particular religious community. Moreover, the protesters belonged to all the religions. Pandit Nehru sent CBI to the valley and the relic was recovered. Yet the damage was already done. The Pakistani "religious authorities, usually so quick to condemn idolatry, declared that the theft of the relic was an attack upon the identity of Muslims. Karachi observed 31st December as a 'Black Day', and soon other cities followed suit. The Pakistani newspapers declared that the theft was part of a deep-laid conspiracy for uprooting the spiritual and national hopes of Kashmiris, and rumbled darkly about 'genocide'" (*TSL*, 136).

In the East Pakistani town of Khulna the demonstrators against the disappearance of the relic turned against the minority Hindus and many lives were lost. As Trivedi reports, the riots soon spread all over East Pakistan. The whiplash was soon felt in Calcutta as refugees from East Pakistan fled to India. On 10th January, mobs went on a rampage, killing Muslims and destroying their property. Army was called when the situation went out of control. The violence was stopped and everything went back to normal, as the narrator declares: "By the end of January 1964 the riots had faded away from the pages of the newspapers, disappeared from the collective imagination of 'responsible opinion', vanished without leaving a trace in the histories and bookshelves. They had dropped out of memory into the crater of a volcano of silence" (*TSL*, 138). Individual paranoia, worked onto a feverish pitch, had been and can be conjugated at macro level to create concerted and planned violent action called a riot. The Indian subcontinent had been a witness to many such planned blood baths whose origin lies in the establishment of the two nation theory in the collective psyche. Such were the fruits of the tree of hatred whose seed was sown around the beginning of the twentieth century.

WORKS CITED

"1964: Riots in Calcutta leave more than 100 dead". Bbc.co.uk. n.d. Web. 27 November 2011.

Anderson, Benedict. *Imagined Communities: Reflections on the Origin and Spread of Nationalism*. Verso: London, 1991.

"Chronology for Hindus in Bangladesh". unhcr.org. n.d. Web. 25 February 2012.

Ghosh, Amitav. *The Shadow Lines*. ebookee.org. n.d. Web. 27 November 2011. DOC.

"The Ideology of Pakistan: Two-Nation Theory". storyofpakistan.com. 1 June 2003. Web. 23 February 2012.

Trivedi, Rabindranath. "The Legacy of the Plight of Hindus in Bangladesh—Part-VII". asiantribune.com. 23 July 2007. Web. 23 February 2012.

25

The Hungry Tide: Globalization and Beyond

Rupali Jain

In the novel, *The Hungry Tide*, Amitav Ghosh seems to have brought a fresh perspective on the East-West theme. In his other novels, *The Shadow Lines* and *The Glass Palace*, for instance, such theme is implicit, or presented as 'involved' with other themes, but in *The Hungry Tide*, it seems to have been played out, unwittingly, against the backdrop of an awesome environment of the Sunderbans. In this case, East and West are not involved in a conflict or synthesis but simply come together and even look beyond. It is globalization in the sense of coming together. The Sunderbans is not only beautiful and awesome in its physical sense, but it is also beautiful in its social and metaphysical sense. Here was a place where, "it was impossible to tell who was who, and what their castes and religions and beliefs were" (79).

It should be clear, then, that the Sunderbans is place, a kind of "Utopia", where one's familiar markers for identity-caste, religion, etc.—stand obliterated and Nature seems to create, undo and recreate a borderless region. We are told that the tide comes in twice daily at the Sunderbans, resulting in an invariable shaping and reshaping of the land, and threatening or demolishing of any permanent structures. Moreover, as already mentioned, "There [were] no borders here to divide fresh water from salt, river from sea" (*The Hungry Tide*, 7). Besides, the tide country is presided over by Bon Bibi, a goddess—at once a redeemer and a destroyer, one who also represents a syncretic local cult.

Here, it would be interesting and appealing to mention Sir Daniel Hamilton, a Scottish visionary, who had bought ten thousand acres of the Sunderbans and invited impoverished people from near, and far to come and populate the place, on no-charge basis. The only, but vital condition that he laid down for his proposed commune was that they would not practice casteism, or tribal nationalism of any kind there. And people, mainly farmers, heeded his call and moved to his commune—in the 1920s, in 1947 after partition, and, again in 1971 after the Bangladesh War. He named the place Lusi Bari, the home of Lucy, after the name of his deceased wife, where some Western and eastern ideas or values like a casteless society that seemed to coalesce, were practiced. The theme unfolds itself in terms of the interactions of the characters, their values, attitudes or ideas.

These interactions, mainly, takes place between Piyali Roy —an American citizen of Indian parentage and a scientist—and Kanai Dutt, a sophisticated and westernized businessman from Delhi. Equally important are the interactions between Piyali Roy and Fokir, an illiterate and proud local fisherman, whom Roy has hired to guide her through the backwaters of the Sunderbans. Piya (Piyali Roy), a graduate student in Cytology at the Scripps institution of Oceanography in California, is on the track of the rare Dolphins that are unique to the Sunderbans.

As Piya does not know Bengali, Kanai (Kanai Dutt) offers to be her translator. But Fokir manages to communicate with her, even though he knows no English. It seems as if Ghosh is trying to emphasize the theme of unity—unity of religion, of communities, of people, etc. He tries to achieve this unity through communication. Therefore communication plays a vast role in his narratives. In *The Hungry Tide* the central metaphor for the notion of communication in a multilingual world is provided by the theme of translation. Significantly, Kanai is a translator by profession: he knows six languages, runs a translation and interpretation agency, and offers to act as interpreter for Piya, who knows only English and has no means of communication with the local Bengali speakers whose knowledge is vital for her research. Kanai interprets between Piya and Fokir.

Here, it must be noted that multilingualism has always been a part of the Indian context, Ghosh himself is multilingual, and his earlier novels contain episodes reflecting a keen awareness of the complexities and difficulties of language interaction, both among Indians and between Indians. These complexities are reflected through the interaction among characters. For instance, Kanai interprets for Piya for a portion of her expedition, but at a certain point he concludes that she does not in fact need his services, apparently supposing she can communicate intuitively with her guide Fokir, "I think you'll be able to manage perfectly well without a translator" (333). Fokir can read the secrets she is searching for; he, the child of the river, can see them before her binoculars reach out to them. They have no words in common. Silence and gestures, movements of eyes and fingers, translate their emotions for each other and dramatize the tension, both elemental and erotic.

It may be mentioned in the passing that Piya's destination, when the novel opens, is the town of canning, the train stops for that region; whereas, Kanai's real destination is Lusi Bari, the farthest of the inhabited islands in the Sunderbans, where his seventy-six-year-old aunt, Nilima runs a charitable organization called The Badabon trust. They travel together in the same compartment from Calcutta to canning and then depart for their respective destinations. But their chance meeting develops in to a kind of kinship that knows no cultural differences, no age bar, and is sustained all through the novel.

Fokir is, initially, drawn into the plot, because of his having been hired to guide Piya to the Dolphin region. But his sense of sacrifice, his commitment to his vocation and his attitude of gay abandon to life's dangers, wins him to Piya and she falls in love with him—a kind of love which knows no understanding; it is purely spiritual. This kind of intimacy between the characters is purely eastern. However, taken by her, Piya is, initially, stubbornly American—it can be said, western. Let us note, how Piya describes her proposed science project in the Sunderbans:

> It would be as fine a piece of descriptive science as any. It would be enough; as an alibi for a life, it would do; she would not need to apologize for how she had spent her time on this earth. (127)

To Piya the study of Biology is mystical, as Ghosh refers to the myths of her interests. Perhaps the "loyal but loose—knit community" is the harmonious connection that Piya feels with nature as she studies the mystical animals that she encounters in the exotic places she visits. By being a biologist, Piya can feel more in touch with nature as she studies its habits and can slowly understand more about the subject that intrigues her most. And, another declaration of Amitav Ghosh pertaining to her characterization is pretty conspicuous in the following paragraph:

> As with many of her peers, she had been drawn to field biology as much for the life it offered as for its intellectual content—because it allowed her to be on her own, to have no fixed address, to be far from the familiar, while still being a part of a loyal but loose—knit community. (126)

Finding salvation in the pursuit of a realized science project is, basically, a Western attitude. But, midway through the novel, there is a slight change of heart, through she is still sceptic of human relationships and yet how different she is towards the end of the novel. It is a situation when a fierce storm was upon Piya and Fokir and, "the air was full of hurtling projectiles"; and "the wind was now coming at them from the opposite direction. Where she had had the tree trunk, to shelter her before, now there was only Fokir's body" (389).

It is in this extraordinary situation that she is transformed altogether; she has had her education of heart, so to speak, and she becomes a very intimate person. This ability to completely indentify with the other person reveals her class and the education of the heart. It is an eastern value, and Piya acquires this in some measure in a formidable, extraordinary situation.

Piya also has her education in the Indian folklore in the form of a legend of the tide country; the story of Bon Bibi, the Sunderban's protectress: A part of the story has to do with Dukhey's redemption. Bon Bibi redeems a poor boy called Dukhey when he is betrayed by Dhona, a ship's captain, and is offered to the tiger demon; Dokkhin Rai. Kannai has translated this part of the legend for Piya and presents it to her as a priceless gift.

Another characteristic of the postmodern novel is that myths, fairy tales, legends and contemporary reality homogeneously merge together. It becomes impossible to distinguish between reality and illusion. The cult of Bon Bibi occupies a significant place in the life of the people of the tide country. The legend of Bon Bibi carries history within its fold, as Kanai rightly identifies, "In those words, there was a history that is not just his (Fokir's) own but also of this place, the tide country" (354). In a letter which he addressed her, Kanai brings out the significance of the legend for the people thus:

> This was the story that gave this land its life. That was the song you heard on Fokir's lips yesterday: it lives in him and in some way, perhaps, it still plays a part in making him the person he is. This is my gift to you, this story that is also a song; these words are a part of Fokir. (354)

The legend inspires the people of the land to live a life of self-sacrifice, which is clearly a significant aspect of our culture. The legend has revolutionized Kanai's thinking; it has forced him to take stock of the (Westernized) kind of life he has been living.

Kanai's uncle, Nirmal, had a similar kind of soul-searching when he realized that his Western leftism had failed to inculcate in him subaltern consciousness which the squatters, the "dispossessed" refugees at Morichjhapi did. They had refused to budge when the police was forcing him to move out, and had acted in unison. Although the squatters of Morichjhapi never envisioned themselves as revolutionaries, the poet Nirmal finds them to be the finest of such breed:

> ...between what was happening at Morichjhapi and what Daniel Hamilton had done there was one vital aspect of difference: this was not one man's vision. The dream had been dreamt by the very people who were trying to make it real...how astonishing it was that I, an ageing, bookish schoolmaster, should live to see this, an experiment, imagined not by those with learning and power, but by those without . (171)

Piya, the Western woman she is, won't leave her science after this encounter with the east, and she continues to be very enterprising. She spent quite some time on the internet and has contacted her friends and colleagues in connection with the cause of raising money for Moyna and Tutul—Fokir's immediate family. As a matter of fact, she has already collected enough money to buy them a house of their own, and may be it also takes case of Tutul's education. Her mind, after discharging this obligation, is concentrated on her project. Fortunately for her, a monitor who is connected to the satellites of the global Positioning System was in her pocket on the day of the storm and that was the only equipment that has survived, "All the routes that Fokir showed me are stored here...." At the touch of button, Piya has access to the memory, and she points to a serious zigzag line that had appeared on the screen:

> That was the route we took on the day before the storm Fokir took the boat into every little creek and gully where he'd ever seen a dolphin. That one map represents decades of work and volumes of knowledge. It's going to be the foundation of my project that's why I think I should be named after him. (398)

A remark by Makarand Paranjape in the context of the Diaspora will be worth considering here as it throws light on the kind of diasporic character Piya is. Paranjape talks of generational differences that discriminate the younger Diaspora from the older one. Since the older people could never return to the mother land, as travel was difficult, expensive, time-consuming, this led to a greater rootedness for them in the new country. As for the younger generations, they were cosmopolitan, and so, they could afford to 'indulge' in a sense of double consciousness, nurtured by trips to the motherland. But Piya does not belong to this category of younger Diaspora. She went to America when she was only one and her parents were not keen that she learnt Bengali: for all practical purposes, she is an American, whose first language is English. She simply becomes aware of the 'roots'. Ultimately, she belongs to the West, and "her home is where the Oracaella are" (400).... After all she is from the West, and so, and 'outsider'.

As for Fokir, he truly represents the east. He has crossed the realm of the evil, represented by Dokkhin Rai and her demons; and he now dwells in the realm of humans, protected by Bon Bibi. As a settler of the Sunderbans he believes that anyone without a pure heart who ventures into the watery labyrinth will never return; and he has kept the sanctity of his heart by leading a life of self-sacrifice and love. It is ideal characters like him who leaves some trace, some hold upon the memory of the world, and are capable of transforming others by their very example. In the early portion of the novel, she brings a Western perspective to the question of the preservation of wild animals. She is furious when she sees a tiger being killed. She is unable to understand that the dispossessed of the Sunderbans have to kill a man-eating tiger, or else their precarious existence will be jeopardized.

As the spirit of the book is quite intimate, Amitav Ghosh has employed the traditional method of narration and struck a chord with the reader, unlike his Western counterparts who keep the reader perplexed in the act of deconstructing the text. Again, unlike the Indo-Anglian writers of the fifties and sixties, his novel does not end up being a pro-eastern text. He has presented a fairly dispassionate view of both the cultures in literary terms and has left it to the readers to make his mind about it. But *The Hungry Tide,* looks beyond the question of East and the West. Through Nirmal, for instance, he not only speaks for the dispossessed of the Sunderbans but the wretched of the entire earth and in the following passage the 'place' refers to any place where the wretched of the earth live without a home:

> ...Who was I? Where did I belong? In Kolkata or in the tide country? In India or across the border? In prose or in poetry?...where else could you belong, except in the place you refused to leave.... (Hawley, John C., 136)

Ghosh's purpose is not merely to deconstruct the binary that holds home and homelessness as counterpoints, but to unite them as parts of an integrated whole. In this way, his work can be called deconstructive, but his objective is to create an independent discourse, where terms such as home and homelessness can have meaning only when they are seen as containing each other. The Utopian goal of mutual understanding, implicit in the novel's recurrent theme of translation, begins to appear as something actually possible. *The Shadow Lines* reveals the crisis of the cultural divide and communal struggle in India. *The Hungry Tide* tries to resolve these issues through mutual understanding, to think transculturally and to build new bridges across the world.

Through the examples of Piya (home is where the Orcellas are) and Nilima (home is where I can brew a pot of good tea) (*The Hungry Tide*, 400), Ghosh tries to show that home is not a fixity. It can be anywhere in the world, wherever you make friends and it becomes home. It is just a matter of warmth and bonding not of borders and lines. Ghosh attempts to find the links between people rather than dwelling on the differences and the myth of separateness that keep them divided across borders, across cultures and across languages.

The tide country itself acquires a symbolic significance. It does not merely remain an immense archipelago of islands where there are no borders to divide fresh water from salt, river from sea, even land from water. The tide country ultimately signifies our brief time on earth. It sends the intelligent minds thinking. After his experience of the Sunderbans, Kanai is an enlightened person and admits to himself that being a translator and interpreter, he can make one person understand by another, but he does not understand himself. Similarly, Piya, after similar experiences at the

Sunderbans feels unsecure and perplexed: "She had no more idea of what her own place was in the great scheme of things that she did of people she did not know" (35).

The difference that separate nation, race and class drove Amitav Ghosh to write *The Shadow Lines*, but in his fifth novel, the emphasis has shifted. In *The Hungry Tide*, he is not talking of differences but of connections. The borders, lines and nations, instead of their shadow appearance as in *The Shadow Lines*, disappear in *The Hungry Tide*. As for superficial westernization, in terms of dress and mannerisms, Ghosh seems to scoff at it, but he is for such westernization which provides the beginning of a modern new era. For instance, one such idea is a healthy and open attitude towards sex, clearly seen in *The Shadow Lines*, which traditionalists might find offensive.

Being modern, in Ghosh's eyes, is a desirable attitude as it brings about social change and takes the regions into the stream of modern international life. But, all said and done, Ghosh is rooted in Indian culture, and is essentially, an Indian writer, with an international readership. The kind of writer Amitav Ghosh is, has been clearly brought out by A.K. Ramanujan, thus. Ghosh, to says, "evokes things Indians with an inwardness that is lit and darkened by an intimacy with Elsewhere..." (6). 'Elsewhere', here, primarily, refers to the west. Though Ramanujan had made his criticism in the context of *The Shadow Lines*, it is very much applicable to some of his other works as well.

In the context of *The Hungry Tide* Amitav Ghosh seems to have brought a fresh perspective on the East-West theme. In *The Shadow Lines*, the theme is implicit, or presented as involved with other themes, but in *The Hungry Tide*, it seems to have been played out, unwittingly, against the backdrop of an awesome environment of the Sunderbans. In this case, East and West are not involved in a 'conflict' or synthesis at all, neither are they presented as contrast, but come together and even look beyond.

WORKS CITED

Ghosh, Amitav. *The Hungry Tide*, Ravi Dayal, p. 35.

Ghosh, Amitav. *The Hungry Tide*. Delhi: Ravi Dayal, 2004. The textual references from this edition with page number(s) are cited in the article.

Google. http://www.makarand.com/index.htm

Hawley, John C. *Amitav Ghosh: Contemporary Indian Writers in English*, Foundation Books, House, 2005, p. 136.

Ramanujan, A.K. www.amitavghosh.com/shadowline_r.html

Rollason, Christopher. "In Our Translated World: Transcultural Communication in Amitav Ghosh's *The Hungry Tide*", 01 Aug 08 <http://www.trucoto.com.ar/ghosh>.

The Diaspora in Indian Culture. *Public Culture*, 2.1 (1989): 73-78.

Zaidi, Nishat. "Myth-History Interface in Fiction and Nation: A Reading of Amitav Ghosh's *The Hungry Tide*." *Litcritt*, 33.2 (2007): 105-20.

26

Elements of Love and Sensuality in Amitav Ghosh's *River of Smoke*

Vivekanand Jha

The novel, *River of Smoke*, profoundly diffuses fragrance and is redolent of immorality, sensuality, passion and love. The theme of love, sensuality and immorality in the novel is circling on one and only one reason of not allowing foreign women in Canton. This being the reason Canton is flooded with bachelors of variegated kinds, conditions and cultures. These bachelors remain with no option other than doing many things with local women of easy virtue popularly known as sing-song-girl. Such is the havoc of sing-song-girl in canton Ah Fatt, a friend of Neel is observed warning him before Neel was likely to set out for Canton: "In China people say 'everything new comes from Canton'. Better for young men not to go there—too many ways for them to be spoiled".[1]

The phrase 'sing-song-girl' is reverberating in Canton where entry of foreign women are strictly prohibited and foreign traders miles, years and countries away from their wife or girl friends fulfil their bodily needs with sing-song girls. The banning of foreign women in Canton is the chief reason for all the incidents of immorality and vice that took place in the novel. What can a man do living away for years from his children and wife? How will he quench his bodily needs that hang about in hibernation like volcano? Under such circumstances the role of the sing-song-girl is prominent in Canton. This term has been amply used by Amitav Gosh in the novel and such title stands for the girl or woman of easy virtue who indulges in flesh trading for the sake of money and merriment:

> 'Fanqui-town', as old hands called it, was a place at once strangely straitened yet wildly luxurious; a place where you were always watched and yet were free from the frowning scrutiny of your family; a place where the female presence was strictly forbidden, but where women would enter your life in ways that were utterly unexpected: it was thus that Bahram, while still in his twenties, found himself gloriously and accidentally entangled with Chi-mei, a boat woman who gave him a son child who was all the more dear to him because his existence could never be acknowledged in Bombay.[2]

Bahram was not immoral by his heart, soul and mind but it was the situation that compelled him to turns towards extra marital sexuality. He was not a kind of person who was looking for every new girl for every new night. His relation other than wife was limited to Chi-mei who was also for him no less than a wife as he could enjoy real pleasure of wife and companionship with her only. Though Bahram got indulged in extramarital affair to quench his bodily requirements when he remained in Canton but he was shying to discuss such things with friend, Zadig Bey and he convinced Bahram to let the things come out hidden into the core of his heart:

> There is nothing shameful in this, you know, said Zadig; it is not just the jism that has its needs but also the rooh, the soul—and a man who feels himself to be alone in his own home, does he not have a right to seek companionship elsewhere?[3]

When he for the first time visited Canton he falls in love with a washerwoman and widow, Chi-mei who was dwelling on a boat with her mother and daughter. He met her first time in her laundry and after that her face kept flashing before his eyes and a strong bond of affinity and love was drawing him towards her. Bahram was not himself while depicting the beauty of Chi-mei to Zadig Bey when first he came across her and how he was caught into the net of her beauty:

> She was scrubbing clothes in the flat stern of her boat. A scarf was tightly tied over her hair, but a few ringlets had escaped their bindings and lay curled on her forehead. Her face was pert and lively, with glinting black eyes, and cheeks that glowed like polished apples. They locked eyes briefly and then she quickly turned her face away. But later, when he was about to head back to the factory he glanced at her over his shoulder and caught her looking in his direction again.[4]

Bahram couldn't get real love and affection from his legitimate wife, Shireenbai due to unequal and lopsided marriage. The sex was not a kind endearment and enjoyment for them rather it was a means of producing children and successor of their family. As for Bahram, "lovemaking with Shireenbai was a clinical affair and their bodies seemed hardly to touch except where necessity demanded".[5] It was Chi-mei who catered bodily requirement of Bahram with utmost freedom and contentment and thus she became de facto wife of Bahram as far as conjugal and carnal pleasure and bliss are required in one's life. This was the reason Bahram was like a parrot in the open sky with Chi-mei and he enjoyed freedom of sensuality and revelry with her. He remained prepared to let loose her restrained passion with her that remained buried inside over the years. Bahram presents passionate accounts of initiative taken by him before successfully copulating with Chi-mei:

> She was sitting close to him, with her shoulders half turned in his direction. He dropped his head on the curve of her neck and to his astonishment she did not push him away. Instead she began to stroke his back with one hand.
>
> Never before had he taken so much comfort in being touched: desire and lovemaking were nowhere in his thoughts; what he felt above all was gratitude.[6]

The entanglement between Bahram and Chi-mei was not a flesh trading rather it was a kind of love begotten by union of hearts and proposal initiated by a man who remained love-lorn in his life. Unlike other boatwoman of Canton, Chi-mei was not indulged in exploiting money in substitute of bargaining her flesh. The relationship between the two advanced ahead after adequate observation and scrutinizing. Bahram tried to test her more often than not by paying unwarranted price to her gratitude and every time she was successful in her ordeal. Allow, an itinerant, impoverished and relative of Chi-mei, was a messenger for the furtherance of love story between her and Bahram. It was he who, first time, rowed them on board of sampan to safest and secluded place, White Swan Lake, where script of their love making was begun. Though Bahram was a married man yet it was very unprecedented experience for him and he enjoyed it in a consummate finish with an initial hitch and hesitation:

> He had never been with any woman other than his wife: to almost the same degree that he was assured and combative in his business dealings, he was shy and reticent in all matters intimate or personal. His previous undressing had been solemn and silent; here Chi-mei kept giggling as she helped him take off his turban, slip off his choga and untie his pyjamas. When she tried to pull off his sacred waist-strings he whispered: 'This piece thread blongi joss-pidgin thing. No can take off'.[7]

Canton is forbidden to foreign women and the most victim of such policy in the novel is Miss Paulette whose eyes trickle with tears when she came to know through Fitcher Penrose that she would not be able to visit Canton. This is the reason while she remained stranded in and restricted to the Outer Islands, she is updated about every goings and happenings of Canton through letters from his childhood friend, Robert Chinnery. A great chunk of novel is flooded with letters that Robert Chinnery sends to Paulette describing vivid pictures of why, how and whereabouts of Canton. The novel, *River of Smoke*, is replete with both platonic and physical affiliation and association. The physical affiliation is amply observed through the characterization of Bahram who is shown to be in love making with Chi-mei and some sing-song-girl in dream. The semblance of platonic love is portrayed when Paulette

Lambert and Robert Chinnery came across in their adulthood after their separation from childhood intimation:

> Paulette threw her arms around him and the feel of his soft and bosomy embrace was like a remembered taste dissolving upon the tongue; she recalled the savour of the times they had spent together, bantering, teasing arguing and gossiping and she understood, all of a sudden, that robin was perhaps the closest friend she had ever had for Jodu was more a sibling than a friend.[8]

Amitav Ghosh has presented Indian womanhood for which they have been emblematic, exemplary and known the world over in the guise of Neel's wife Malati who has been shown as deeply observant of Hindu custom. Neel escaped successfully from the Ibis in the midst of storm but a rumour was spread that he perished and died due to capsizing of the boat on which he was escaping. Though this message was conveyed to his wife but she didn't believe it as she had not seen him dead with her naked eyes and her soul was informing and telling her that it was only a rumour. Such was her pious dedication and devotion for her husband that she didn't lose hope and she remained in the robe of blessed woman. She adopted no sign of widowhood, she never wore widow's whites, she kept applying vermillion into the parting of her hair and she didn't break her bangles. She even convinced her son, Raj Rattan that his father was surviving and he educated his son better than any other children of her locality. Neel was updated about his wife and son by Baboo Nob Kissin in Canton and the news of his wife and son turn Neel emotional and sentimental and have reminded him of his wedding days:

> Tears came into Neel's eyes now, and he lowered his head to blink them away unseen. He remembered Malati's face as he had seen it the first time, on the night of their wedding, when he was fourteen and she a year younger. He remembered how she had hidden behind her veils, even when they were in bed; he remembered how she has turned her face away from him when he tugged at the coverings. He remembered also the day she came to see him in jail, in Calcutta: her ever-present veils

> were gone and it was as if he were seeing her for the first time. Not till then did he realize that the girl he had married had grown into a woman of uncommon beauty.[9]

Another woman who represents Indian womanhood in true colour, religion, conviction and faith is Shireenbai, the wife of Bahram. Though she was despondent and depressed for her wedding with Bahram but that didn't diminish her from the path of loyalty and devotion for her husband. Like most of the Indian women she is superstitious and has deep conviction in the prophecy of miracle-monger. Her every bad and good decision is based on ominous and auspicious signs in her vicinity respectively. For example at the time of his final and last departure for Canton, the bangles of Shireenbai are inadvertently broken and she desperately and unsuccessfully convinced him to defer his journey: "You know what it means for a wife to break her bangle, don't you? Even if you care nothing for me: what about the family? Do you care nothing for your daughters and their children?"[10] Her skepticism came true as it remained the last meeting and interaction between Bahram and Shireenbai and he died before he could return to Bombay. Indian woman can tolerate anything but not an indulging of her husband in extra-marital affair and this is one of the prime reason Bahram extremely abstaining from telling her truth about himself, Chi-mei and Ah Fatt. Just before his last visit to Canton though he made up his mind to tell her all truth about Chi-mei and Ah Fatt but he thought she should not be told about such sensitive issues in hot haste and he abruptly deferred his mind:

> There was something in her voice that made it impossible for Bahram to answer her in his usual indulgent way: in her pleas there was an urgency and despair which he had never heard before. It was as if she had at last accepted him as something more than a substitute for the husband she should have had; it was as if, after forty years of performing her marital duties with a pathetic punctiliousness, her feelings for him had suddenly ripened into something else.[11]

The anguish, aggravation and nervousness in mind-set and deportment of Ah Fatt against Bahram is obvious for not getting lawful name and right for being the son of his well heeled and reputed father. Ah Fatt was inquisitive to trip Bombay and India but Bahram was no way prepared to accompany him into his ship as he was afraid that his elder wife and in-laws would come to know about all these immoral and unbearable affairs. But Neel makes every attempt to convince and persuade Ah Fatt that his father is right in his position and disposition as Neel belonged to Zemindar family and extra marital indulgence was not uncommon and bizarre things in his knowledge. He cites many such example to Ah Fatt that were pretty easy for the man like Bahram but he still remained distinct and diverse from other people of his cadres and "Bahram's conduct in relation to Ah Fatt and his mother was not just unusual but quite exceptional for a man of his circumstances"[12] Neel recalls some incidents of his previous life in Calcutta where his own father was indulged in such a malicious and immoral activity:

> In his previous life, in Calcutta, Neel had known so many men who had fathered illegitimate children: not one of them, so far as he knew, had shown any trace of kindness in their treatment of their mistresses and their progeny; he even knew of some who, fearing blackmail, had had their babies strangled. His own father, the old Zemindar, was said to have begotten a dozen bastards, with a succession of different women: his method of dealing with the situation was to pay the women a hundred rupees and pack them off to their villages. Amongst men of his class this was considered normal and even generous; Neel himself had taken it so much for granted that he had never occurred to him to think of his father's bastards as his own half-siblings.[13]

Despite Ah Fatt being illegitimate, illegal and bastard son of Bahram, he provided him all the facilities and love that a father is supposed to give his son only other than taking him to Bombay due to some uncompromising and compelling circumstances that he could have faced by her elder wife and her family members. All clandestine measures were taken by Bahram to make life of Chi-mei luxurious and facilitate Ah Fatt with all better educations and upbringings and that he could have easily averted and settled with some silver coins like some instances cited by Neel in the novel. Neel further goes on to persuade Ah Fatt on these aspects of humanity and inhumanity and counsels in defence of Bahram: "But believe me, most men in his situation would just have abandoned you and your mother. That would have been the easy thing to do; it is what ninety-nine men in a hundred would have done. It says something for him that he didn't do it. Don't you see that?"[14]

Another man who is exhibiting craving for sensuality and love is Mr. Jardine who is in his late forty and still bachelor and has been in Canton for more than a decade. He is powerful and influential man in Canton and the largest player in the trading of opium in Chinese market. He is not only an adept trader but also skillful and proficient in setting up approach and rapprochement with the people of various class and cadres. Since Chinese government didn't allow entry of any European woman in Canton, he decided to return to England to solemnize his marriage with suitable bride. All members of Canton's General Chamber of Commerce wish him best of luck in finding the suitable and belle bride and he acknowledges his well wishers thus:

> Thank you, gentlemen, thank you: I will certainly need your good wishes. I have so little experience of the petticoat company that I should consider myself fortune if I succeed in finding a lady who is fat, fair and forty. It is as much as a man of my age has a right to expect.[15]

Bahram was upset with the sudden and unprecedented development in Canton which is caused by the arrival of new commissioner in Canton, Lin Zexu who has been famous for his dry honesty and absolute integrity and is determined to root out the trading, transporting and smuggling of opium into Canton. He feels heat of heavy pressure from his investors in Bombay and other parts of India for disposing of the large amount of opium on board of his ship, Anhita. Amid hue and cry of embargo on the trading of opium, Bahram came across

Allow who is now deeply involved in small scale smuggling of opium and by the time this meeting of Bahram with Allow took place Chi-mei had already died. Bahram was such a long trader of opium he didn't want to take any notice of the small fry like Allow. But Allow was well aware of his caliber, so he was adamant to follow and flatter Bahram like shadow. One day Bahram was stranded in such situation that he had left no option other than talking the help of Allow's boat. Allow was well aware of the weakness of Bahram and she was none other than Chi-mei and he tried to push Bahram into flashback of his meeting with Chi-mei. When Bahram was not melted through this malicious and nefarious design, he was given an offer of another sing-song-girl to quench his corporeal requirements but Bahram vociferously rejected such proposition of Allow. Stressed and strained by relentless news of opium imbroglio, Bahram gives in to the last offer of Allow: "Seating himself on the divan, Allow plucked the cloth cover off the tray to reveal a finely carved ivory pipe, a long needle, and a carved opium Box".[16] Inhaling of opium set him into a world of sensuality in a dream:

> Something stirred in Bahram, some deep need, some yearning that had gone so long acknowledged that he had forgotten its very existence. He tugged at her arm and when he seemed to resist, he turned his body around and laid his head against her. It was almost as if he were back with Chi-mei now, in that bubble of impossible absurdity they had once inhabited together, floating side by side in that coracle which had no proper name, which wasn't love but wasn't quite 'lob-pidgin' either.[17]

He was deeply involved in love making in a dream with some sing-song-girl but mannerism and fashion of sex was same as he and Chi-mei had been enjoying for years. At the time of love making with Chi-mei too, he had resorted to some foreplay to know what was going in the inner core of her mind and heart and when she exhibited no opposition then only Bahram advanced ahead on path of profound lovemaking. Dream is nothing but a translation of what one thinks in his consciousness and similar course of lovemaking is noticed in

Bahram while he is in a romantic dream administered by a heavy dose of opium:

> When she made no move he was seized with the fear that she would refuse him. To test her, he brushed her cotton-clad nipple with his lips; there was a wetness in the cloth that surprised him, but he was so glad she hadn't pushed him away that he thought nothing of it. He undid the buttons and laid his face between her small, firm breasts and breathed deeply, sucking in the smell of smoke and water.[18]

The dream of Bahram that perpetuates in the chronological order is copy cat of what both had been earlier and is mere a recurrence of old love story. But this love making dream is different in only one respect as it is well supported by the intoxication of opium where as real love making was totally based on spiritualism and corporeal amalgamation of two passionate souls. Even though it was in dream but he experiences a consummate sex full of contentment and bliss and he feels himself in such union with girl as if both were two souls in one body and he were embarking his journey into uncharted sea of sensuality. He was drowning in such a water of love-making with a sing-song-girl that it was now impossible for him to let her go and the girl was in his arms like a drowning man catches at a straw:

> Her hands were on him too now roaming through the folds of his clothing with the ease of familiarity, parting his choga, undoing the ties of his angarkha, gently lifting the sadra from under the strings of the kasti, loosening the top of his leggings and slipping down, to touch him in his secret places. Almost without effort, she drew him into her, pivoting her body so that her covered face was turned away from him, and his cheek was pressed against the back of her wet, moist neck.[19]

But as every climax is followed by anticlimax, when Bahram suddenly wakes up from his dream-dipped-sleep he finds himself alone and his hands were empty. He was surprised to recollect all that have been fresh in his mind and memory. In sheer surprise he asked Allow where is the girl she had been with him throughout night? Allow had to take pain in convincing Bahram that there was no girl but it was an opium pipe and opium fuelled smoke dream. The following passage of the novel has special and specific significance in the light of the fact that the very title of the novel under discussion, *River of Smoke*, is seemed to be extracted from the same passage:

> Bahram closed his eyes and laid his check against her neck; once again he was weightless, afloat in the mist. He allowed himself to drift along, on the river of smoke, and when his sleep broke he was amazed to find that his arms were empty and she was gone.[20]

Like first Novel of Ibis trilogy, *Sea of Poppies*, the second of it, *River of Smoke*, too ends on tragic note. Commissioner Lin made all the opium of foreign traders on board of their ship damaged under his watchful supervision and he kept all foreigners confined to camp until all opium was surrendered. Before we move further on the issue of tragic end of novel, it is interesting to note here the prediction and proclamation that Neel once made before Compton, an owner of Canton's press: "But you know, Compton, it is also true that amongst those who are close to Seth Bahramji there are very few who do not love him. And I am not one of them—for if there is one thing I know about the Seth it is that he has a large and generous heart. This is what makes him different from the Burnhams and Dents and Ferdoonjees and the rest of them. You mark my words, those men will lose nothing in the end. It is Seth Bahramji who will be the biggest loser—and the reason for that is just this: he has a heart".[21] And prophecy of Neel came true in the end of the novel and in the very subsequent of losing of large amount of opium he lost his life itself but he didn't forget to remember her true love, Chi-mei who was giving him a clarion call:

> Afterwards, as so often before, they crawled out on the prow. Lying flat on their bellies they looked at the moon's image, shimmering in the water. It was shining so brightly that her face too was illuminated by its reflected glow: she seemed to be looking up from under

> the water's surface, smiling at him, beckoning with a finger.
>
> 'Come, Mister Barry. Come. Ha-loy!'
>
> He smiled. 'Yes, Chi-mei, I'm coming. It's time now.'
>
> The water was so warm that it was as if they were still on the boat, lying in each other's arms.[22]

Ghosh paints such a picture of amorous, quixotic and romantic loves through the characterization of Bahram and Chi-mei that even the readers found themselves swimming across the river of sensuality. He has also exhibited a testimonial through relationship between Bahram-Shireenbai and Neel-Malati Indian version of dedication and devotion that a wife has for her husband. The passion for physical love and wedding palpitates in every youth and adult which is embodied through the characterization of Mr. Jardine. The terms platonic and spiritual truly defined the word 'love' which is depicted in the association of Mr. Robert Chinnery and Miss Paulette. To conclude, the novel, *River of Smoke,* is a marker of great deal of love and sensuality where passionate, physical, platonic and spiritual love together matter much in measuring and magnifying the magnanimity, majesty and magnificence of the novel.

NOTES

1. Ghosh, Amitav. *River of Smoke*, Hamish Hamilton an Imprint of Penguin Books, 2011, p. 145.
2. *Ibid.*, p. 52.
3. *Ibid.*, p. 66.
4. *Ibid.*, p. 67.
5. *Ibid.*, p. 71.
6. *Ibid.*, p. 70.
7. *Ibid.*, p. 71.
8. *Ibid.*, p. 165.
9. *Ibid.*, p. 398.
10. *Ibid.*, pp. 112-13.
11. *Ibid.*, p. 113.
12. *Ibid.*, p. 144.

13. *Ibid.*
14. *Ibid.*
15. *Ibid.*, p. 236.
16. *Ibid.*, p. 298.
17. *Ibid.*, p. 300.
18. *Ibid.*
19. *Ibid.*
20. *Ibid.*, p. 301.
21. *Ibid.*, p. 542.
22. *Ibid.*, p. 546.

27

The Author with an Author

AMITAV GHOSH IN A CONVERSATION WITH LILA AZAM ZANGANEH

Lila Azam Zanganeh: I'm curious to know if in your studies, when you went to Oxford, and in your anthropological studies, if somewhere in the back of your mind you knew that the path was going to lead to writing novels, or how you came to it—how the little throb came.

Amitav Ghosh: It was absolutely my first love. It was what I always wanted to do. But for us in India, certainly when I was a kid—when I was in my teens and so on—there was no such thing as a literary career. It was not something you could aspire to. Because the possibility of making a living by writing was unthinkable. And I thought, what do I do which is close enough? So I became a journalist. In fact when I was eighteen, I took my first job. First, I worked as a journalist, and at a certain point I realized that it wasn't going to let me do my writing. So then I went to the University to do a master degree, and somehow I ended up with a scholarship to go to England, which was wonderful because mainly I just wanted to travel. So that's how it happened. It was just a set of accidents really.

Lila Azam Zanganeh: When did you start writing fiction?

Amitav Ghosh: I wrote when I was in my teens. But I started really, in earnest, when I was twenty-four.

Lila Azam Zanganeh: And was that your first novel?

Amitav Ghosh: Yes, that was the *Circle of Reason*, which won the Prix Médicis Etranger.

Lila Azam Zanganeh: In France, you have quite a following, and you have had it for quite a while.

Amitav Ghosh: Well it was wonderful! It was just magical; the book did amazingly well in France, it got the Prix Médicis Etranger, it sold a lot. So I felt very, very grateful to France for that.

Lila Azam Zanganeh: As a Nabokovian, what's incredibly important to me as I read literature is to envision the details and to visualize the concreteness of things. Of course with your background in anthropology, you're always giving a sense of concreteness of images, of things—the way boats look, or canals. How do you think [anthropology] informed your writing from the beginning—if at all?

Amitav Ghosh: I was an anthropologist for two years.

Lila Azam Zanganeh: In Egypt.

Amitav Ghosh: In Egypt, yes. The time I spent there was absolutely the fundamentals of my education as a writer.

Lila Azam Zanganeh: How so?

Amitav Ghosh: What does an anthropologist do, really? You just go and talk to people, then at the end of the day you write down what you see. So what it really does it trains you to observe, and it trains you to listen to the ways that people speak. So it's really a very important thing to teach yourself: to observe, as a writer. And I think basically that was where I learned that. The other thing was that I also read a lot when I was there, and that also very influenced me.

Lila Azam Zanganeh: What did you read?

Amitav Ghosh: I read Marquez for the first time while I was living in the village. I read *One Hundred Years of Solitude*, which really in some strange way had a very powerful impact on me at that time.

Lila Azam Zanganeh: How?

Amitav Ghosh: When you're living in this very tiny place, [with] a thousand people or something, your temptation is to think of it as being outside the flow of history. In reading Marquez you begin to think of all the ways in which the whole world is visible in the microcosm of this one small place, like Marquez's Macondo. Another writer who had a very powerful influence on me at that time was James Boswell. I read the whole of the *The Life of Samuel Johnson*. And it had this enormous influence on me because what Boswell really does, what is so miraculous about the *Life of Johnson*, is that he listens to people speak. And I see when I look back on my writing of those years that there's a pre-Boswell period and a post-Boswell period. In the post Boswell period, I'm just listening so much more closely to what people say. And I think that was a very powerful thing for me; it got me to listen.

Lila Azam Zanganeh: Salman Rushdie is nine years older than you. There's this idea that *Midnight's Children* was the door that opened the path to Indian [fiction in English]. Is that so? Was Indian literature thriving before *Midnight's Children*? Did that book influence many would-be authors to dedicate their lives to writing? Did it make it more accessible? And did Rushdie influence you in many ways?

Amitav Ghosh: I think *Midnight's Children* was very important in the sense that it suggested the existence of a market. It was a curious thing, if you remember what it was like in the late 1970s, early 1980s; there was a whole wave of books from Latin America, from other parts of the world, and *Midnight's Children* was a part of that. So suddenly people from Africa, from Asia—we could see a new audience coming into being. In that sense, yes. It was a set of books. Again, Marquez was an important writer, and Mario Vargas Llosa, who indicated the possibility of telling the sorts of stories that we could tell. So in that way, yes, I think it was very important.... But personally, I think much more important to my development as a writer were writers like V.S. Naipaul. I mean [in terms of] the people that [I] read when I was in my teens and twenties.

Lila Azam Zanganeh: You're constantly compared to V.S. Naipaul.

Amitav Ghosh: Whether one agreed or disagreed with it—and I never did agree with it as such—his project was to claim the world from a point of view other than that which has been handed down from the West. So he was a traveler. He was seeing the world. He was writing about the world. He refused to be limited by Trinidad, as it were. Which is in some ways a strength and in some ways a weakness. But it was the nature of what he was doing which was so powerful, so interesting. I can see [this] very much in myself: my interest in going to Egypt, my interest in writing about Egypt and Burma and Cambodia and so on. In some sort of complicated way they all link back, and Naipaul is very much a kind of important figure, an important figure to depart from, as it were.

Lila Azam Zanganeh: But how so? Depart from how exactly?

Amitav Ghosh: Especially in his essays and his nonfiction writing. I don't think I would agree with more than like ten or twenty things that he says. I think he's completely wrong about a lot of things.

Lila Azam Zanganeh: Like what?

Amitav Ghosh: His representations of India, his representations of Islam. I think very often they're just mistaken. They're just in fact a sort of perverse kind of autobiography rather than representations of what he sees. But the thing that I respect about Naipaul is that he was struggling with something. He was struggling with something that he was trying to do truthfully, pushing himself. He was never doing what's comfortable, or what's easy. He was always pushing himself.

Lila Azam Zanganeh: You mention his traveling as somehow containing a form of weakness. You also write about such an extraordinary variety of places. How are you able to overcome that weakness? I mean in the midst of traveling, did you still attach yourself to roots?

Amitav Ghosh: Very much so. I was very lucky in that unlike Naipaul I was from a large country—a large, increasingly self-confident country. Often I think the weaknesses of Naipaul's work come from the fact of his having grown up in a circumstance where there were very intense small conflicts. Where he, I think, could never really claim Trinidad for himself, and never felt enabled to claim it for himself. But I felt very much that I was looking at the world as an Indian. So I think that was certainly one of the huge differences.

Lila Azam Zanganeh: What did your parents do?

Amitav Ghosh: My father was a bureaucrat. But he also worked for a while for the Indian External Affairs Ministry. So with him, in my childhood too, I traveled a lot. In fact I spent two years of my life in Iran.

Lila Azam Zanganeh: Where?

Amitav Ghosh: In Tehran.

Lila Azam Zanganeh: Then you know Iran better than I do.

Amitav Ghosh: May well do, but it was a long time ago.

Lila Azam Zanganeh: Was your father part of the elite that came out in some of your novels, of the English-speaking, educated upper middle class, that was created by the Raj?

Amitav Ghosh: No, he was very much a middle-class boy who actually during the Second World War ran away from home and joined the army. But that gave him a certain kind of mobility.

Lila Azam Zanganeh: The Indian army?

Amitav Ghosh: Then the British-Indian army. Which I write about at some length in *The Glass Palace*. But no, at home we always spoke Bengali. So I feel myself very lucky in that unlike many Indian writers, I'm very much part of two cultures: the Bengali-speaking culture and an English-speaking culture. That's one of the wonderfully liberating things about India; it lets you be exactly who you want to be.

Lila Azam Zanganeh: In my reading I found that so many people want to attach little categories onto you or your family, you yourself come from this kind of India, and therefore it influences your writing in such and such a way. But with India being such a complicated place, my sense is that this kind of judgment is hasty and ill-conceived. But I know one of the things that come up constantly in your books is the question of "who are we?" When I read your *New Yorker* essay, "The Town by the Sea", what struck me is that it's as though this idea of a tsunami could also almost work as some sort of powerful metaphor for the identity of a country being completely washed away. And because there's always this idea of struggling over who we are: Are we the colonization imposed on us, are we something else altogether? Could we ever wash ourselves free of the stamp of civilization? And all of a sudden there's this idea that well what if we do, what if civilization is washed away and we start from scratch?

Amitav Ghosh: People often talk about identity. It's not one of the things which really is washing about in my head at all. One of the reasons why is because anybody who's lived in India knows that India is incredibly, incredibly diverse. I mean it would be almost impossible to define what it means to be, moreover to say that everyone who identifies themselves as Indian is [the same as] what they are. That's one of the wonderfully liberating things about India; it lets you be exactly who you want to be. And in many, many different ways. At the same time it also offers you these incredible civilizational resources. Myths and poetry and....

Lila Azam Zanganeh: So much of the critical literature on you pigeonholes you as a writer who is interested in the question of identity. Do you think that's the curse of the Indian writer in the post-colonial age?

Amitav Ghosh: I never read critical writing, because if you start doing that you just get very caught up in that. I don't think it's anything to do with my work, because, I've noticed, that especially people who come out of a literature background in America, I think they're taught to think primarily about identity.

Lila Azam Zanganeh: That's true.

Amitav Ghosh: I mean from the age of like fourteen onwards when they first read *Catcher in the Rye* or whatever, they're taught that that's what literature is about. So that's what they think it's about.

Lila Azam Zanganeh: You don't like *Catcher in the Rye*?

Amitav Ghosh: It's not that I dislike it. But it's not something which I respond to very powerfully. But no, I'm not talking about *Catcher in the Rye*. I'm talking about the pedagogy of literature in America—and I think increasingly around the world—is one which is about identity, whether it's relevant or not. I don't know why that should be the case but so it is.

Lila Azam Zanganeh: What do you think of the whole post-colonial studies movement in the U.S.? Because it has certainly helped the emergence of Indian writers.

Amitav Ghosh: Very much so. And that's mainly what I think about it. When I started writing twenty years ago, writing in English was seen as a tenuous thing [for writers like me] to do, a marginal thing to do. And the sorts of reviews we would get, it would be like, you know the singing dogs? It's just interesting because they do it. But I think that's what really changed.

Lila Azam Zanganeh: Only 20 years ago?

Amitav Ghosh: I would say. I think that's what really changed with people like Gayatri Spivak and Homi Bhabha. I think they really changed the grounds of the debate so that it was no longer possible to take that position in relation to us. So I really respect what they've done. Does it in any way inform my writing? I don't think so.

Lila Azam Zanganeh: You embody such a remarkable diversity especially in your nonfiction. I mean aside from someone like, say, John Updike, it's rare to see someone who writes so much fiction and substantial books in volume, who is also very much involved in writing essays as well. I mean your *New Yorker* pieces seem like they require a lot of research and travel and observation. So do you feel like there's a driving obsession, or unifying force behind your work?

Amitav Ghosh: One thing I will say is that if you were to divide writers, like people do divide painters—between the abstractionist and the figurative painters—I'm definitely a figurative person. *I mean it's the world that interests me.* The world completely fascinates me. I want to see it, I want to know it, I want to write about it. It gives me pleasure, you know? Even when I'm writing about something completely horrific, it engages me. So yes, it's in that sense that I suppose writing nonfiction was something I did. But I do it less and less now.

Lila Azam Zanganeh: Why is that?

Amitav Ghosh: I just enjoy writing fiction more. And nonfiction, yeah, it's faded a bit for me.

Lila Azam Zanganeh: Fiction is so sensual and sprawling, and all kinds of characters come up, and there's almost a fairy tale element. Nabokov always said that the best novels are fairy tales. Good novels are fairy tales. And he even called *Remembrance of Things Past* a fairy tale, Proust's fairy tale. In that sense, are you a Nabokovian, are you interested primarily in aesthetics? It doesn't seem so. Do you think your writing is also driven by a political quest?

Amitav Ghosh: I think all important writing comes out of some sort of passionate engagement with the world around it. I mean even with Proust, you see so much his engagement with the famous Dreyfus case, and that was so central to everything he did. So yes, I mean I think you know the political world is very important. And that's also a part of being Indian. Whenever I'm in India, just growing up in India, half your conversations are political, as it must be with Iranians.

Lila Azam Zanganeh: Yes, always.

Amitav Ghosh: Always! It amazes me when you see in Western reviews people saying—ohhhh as people talk about politics it's so strange. I think maybe in the West they don't, but we do all the time.

Lila Azam Zanganeh: So your literature you say will be innately political as well?

Amitav Ghosh: It is. But I think for me, my great heroes of writing are.... One of the great sources I draw from is Balzac. In some very important way my engagement in writing comes from a very Balzac-ian source; it just interests me. What I see around me interests me, this human comedy. I'm interested in the literary part of it, I'm interested in every aspect of it. That's why I think I'm drawn to the novel even more than writing nonfiction, because only the novel allows you the completeness of representation. To me, the novel is important because it's such a complete form of utterance. It allows you to represent your utterance in all its nuances, in all its representative possibilities, in all its expressive possibilities in a way that nothing else can.

Lila Azam Zanganeh: I agree. Even if you love music or architecture or sculpture, nothing comes quite as close to this satisfaction, in terms of absorbing consciousness, as the novel. But to circle back to the criticism of your work, it's really quite extraordinary how everybody had a different opinion as to why you're writing, where you're coming from—

Amitav Ghosh: Yes, and they often send me these questions and things, and I mean, you know....

Lila Azam Zanganeh: I mean half of the things I read about you recently said that Amitav Ghosh is a writer basically obsessed with identity. It made me wonder somehow about the diaspora. Is there a rift between people writing outside India and people writing within India? One thing I will say is that if you were to divide writers, like people do divide painters—between the abstractionist and the figurative painters—I'm definitely a figurative person.

Amitav Ghosh: I think the question of the diaspora is very, very interesting. I'm not really a diasporic in the sense that I grew up in India. I'm returning to India. So I've been away for a while. But the trajectory of my life is really one of travel rather than being in the diaspora. But being in the diaspora completely fascinates me and I think this has been the most important thing to me about being outside India. I've really come to realize that the most interesting thing about being Indian is that India is not in one place. I think this is in some very important way the pattern of the future. What we see today in that nation-state is fading to be replaced by these enormous diasporic civilizations. India is one, China is one, England is one, France is one. Today it's in fact those countries which are more and more tied to the model of the nation-state that seem more and more parochial—like America. So I think that's a very interesting thing that is so striking. When I started writing, if you were invited to Europe or America you went in to do a reading, and you would see maybe one Indian face in the audience, and it would be all Europeans. Now it's completely changed. I mean anywhere you do a reading, it's like 60 to 70 per cent of your readers are diasporic people, are Indians!

Lila Azam Zanganeh: Really, 60 to 70 per cent are diasporic or Indian?

Amitav Ghosh: Well, I don't think you can make that distinction anymore. That distinction has faded, most of all in the work of cultural production. Almost every major Hindi film that's now produced in Bollywood is actually aimed, the whole cultural effect is defined by the diaspora. They are produced by the diaspora, they have diasporic themes. So twenty years ago it was the other way around. India was exporting to its diaspora. Now that whole relationship has changed very much, the relationship between India and the diaspora.

Lila Azam Zanganeh: You mean twenty years ago—India was exporting or importing?

Amitav Ghosh: Exporting.

Lila Azam Zanganeh: So now?

Amitav Ghosh: Now the diaspora is exporting *to* India. The diaspora is determining the ways in which cultural products in India are shaped. Which wasn't the case twenty to thirty years ago. But again, it goes in cycles: I mean the entire Indian national movement was invented in the diaspora. Gandhi in the diaspora, Gandhi in South Africa, even, say, what I describe in *The Glass Palace*, the garden party in America. When I was growing up in India you thought of the diaspora as being way out there, as just being very far away. You thought of them as a kind of periphery to your metropolis. But it's actually a much, much more intimate relationship. To me, to explore that relationship has been something completely absorbing.

Lila Azam Zanganeh: When you talk about cultural production, obviously you're talking about writing as well. Do you have a large readership in India? You just said that you are receiving the *Légiond'honneur* in India? I'm sure that's also a seal of popularity.

Amitav Ghosh: Yes, my books are very well received in India. That's in some sense my primary audience. Now, every school child reads one of my books or essays, so I get a lot of questions.

Lila Azam Zanganeh: That's wonderful.

Amitav Ghosh: It is wonderful.

Lila Azam Zanganeh: It's really fascinating that your main readership is in India now.

Amitav Ghosh: I think of it as such. Yes, I mean, India and the diaspora, I would say. I mean, take this café I come into. One of the men who runs it came to me the other day. He didn't know that I'm a writer or anything. So he said, "I know this girl, she's Indian, she said to me, 'Oh, you must read this book, it's so important to me.'" And it was one of my books!

Lila Azam Zanganeh: Which?

Amitav Ghosh: *The Glass Palace*. But [when] he saw it, he recognized me from the picture.

Lila Azam Zanganeh: That's incredible.

Amitav Ghosh: The Indo-Burmese diaspora is now spread out around the world. And you know, when they read *The Glass Palace*, it gives them something to recognize who they are, where they came from, what happened, the entire history, because they didn't know. Because what I do think is true is that human beings live life in narrative. Where the narratives don't exist, in some way life doesn't exist. So I wish I could tell you how often I get letters from here, there, everywhere, saying thank you, you've given my life a shape.

Lila Azam Zanganeh: Salman Rushdie coined the phrase "the Empire writes back." Could we say that now the diaspora is writing back to India?

Amitav Ghosh: I think it's a much more dialogic relationship—not one way or the other. In this generation, I don't think one can even talk of diaspora anymore. I think the myth of countries of immigration like America is that when people come here they renounce their other identities and become American. But in fact what we see today is exactly the opposite. I think that's what Americans just don't understand.

Lila Azam Zanganeh: Not giving up their identity.

Amitav Ghosh: They're not. In fact, they're not even moving. They're just taking planes.

Lila Azam Zanganeh: You mean, like you they're moving constantly....

Amitav Ghosh: Constantly. I mean that's true of almost everyone I know. I mean there's no sense in which you suddenly say to yourself that I'm remaking myself into another citizen. What you actually do, is you do become a citizen off this moving entity called the diaspora.

Lila Azam Zanganeh: But when you said that in the seminars where you were invited to speak, in America or Europe, you used to see only one Indian face, and now they are 60 to 70 per cent diaspora, you mean 60 to 70 per cent of the audience is Indian diaspora?

Amitav Ghosh: What I'm saying is this: it's not that the diaspora wasn't there before. It's just that twenty years before, if you went to a town in America, or you went to a town in Europe, the local Indians wouldn't care about a writer coming. But now it's completely changed. Throughout the world now you have these Asian literary festivals, people go to them. It's one of the very interesting things that I find in looking at the Indians who are abroad. You go to any small town in America, the local college, one of the English teachers will be Indian. People always think of Asians as being just involved in addressing science. Actually what you see is that this whole Asian diaspora is very profoundly involved in the production of ideas, in literary production, cultural criticism.

Lila Azam Zanganeh: But still, isn't there a difference between a writer living and writing in India, and you?

Amitav Ghosh: Sure. One of my friends who does live there wrote a very powerful piece saying, unless you're dealing with the old business of coping with the bad traffic and this and that, it doesn't really seep into your work.

Lila Azam Zanganeh: What doesn't seep into your work—India?

Amitav Ghosh: Yeah, just the frustrations of daily life or you know, maybe it doesn't, I don't know.

Lila Azam Zanganeh: So he was claiming that he was more Indian than you in a way.

Amitav Ghosh: *She*, in fact. I don't know if she'd make that claim. But yeah, I think location does have something to do with it. Location is important. But I think much more important than location, actually, is language. For example, the idea that what you see increasingly nowadays, of say Englishmen, or English Indians living in India, writing about India without knowing the language, or any of the languages, it just seems so odd to me. I mean I think language is much more important than location.

Lila Azam Zanganeh: Do you think your vision is more global so to speak—since you write about Burma and you've written about so many different places—than somebody living in India? There must be a difference between the way you perceive even the diaspora or India from a distance living here nine months a year, and somebody who is sitting in Calcutta all year long. Rushdie, for instance, seems to be much more global. Yet in most of his well-known books, he is also deeply grounded.

Amitav Ghosh: His books are national projects. One book was sort of like a modern history of India, the other is modern history of Pakistan. But I don't think one can write about India like that. So, yeah, that project has no reality to me. Because India is either something you see absolutely at a ground level, or you see it in the way it spills over. But the project of writing about the Indian state—or of any of those states—it just seems to be, in an imaginative sense, a strange thing.

Lila Azam Zanganeh: Why?

Amitav Ghosh: Because no one experiences India like that, I don't think, except politicians, really. I don't think one can even talk of diaspora anymore. I think the myth of countries of immigration like America is that when people come here they renounce their other identities and become American. But in fact what we see today is exactly the opposite.

Lila Azam Zanganeh: Recently a specialist of American and English literature in Paris, one of the most prominent, told me she's not impressed with the likes of Philip Roth or John Updike. But she's actually very impressed with Indian writing. In her opinion, right now, Indian writing is at the helm of the English literary world.

Amitav Ghosh: To me there's no doubt about it. I look around at my contemporaries, and it would be hard to think of a group of writers who are more productive or interesting, and I think that's why people read us.

Lila Azam Zanganeh: Whom do you admire?

Amitav Ghosh: Vikram Seth, Michael Ondaatje—his work is incredibly interesting to me. There are just so many. When I walk into a bookshop in India, I just think, I could spend, you know just the day....

Lila Azam Zanganeh: And is that new? Has this happened in the last twenty, thirty years?

Amitav Ghosh: Yeah, I think it's happened in the last ten or fifteen years. But you know, people often say to me, "Why is it that people around the world want to read Indian writing?" I tell them that there's no trick to it: people want to read it because it's good. And I think it's even more than that:

what I would say about Indian writing is that it speaks to people.

Lila Azam Zanganeh: Why?

Amitav Ghosh: Take a writer like Arundhati Roy. She's not afraid of talking about emotion. About very essential, powerful, human emotions. And that's what you don't find in American writing anymore.

Lila Azam Zanganeh: Playful high jinks and post-modern....

Amitav Ghosh: It's just so ironicized, it's just boring. I can't read any American writing anymore; it's just not interesting to me. So I think that's what happened really.

Lila Azam Zanganeh: Perhaps there's a complex in America about narrative. You have to make it so contrived for it to be intellectually acceptable.

Amitav Ghosh: I think, in a way, a certain condition of American life where people become very isolated from other people eventually reflects itself in the work. Often when you read it, you just get a sense that people are not curious about other people. Or else that they are so curious that it becomes obsessively concerned with the sort of psychologizing of people. But you know emotion, and passion, and all those things, I think that's why people all around the world read us, because people know that those are real things and they respond to them.

Lila Azam Zanganeh: Who are the women writers from India you like? You've mentioned Arundhati Roy. Do you like Jhumpa Lahiri?

Amitav Ghosh: Anita Desai, she's a great favorite. Kiran Desai, who's a very dear friend.... You know, it's such a long list, I could just go on. It's a very fortunate moment to be an Indian writer.

Lila Azam Zanganeh: Is Indian writing—just by virtue of its contact with so many different cultural layers—enriched constantly by the language of....

Amitav Ghosh: Constantly!

Lila Azam Zanganeh: In your writing too, there are all these words that you weave in, and it always enriches the texture of the language. Even to foreign ears. For me as a Persian-speaker, there are some words I understand, but....

Amitav Ghosh: Sure. Absolutely. It varies from parts of India. I mean if you go to Delhi, the writers who write in English and the writers who write in Hindi don't have much to do with each other. But in Calcutta, this is a very fortunate thing. I mean, I'm close friends with most of the major Bengali writers, their work influences.... I read them, they read me: I feel a very deep sense of connection and gratitude.

Lila Azam Zanganeh: How does their work in Bengali, how does that influence you?

Amitav Ghosh: Oh! Very much! It's something I've often tried to explain to people. The Bengali storytelling voice is a very inviting and warm voice. I don't really know how to explain it to you but it's a very intimate voice which invites you into the story. And whenever I get stuck in my work, I always try to listen to that voice.

Lila Azam Zanganeh: I understand, I love it. But is there also, by virtue of writing in English, the fact that you want to be exposed to a larger readership and a larger market? So is there also a rift there within India between those who decide to write in Indian languages and those who write in English?

Amitav Ghosh: There has been in the past. But it's another thing that's completely changing. Because with the development of the Indian economy what's actually happening now is that three or four major publishing houses have launched these enormous translation programs. So actually if you go into an Indian bookshop today, the books that are next to mine may have been written in Bengali, you wouldn't know. [Updike] can write about Connecticut, which he knows. But clearly he himself feels it's not enough. He has to reach out to the world. It's pathetic.

Lila Azam Zanganeh: And it works? Are they sold?

Amitav Ghosh: Yes! They sell enormously.

Lila Azam Zanganeh: I'm always interested to know, this is a question I asked Updike a couple of months ago.

Amitav Ghosh: Oh my God, I reviewed that book of his....

Lila Azam Zanganeh: Oh you did, which one, *Terrorist*?

Amitav Ghosh: Yes. It was just trash. TRASH. It was completely racist. I reviewed it in the *Washington Post*. I just made a list of all the skin colors.

Lila Azam Zanganeh: Brownish this, brownish that?

Amitav Ghosh: You know you look at that stuff and you suddenly realize....

Lila Azam Zanganeh: He was disconnected.

Amitav Ghosh: Completely! His obsession is basically a nineteenth-century obsession with race. The strange thing is you can't help [thinking] Updike doesn't have to write about this. He can write about Connecticut, which he knows. But clearly he himself feels it's not enough. He has to reach out to the world. It's pathetic. The narrative voice, it was pseudo-Arab!

Lila Azam Zanganeh: Now that you're more drawn to novels and fiction, I'm interested to know how you are able to combine fiction and nonfiction—are those two different toolboxes? You know, how, what draws you to go to Egypt and all of a sudden to come back and write a novel [about] that—how does it coexist?

Amitav Ghosh: They're not really different toolboxes. But it's also true that there's a difference between writing fiction and nonfiction. With nonfiction you always do have a responsibility to what's out there. You can rearrange, but it's like the clay; it's like being a potter; the clay is out there and it resists you and you have to shape it. Whereas writing fiction is more like music—you shape it, it's in your head, by the time it comes out of your mouth, it's already shaped. There is a huge difference, but they inform each other.

Lila Azam Zanganeh: I know that you're moving away from it. Yet I still hoped to discuss your nonfiction and the pieces you've done. You've written about the U.S. intervention in Iraq.

Amitav Ghosh: Yes, when the Iraq war was beginning in 2003, before it started, I was so disturbed and so upset, I wrote this piece on why this kind of imperialistic venture is doomed to failure. It came out in *The New Yorker* in March 2003, literally weeks before the war. So I wrote it and sent if off. They wrote back and said yes, we like it, we'll run it. Then for the next week we had these violent arguments, they wanted me to change it completely. They actually wrote out [their own] paragraph and sent it to me.

Lila Azam Zanganeh: They wrote a paragraph in your essay?

Amitav Ghosh: They dictated a paragraph to me and said we want you to put this in.

Lila Azam Zanganeh: Really?

Amitav Ghosh: Yes, I remember it. It said, "The modern connotations of the word 'empire' also show how the context of imperialism has changed. For many, especially in America, it is a reminder of an image that played a significant part in discrediting the Soviet Union: the 'evil empire'. This is not a purely rhetorical anxiety; the unease goes deeper than that. A substantial proportion of America's population remains unconvinced of the need to undertake a new version of a 'civilizing mission'. This is what distinguishes America from the imperial nations of the past."

Lila Azam Zanganeh: I assume you're writing a new novel right now. Can you tell what it's about?

Amitav Ghosh: No, I never feel comfortable talking about these things.

Lila Azam Zanganeh: What's your writing schedule?

Amitav Ghosh: Some days it's 10 to 6; some days it's maybe 9 to 5, some days it's like 7 to 4. But for me writing is like music. It's not just that you're working towards the book. But if you're not writing a sentence, you lose your pitch.

Lila Azam Zanganeh: Where does inspiration usually come from?

Amitav Ghosh: It comes from lots of things: from traveling, from speaking to people, from my family. You know I have a *huge* Indian family. I listen to their stories; I listen to what people say. But one of the great things about being from India is that you know there are so many stories to tell you could go on forever and I think people will go on forever. It's one of the things which I really do realize now that I look back on the past—this has been India's great strength: storytelling, always. India's influence on the world such as it was has always been through stories.

Lila Azam Zanganeh: Even from *The Mahabbharata*.

Amitav Ghosh: So many of the *Arabian Nights* come from Indian stories. Aesop's *Fables* come from Indian stories.

Lila Azam Zanganeh: That's right.

Amitav Ghosh: If you look back on that past, it's so humbling. Really as a contemporary Indian writer, you look back on that history and you feel: nothing I could do could even come close.

Lila Azam Zanganeh: Is there such a thing as Indian-ness?

Amitav Ghosh: No.

Lila Azam Zanganeh: Being Indian?

Amitav Ghosh: No, one of the wonderful things about being Indian is it gives you this wonderful chameleon-like quality. I always tell my wife: any statement you make about India, whatever you say, the opposite is also true!

Lila Azam Zanganeh: Would you say that your work has in any way been informed by thinking on the consequences of colonization in India?

Amitav Ghosh: Absolutely. Certainly with *The Glass Palace* I thought of that very much.

Lila Azam Zanganeh: And do you think that formerly colonized Indians are finding their own independent voice or is their voice always fraught with "Englishness"?

Amitav Ghosh: One of the interesting things about the Indian voice is that it's always been a composite voice. As late as the nineteenth century every Bengali learned Persian; it was normal! We've always learned Sanskrit. No one in India has ever spoken in one voice; it's not something anyone thinks of. But this much is clear: India and China in the eighteenth century controlled 50 per cent of world trade. After the end of colonialism they controlled less than 2 per cent of world trade. But what is happening? The balance is being righted. India and China will again control 50 per cent of world trade. And it's taken us.... We're just now awakening from the long night of that colonial experience.

Lila Azam Zanganeh: The *New York Times* review of *The Glass Palace* said that you seem to be very much concerned with the idea that Indians have to find this new voice that was no longer fraught with the paradigm of the colonized. The reviewer claimed that *The Glass Palace* was just posing the question: how can we be human? Would you agree with that?

Amitav Ghosh: Yeah, I think so.

Lila Azam Zanganeh: A question about influence—as Harold Bloom would call it "the anxiety of influence". In the post-colonial world many say that an Indian writer or, for instance, an Iranian writer should be concerned primarily with Indian or Iranian writing. But in fact you seem to be just as influenced, just as inspired, by Bengali writing as you are by the likes of Marquez.

Amitav Ghosh: Very much so. I mean the filmmaker Satyajit Ray, for example, was a huge influence on me, it was an enormous influence, completely formative for me. That's exactly where I come from. But equally I think for me, three or four other writers have been very important. One is Balzac, one is Proust, and I think most of all: Melville.

Lila Azam Zanganeh: Really? Which Melville? Melville of "Bartleby", Melville of *Moby Dick*?

Amitav Ghosh: All of them, actually. But most of all I suppose *Moby Dick*.

Lila Azam Zanganeh: I can see that, also your anthropological background—the boats and the whaling. But precisely how so, *Moby Dick*?

Amitav Ghosh: Oh I think it's just a magnificent, magnificent book.

Lila Azam Zanganeh: You spoke at the very beginning of this conversation about how you learned to be a writer in Egypt while doing anthropology because it was mostly looking and listening. So is that why perhaps in your writing you don't feel that there's a frontier between so-called anthropology and narrative because they're constantly interconnected?

Amitav Ghosh: Yes, absolutely. That's one of the things which always interested me so much about Melville, that for him the real and the imagined are always on the verge of interpenetrating each other. And so much of *Moby Dick* is just nonfiction. Melville was a great observer. Other books like *Typee* are so finely observed. I think he was the one 19th century English-language writer who really was able to write about other peoples in a genuine [way]. You can see what drives him is a genuine interest in Polynesia.

Lila Azam Zanganeh: And like you perhaps he chose fiction in the end because fiction is a far better tool and texture to explore metaphysical issues.

Amitav Ghosh: In a way it is. I recently re-read *Moby Dick* and—especially considering all that's now happened—he uniquely understood the kind of strange and crazy compulsions that his country was and still is capable of.

Contributors

Vivekanand Jha is a Translator, editor and award winning poet from India. He is Diploma in Electronics and Communication Engineering, Certificate in Computer Hardware and Networking, MA and PhD in English. He is a contributing poet to Wavelengths—2011 Savant Anthology of Poetry (USA) which has won first place in the 2011 London Book Festival. He has been Poetry Contest Winner-Third Place Winner for the poem "Hands Heave to Harm and Hamper" conducted by Beginners®, a documentary, graphic, nonfiction book series (USA). He is the author of five books of poetry. He has also authored one critical book on the poetry of Jayanta Mahapatra and edited two critical anthologies on Indian English Novels. His works have been published in more than seventy magazines round the world. Apart from that his poems have been chosen and published in more than fifteen poetry anthologies. He has more than twenty research and critical articles published in various national and international anthologies and referred journals. He is son of noted professor, poet and award winning translator Dr. Rajanand Jha (Crowned with Sahitya Akademi Award, New Delhi).

Neerja Arun is a Principal, Senate member and Coordinator for 9 programs at Gujarat University. She is also on panel of fourteen International and Indian Universities. Her area of specification are Indian Poetics, ELT, Modern Literature, Indian Diaspora Studies, Indian Culture and Religion, Gandhian Philosophy, Indian Heritage, Comparative Poetry/Drama, Nationalism and Indian

Diaspora, tribal art and culture. She is affiliated with a number of International journals as editor and reviewer. She has authored 9 books and has widely travelled in India and abroad to follow academic pursuit in National and International Conferences. Her major publications of the books are: *Going to Wipe their Tears: Gandhi's Biography, Ecology and Literature: A Global Perspective, A Handbook of Indian Aesthetics and An Anthology of Criticism of Amitaav Ghosh, An Anthology of Contemporary Writings of Indian Diaspora, Summarizing History of Indian Diaspora, An E Card from Across the Border-Writings of Diaspora, GOPIO Writing Series, Human Rights Related to Women and Children.* More than 40 critical articles and research papers of her are published in various national and international publications and journals.

Indira Nityanandam, Principal Smt. S.R. Mehta Arts college, Ahmedabad has been teaching English language and Literature since 1974. With six books to her credit, she has published more than 40 articles in leading journals as well as books. Her main areas of interest are ELT, Translation Studies, Diaspora, Women's Writing and Comparative Literature.

Deepak Thakur is a Principal, Govt. PG College, Nalagarh, Himachal Pradesh, 174101. He has been teaching English language and literature to both UG and PG Classes for the last 29 years. He earned his doctorate on the novels of Amitav Ghosh.

Anju Bala Agrawal is a Reader and Head, Department of English, R.C.A. Girls' P.G. College, Mathura.

Dinesh Kumar is an Associate Professor, Department of English, V.G. Vaze College, Mulund East, Mumbai. He has a Doctoral degree in African American Literature, from the University of Mumbai. His areas of Specialization are Literary Theory and African American Literature. He has presented about 20 research papers and published articles in University News and in Critical Anthologies on Amitav Ghosh, GV Desani, Amitav

Ghosh and Kamala Das. He has co-authored and edited three books for the University of Mumbai—Stylistics, Translation Studies and Literary Theory. He has 19 years of undergraduate and postgraduate teaching and has a guided 16 students for their M. Phil Degrees.

Rajnish Mishra is an Assistant Professor in the Department of Applied Science and Humanities in IMS Engineering College, Ghaziabad. He is PhD on Role of Villains in Shakespeare's Tragedies and he is also UGC-NET qualified. His areas of interest are postcolonial theory and literature.

Vishwanath Bite is Translator, Writer, Critic, Editor and Assistant Professor in English, Government of Maharashtra's Ismail Yusuf College, Jogeshwari, (E), Mumbai. He is also an Editor-in-Chief of *The Criterion: An International e-Journal in English*. Besides publication of numerous critical and research articles in various anthologies and referred journals he has authored and edited seven books of English literature.

Vandana Rajoriya is a Lecturer of English, Government Polytechnic College Khurai, Sagar, Madhya Pradesh, India. She is author of four books and her critical and research articles have published in various anthologies and referred journals. She has also a working experience as Soft Skills Trainer in ICFAI National College and Guest Lecturer Communication Skills in Indira Gandhi Engineering College Sagar, Madhya Pradesh.

A. Sujatha is an Associate Professor, Department of English, Mahalakshmi Engineering College, Trichy. She has been teaching for the past 16 years and is an ardent lover of Literature and Language Teaching. She refuses to acknowledge the divide between these two disciplines and affirms that they are complimentary. Her areas of interest include Feminism, Postcolonialism, Designing Learning Materials, Task-based Language Teaching, Participatory Learning, and Teacher Training and Development. Her passion is storytelling on which her doctoral research was based.

Ch. Swathi is a Lecturer, Department of English, GITAM Institute of Technology, GITAM University, Visakhapatnam, Andhra Pradesh, India. She has a number of research articles published in reputed referred journals and critical anthologies. She is also member of Guild of Indian English Writers, Editors and Critics (GIEWEC), Thodupuzha, Kerala; International Congress of Language, Literature, and Culture (ICLLC), Patna and International Journal on Multiculturalism (IJML), Kerala.

Dalvir Singh Gahlawat is an M.A., M.Phil, PhD in English, M.A. Political Science and pursuing PGDJMC. At present he is working in Delhi Police as a Sub-Inspector (Wireless Operator) and also editing a critical anthology on Indian English Poetry. More than twenty research articles of him have been published so far in various critical and referred journals.

Suman Yadav is a Research Scholar, Department of English, Singhania University, Jhunjhunu, Rajsthan.

L.V. Padmarani Rao, P.G. Department of English & Research Centre, Yeshwant Mahavidyalaya, Nanded-431602, Maharashtra.

Githa Bhojane is a Research Scholar, P.G. Department of English and Research Centre, Yeshwant Mahavidyalaya, Nanded-431602, Maharashtra.

Ambarish Sen works as an Assistant Professor of English in Barasat Government College, under West Bengal Education Service (W.B.E.S.). His areas of research interests include Indo English Poetry and Fiction, American Literature and social studies. He is currently pursuing his PhD on fictional works of Amitav Ghosh.

Saykar Satish Govind is head and Assistant Professor, Dept. of English, D.P. College, Goregaon.

Neeta Dhumal is an Associate Professor, Department of English, Kamala College, Kolhapur, Maharashtra.

Shyam Chothani is a Lecturer, Depatment of English, V.G. Vaze College, Mulund East, Mumbai-400081.

Rashi Saxena is Assistant Professor of English, Raj Kumar Goel Engineering College (RKGEC), Ghaziabad. She has attended several conferences and workshops and her various articles have published in the referred journals and critical anthologies.

Somdatta Bhattacharya is currently a Guest Faculty at the Centre for Comparative Literature and the Centre for English Language Studies, School of Humanities, University of Hyderabad. She has been a UGC-NET Senior Research Fellow with Jadavpur University, Kolkata, India and is the author of a volume of poems and several academic papers. She is also currently pursuing her PhD at Jadavpur University and her thesis examines the representation of the city Calcutta in post-Independence literature, cinema and popular arts. Her work and research interests are mainly rooted in urban studies and she has explored urban geography using theories of space and gender and subaltern studies. In 2007, she submitted her study of space in Amit Chaudhuri's fiction for her M.Phil from University of Hyderabad.

Priyanka Vaidya is an Assistant Professor of English, Govt. P.G. College, Nalagarh, Himachal Pradesh.

Rituparna Datta Roy is Assistant Professor, Dept. of English in Kanya Maha Vidyalaya, Jalandhar, Punjab. Her articles, reviews and translations of poems are regularly published in different journals and edited books. She has authored two books.

Rupali Jain is teaching as an Assistant Professor of English in Satyawati College, University of Delhi. She is M.Phil in English and got her NET clear in June 2008.

Lila Azam Zanganeh was born in Paris to Iranian parents. After studying literature and philosophy at the Ecole Normale Supérieure, she moved to the United States to teach literature, cinema and Romance languages at Harvard University. Since 2002, she has been a contributor to Le Monde and has been published in *The*

New York Times, *The Internatitonal Herald Tribune*, *The Nation*, *The Paris Review* and *La Repubblica*. In 2006, she edited a collection of narrative essays on Iran. Her first book, *The Enchanter: Nabokov and Happiness*, has just been published by Norton in the United States, Penguin in England, L'Olivier in France, Contact in Holland, and L'Ancora del Mediterraneo in Italy. In 2012, it will be published by Duomo Ediciones in Spain. She is currently at work on a novel titled *The Orlando Inventions*. Lila is fluent in six languages and serves on the Board of Overseers of the International Rescue Committee. She is the recipient of the 2011 Roger Shattuck Prize for Criticism, awarded each year by the Center for Fiction. She writes and lives in New York City.